CW01496159

YOURS LOYALLY

THE LIFE OF CHRISTOPHER SCLATER MILLARD

Maria Roberts

Published in 2014 by FeedARead.com Publishing

Copyright © Maria Roberts

First Edition

The author has asserted their moral right under the
Copyright, Designs and Patents Act, 1988, to be identified
as the author of this work.

All Rights reserved. No part of this publication may be reproduced,
copied, stored in a retrieval system, or transmitted, in any form or by any
means, without the prior written consent of the copyright holder, nor be
otherwise circulated in any form of binding or cover other than that in
which it is published and without a similar condition being imposed on
the subsequent purchaser.

A CIP catalogue record for this title is available from the British Library.

CONTENTS

PROLOGUE

Spiritum nolite extinguere

It was during the mid-1920s that a young gay man, Michael Davidson, first encountered Christopher Sclater Millard and he recalled their meeting forty years later in his autobiography *The World, the Flesh and Myself.* By then Christopher was in his early fifties, a tall, rather gaunt, but graceful man, whose long face was framed by thick greying curls. He was invariably dressed in a blue shirt and shabby flannel trousers rolled up at the ankles although his red knotted neckerchief added a splash of colour to his outfit. Over one of his shoulders he carried his old haversack which almost always contained a book ot two.

Michael was immediately captivated by Christopher, who proved to be both clever and charming, with an "exactingly fastidious" mind and "a grave and gently sardonic" sense of humour. He talked entertainingly in his deep musical voice of "the fun of literary and bibliographical detection" and was quick to laugh at things that amused him. But at the same time Michael was impressed by how honest and forthright Christopher could be. Indeed he could even be "crushingly plain-spoken." The attraction was mutual and as Michael prepared to leave, Christopher reached out and "tickled the palm" of his hand before inviting him to return. He was soon introducing him to his friends as "my new young man."

****

Christopher's story begins over fifty years before in the late autumn of 1872 when the scattered trees in the grounds of the rectory in the

Hampshire market town of Basingstoke were leafless, the shrubs in the borders were bare and the lawns, kept short over the previous summer, were wet underfoot following days of heavy rain. In northern England gales had caused a number of deaths and even in the south it had been very windy.

Christopher's birthplace —Basingstoke Rectory

On the first of November the vicar, James Elwin Millard, celebrated All Souls Day in St Michael's Church, although his heavily pregnant wife probably rested at home. On the fifth of November the Basingstoke community, like many others up and down the country, took part in the annual celebration of the failure of the Gunpowder Plot and the execution of its Catholic organisers. Then two days later on Thursday the seventh of November, as the wind subsided and the skies cleared, Dora Frances Millard gave birth at the rectory to her second son, Christopher Sclater. He was baptised at his father's church a month later.

****

CHAPTER ONE

CHRISTOPHER'S FATHER

"Fathers should be neither seen nor heard. That is the only proper basis for family life." from An Ideal Husband by Oscar Wilde

Even though Christopher frequently disagreed, not only with his father, but with most of his other relatives, he was considerably influenced by them and his personality was shaped, at least in part, by the family from which he came. It was not only his father and mother who played their part in developing his character, but also his siblings, his aunts and uncles and his grandparents. He can only really be fully understood if something of his family background is taken into account.

A good place to begin is with his paternal grandfather, William Salter Millard, whose own father was the precentor and chancellor of Norwich Cathedral and whose mother was the daughter of the master of Charterhouse. William might have been something of a family rebel in that he deliberately chose not to follow a clerical career but joined the navy instead and this willingness to go against expectations seems to have been passed on to his grandson even though William died ten years before Christopher was born.

William's naval career progressed as far as midshipman which was considered a suitable position for a young gentleman and from which he could have hoped to progress to lieutenant. At the same time he was nurturing an ambition to write which he transmitted first to his son, James Elwin, and then to his grandson, Christopher. In William's own case this inspired him to produce a vivid account of a major naval battle in which he was involved.

In 1801 he was aboard the *Monarch* as it prepared to take part in the Battle of Copenhagen against the Danish fleet. He was sobered by the sight of the surgeons preparing their medical equipment in anticipation of a large number of casualties, but despite this he was impressed by "the beautiful and solemn spectacle" of the British ships as they got ready to engage with the enemy. When the fighting began the commander of the

Monarch, Captain James Robert Mosse, was an early casualty. Indeed William had been lucky because shortly before he had been standing in the exact spot on the quarter-deck where his captain was killed. There was little time to mourn Captain Mosse in the midst of the battle so he was simply "laid in the stern walk, and a flag thrown over him" whilst the other officers bravely kept up the men's spirits despite their own injuries. As the fighting continued, William was kept busy ferrying shot and wadding to the guns. He was wounded in the cheek but luckily he escaped "the dreadful slaughter… in the centre of the ship" where there were so many injured men that at least one bled to death as he waited for the surgeon to examine him. Still "the sun shining and the old blue ensign flying as lofty as ever" helped him feel more positive and by three o'clock in the afternoon he realised he was both hungry and thirsty. He managed to find some cheese, cold potatoes and biscuits as well as a can of fresh water, which he shared with his fellow sailors, and not long after they had finished their hasty meal, one of the enemy ships exploded in "an immense mass of black smoke" and the Danish fleet soon surrendered.

William was a loyal midshipman who seems to have taken considerable pride in the achievements of the Royal Navy and been a fervent supporter of British patriotism. So he would probably not have approved of his grandson Christopher's later hostility towards British imperialism and his detestation of "anything that savours of Jingoism and 'expansion of empire'." Nevertheless Christopher did inherit his grandfather's love of sailing along with his dislike of injustice and his willingness to challenge authority. These two traits were both evident in William's criticism of the treatment of the first lieutenant of the *Monarch*, John Yelland. He had fought "like a lion" during the battle but allegedly the Admiral, Sir Hyde Parker had not recommended him for promotion and instead had given preferential treatment to his own officers. William must therefore have been pleased that subsequently John Yelland was indeed promoted to the rank of commander for his conduct, whilst Sir Hyde Parker quickly found himself facing a barrage of criticism for making poor decisions during the battle, which fortunately were deliberately ignored by his Vice-Admiral, the naval hero Horatio Nelson.

William himself never advanced beyond the rank of midshipman because he left the navy soon after the Peace of Amiens was signed in March 1802 putting an end to hostilities with France, at least temporarily. Perhaps by then he had had enough of life at sea. He returned to the county of Norfolk where he had grown up and began to farm a small piece of land of his own as well as acting as land agent and surveyor for a wealthy neighbouring landowner. Eleven years after leaving the navy he married in Norwich. His bride was a woman named Philippa Frances Elwin and the Millards obviously knew the Elwins well because William's brother, Philip, married Philippa's sister, Virtue.

After their marriage William and Philippa had six children together. Their first son was Charles William, who was named after his father and grandfather, and he was followed first by a daughter, Frances Maria, and then by another son, Philip Salter. Next came a second daughter, Caroline, followed by a third son, Henry James, who died as a baby. Finally on Sunday 18 May 1823 their sixth child, James Elwin, was born. There were to be no more children because Philippa died just over a year after James' birth. Her young son must dimly have been aware that his mother was no longer around to care for him, but he can't have retained many distinct memories of her. Perhaps her place was filled at first by his older sisters

Four years later James acquired a stepmother called Isabel Shaw who was then only in her late twenties, but was nevertheless prepared to take on the responsibility of looking after five-year-old James and his older siblings. William moved with his new wife to the village of Sprowston near Norwich where he began running Manor Farm. Isabel became pregnant within a few months of the wedding and in 1829 she gave birth to James' half-sister, Charlotte Mary, who was the first of eleven siblings. Nearly all survived into adulthood so eventually James' family became a very large one and Manor Farm must already have been quite crowded by the time James reached the age of twelve although from then on he would spend much of his time away from Norfolk. It was then that, like his father and grandfather before him, he became a pupil and chorister at Magdalen College School which lay on the High Street in Oxford and he would spend most of the next three decades in this university city.

Magdalen College School had a long history and it had been an excellent institution. But when James arrived he found a school that had seen better days and which was finding it difficult to attract pupils. The headmaster was a man called Richard Walker and, although he was considered a fine scholar, he was an ineffective teacher. There was very little discipline at the school and bullying and theft were widespread. The pupils regularly fought in the streets with the town boys and on one occasion they barricaded an unpopular teacher in the schoolroom. The school also found it hard to attract good teachers. During his early years there, many of James' lessons were taught by the usher, George Grantham, an impatient man who frequently lost his temper and who was severe with his pupils. James and the other young boys were not only expected to light the fires, get water and sweep the schoolroom, but to fetch Mr Grantham's beer. He seems to have consumed excessive quantities of this beverage and he had probably been drinking when a few years later he fell out of his study window and broke his neck.

James probably made the best of his lessons with Mr Grantham because, unlike some of his fellow pupils, he took his education seriously and he wanted to learn. He was taught arithmetic by another teacher, Mr Lockey, and as he progressed through the school he must have had lessons with the headmaster too. Despite his failings as a teacher, Mr Walker was an excellent Hebrew scholar as well as a skilled botanist. In 1833, two years before James joined his school, Mr Walker had published *The Flora of Oxfordshire* and he might well have shared his knowledge of wild flowers with James and the other older boys. Perhaps this kindled James' own interest and later led him to pass an enthusiasm for plants on to his own children.

Although the education at Magdalen College School was perhaps not of the best, there were other positive aspects to the school as far as James was concerned. Firstly he was offered the chance to become school librarian and he was delighted by this because it gave him the perfect opportunity to indulge his great love of literature. A love for books and for reading would remain a key part of James' personality for the rest of his life. Secondly James had the opportunity to study for a short time with a Fellow of Magdalen College named William Henderson. This must have fuelled his academic ambitions and encouraged him to go on to university.

It was also during his time at school that James began to develop his writing skills. Like his father he was keen to make his literary mark. In order to give himself opportunities to disseminate his work he established several weekly school papers before in early 1838 at the age of fourteen he launched *The Choristers' New Monthly Magazine* along with three fellow pupils including Richard Humphrey Hill, who became his lifelong friend. Over the next two years the four boys wrote most of the verse and prose that appeared in this magazine with James often winning prizes for his submissions. Later he must have been gratified when five of his poems were selected for publication in a collection titled *Poems by Members of Magdalen College School, Oxford*. James' contributions begin with his piece about *The Battle of Trafalgar* which opens: "Oh! brightly rose the morning sun, and calm the ocean lay,/And nought foretold of battle in Trafalgar's tranquil bay". Perhaps this was influenced by his father's own naval experiences. James' second poem is *June* and his third, *The Enchanted Rose*, recounts the journey of a knight. It is followed by *The Destruction of the Egyptians* based on a biblical story and his final poem is the *Lament of Mary Stuart*. This was a significant choice because it demonstrates James' teenage sympathy with a Catholic monarch. Perhaps he later shared his attitude towards the doomed queen with his son, Christopher, whose own compassion might have been roused by the story of the unhappy queen who mourns her fate: "How brightly beams the summer sun/On Leven's dancing sea,/But am not I the lonely one?/Its beams are not for me."

The *Lament of Mary Stuart* and James' other poems appeared in the year before he and his handsome young friend Richard left school in order to continue their academic studies at Magdalen College. Coincidentally, thirty years later this would turn out to be the college where Oscar Wilde studied and he was to exert an immense influence on the life of James' son, Christopher. Both James and Richard were talented young men who were admitted to Magdalen College on scholarships and became successful university students. In 1845 James was awarded his Bachelor of Arts degree and he was keen to pass his knowledge on to others so in the following year, when he was only in his early twenties, he was appointed headmaster at his old school and brought his elder sister Frances with him to act as school matron. Young James, who was not much older than many of his new pupils, must have been an impressive candidate to have been offered this position and he quickly developed into a much loved and respected teacher. Unlike his own headmaster, Richard Walker, James was a strict, but fair, disciplinarian who effectively supervised his pupils and oversaw the work of the nine other teachers under him who included the usher, William Sawell, two teachers who taught classics, a teacher who taught mathematics and writing, and specialist teachers for French, instrumental music, singing, drawing and drilling. James established a well-structured school day at his school which began with an hour of study before breakfast. The pupils then had a break before lessons resumed at eleven o'clock until one o'clock. After lunch there was another hour of study from quarter to three until quarter

13

to four, and there was one further hour of lessons in the evening before the younger boys went to bed at nine o'clock and the older ones followed half an hour later. Time at school was punctuated by regular holidays. At Christmas the pupils were given five weeks off with another week's holiday at Easter, and then six weeks in the summer.

Part of James' strength as a teacher was his ability to set clear expectations for the behaviour of his pupils. This is evident in the book he kept in which he recorded the rules of the school. It demonstrates both his calm and reasonable approach and his sense of humour. The younger boys were forbidden from setting off fireworks and all pupils were stopped from damaging the trees in the playground by climbing them. Neither were they allowed to enter the local public houses, though James did permit the older boys to visit inns when they were rowing on the river or on long excursions as long as they behaved themselves. At the same time as he gave them clear rules, James also demonstrated his commitment to his pupils in various ways. He gave up his Sunday evenings to read to them and he worked hard to keep up the standard of the school choir. He also insisted on the importance of physical activity. Pupils were allowed to use the garden for half an hour before and after each meal and then in the evenings James had the schoolroom cleared so that he could lead gymnastics sessions there. He joined in enthusiastically with school sports – he had enjoyed the school cricket matches when he had been a pupil himself – and he participated in the regular paper-chases and took the boys for long walks on Sunday mornings. James clearly relished being physically active and believed strongly in the need for both a healthy body and a healthy mind so besides his school activities, he swam regularly all year round at Parson's Pleasure, a site on the River Cherwell which was set aside for male-only nude bathing and which was often used by university dons. For some men this site had a further appeal as it seems likely that one of its attractions was as a place where it was possible to look (if only covertly) at other men's naked bodies.

Although teaching kept James busy, he had not abandoned his interest in writing and in 1847 at the age of twenty four he published a moral tale which he had originally written for the school choristers. *The Island Choir; or The Children of the Child Jesus* deals with the plight of twelve young choristers left alone on an island after the accidental drowning of their elder brethren. It seems likely that James partly modelled the boys in his story on the pupils he taught, but also drew on aspects of his own personality to create these fictional characters, which might explain why some of them seem to anticipate the personalities of the sons he would later father. In the light of the fact that James almost certainly could not accept sexual relationships between men, and that in the future this would probably be the greatest (possibly unspoken) cause of the rift that developed between him and his son, Christopher, it is rather surprising that in this book he describes the close friendship between two of the boys, Hilary and Clement, in rather sensual terms although it must be acknowledged that at the time of writing these no doubt appeared uncontroversial. Nevertheless they are obvious. When Clement sits wistfully on the shore, Hilary "made him rise and walk away with him. So the two boys twined their arms about each other's necks and wandered along the shore." When they sit down to rest "Hilary laid his head on Clement's knee, and the soft waves sang him fast to sleep, but Clement watched the waves…. The moon rose high, and the sun was clear, and the sea very light and smooth … And late at night … he laid his hand on Hilary's hand, and woke him very gently."

In 1848 James followed *The Island Choir* with another book, *Historical Notices of The Office of Choristers*, and in the same year he contributed hymns to a collection called *The Devout Chorister* compiled by a Fellow at Magdalen, Thomas Frederick Smith. In addition James is generally credited with the words of the carol, *The Boy's Dream*, that appeared in a highly influential book, *Christmas Carols Old and New*, which had been jointly edited by another Magdalen Fellow, Reverend Henry Ramsden Bramley, and the college organist, Sir John Stainer. This simple carol flows along easily enough: "Last night as I was laid and slept,/When all my prayers were said:/While still my guardian Angel kept/His watch above my head;/I heard his sweet voice carolling,/Full softly in my ear,/A song for Christian boys to sing,/For Christian men to hear." However three years later (in 1851) the twenty-eight year old James published a considerably sterner piece. *The Christian Knight* was a sermon originally written for the benefit of those boys who were leaving his school and preparing to become "soldiers of Christianity." He urges them to be strong in the face of temptation, to regularly confess and repent of their sins, and to remain vigilant. He warns them, "You have fiercer foes than have ever yet assailed you" and "hotter passions than have ever tried your purity" as well as "society and the world to resist in forms more difficult than you have yet known." He sincerely believed this was an important message to convey and almost certainly he later strived to convince his own children of its truth. But he would fail dismally as far as Christopher was concerned because his son would find the "hotter passions" irresistible and, in any case, he would not consider that giving in to the temptations they posed was particularly sinful.

Not long after the publication of *The Christian Knight*, James was delighted to oversee the completion of the chapel at Magdalen College School and this immediately became the centre of life at the school. James regularly preached there addressing his young pupils in simple and direct language and giving them rules for Christian living telling them to be truthful, to act fairly, and to avoid getting into debt. It was such guidance, rather than any diatribes against the passions, which actually would have an impact upon his son, Christopher, who maintained a keen sense of justice and a commitment to the truth throughout his life.

In 1855 when he was thirty two James received his Doctorate in Divinity and in the same year he inherited some money from his uncle, Philip Millard, but neither event distracted him from his dedication to his school which continued to expand. He oversaw the construction of a new dining hall and kitchen as well as the building of school laboratories and by the early 1860s the school was catering for nearly five times as many boys as it had done in Richard Walker's day with sixty three boarders and twenty eight day boys attending. Because of the high quality of the teaching at the school, many of its pupils were awarded university scholarships. James was clearly a talented educator and school leader and he could well have spent the rest of his life making a success of teaching. However this was not to be. Instead a new opportunity appeared, probably not entirely unexpectedly as it originated from his old university college. James kept up close links with this college throughout his time as headmaster and he was appointed a college Fellow in 1853 and later became both its Junior Dean of Arts and its Bursar.

So it was the Masters and Fellows of Magdalen College who in 1864 invited James to become the incumbent of the parish of Basingstoke. After eighteen years as a headmaster he was ready to move on and he soon accepted the new position and prepared himself to leave both Magdalen College School and the city of Oxford where he had lived for nearly thirty years. He did not entirely sever the ties however. He always returned for Speech Days and he was delighted to be able to leave his school in the capable hands of his old friend Richard Hill, who had previously run Beaumaris Grammar School in Anglesey, and who proved to be another kind, but firm, headmaster who successfully built upon James' achievements.

Basingstoke, which now became James' new home, was a long established and expanding market town in a key location on the route from London to Bristol and the West Country and with good railway links not only to Salisbury and to Reading but to the port of Southampton. The town was surrounded by undulating fertile fields where local farmers grew sainfoin, turnips, wheat, barley, and oats which they sold in the weekly markets held behind the town hall. Once installed as vicar in this busy town, James carried out his various parish duties conscientiously. However, like many academic clerics he also found time to take an interest in the history of the town which would be his home for the next twenty five years. He must frequently have explored the local area and researched its background and eventually he edited a book on the subject. Nevertheless his priority was his parish work and he preached regularly in St Michael's Church and was active in the local Temperance Society, which worked hard to persuade working class men (in particular) to abstain from alcohol. This was probably never an easy task and indeed James own son, Christopher, would prove to be an enthusiastic drinker throughout his life.

James did not carry out his duties in isolation, of course. He quickly became part of a local ecclesiastical network with his nearest clerical neighbour being Reverend Robert Falkner Hessey, who held the living at Basing and who occasionally came into Basingstoke to assist James with the services. For a while Robert had a curate called Hume Skeffington Dodgson who lodged at Four Lane Farm and he sometimes walked over to take tea at the Basingstoke rectory. James had family support too because he was far from being the only cleric in the Millard family. Several of his half-brothers were pursuing clerical careers and James doubtless had many opportunities to discuss church matters with them mainly through letters, but sometimes in person if they visited each other's parishes. His half-brother, Jeffery Watson was the rector at the church of St George in the village of Shimpling near Diss in Norfolk, whilst Henry Shaw was based in Clifton just outside Bristol, and Charles Sutton was the rector at St Giles' Church in the village of Costock in Nottinghamshire. Perhaps James also compared notes with a fourth half-brother, Frederick Maule, whose career was very similar to his own. Frederick, too, went to Magdalen College and afterwards he became the headmaster of St Michael's College in Tenbury Wells in Worcestershire, which had been founded in 1856 primarily to teach choral music. John Stainer (who has previously been mentioned as the organist at Magdalen

College) later played the organ there. Like James, Frederick produced a book of his talks to his pupils – *St. Peter's Denials of Christ: Seven Short Lectures to the Boys of St Michael's College, Tenbury* - which he published in 1869, the same year that his old college offered him the living of the village of Otham near Maidstone in Kent. No doubt James' sisters (Frances Maria, and Caroline) and half-sisters (Charlotte Mary, Barbara Isabel and Agnes Jane) also took an interest in his clerical career. All five women remained single and lived to ripe old ages.

When James moved to Basingstoke he, too, was still unmarried even though he was already in his mid-forties. He seems not to have seriously contemplated marriage up to this point. However he now had a secure career and enough money to consider taking a wife. Marriage would have particularly appealed to him if he was keen to have children of his own to raise and influence.

CHAPTER TWO

CHRISTOPHER'S CHILDHOOD

"Children begin by loving their parents; after a time they judge them; rarely, if ever, do they forgive them." from A Woman of No Importance by Oscar Wilde

It was probably shortly after his move to Basingstoke that James was introduced to a woman named Dora Frances Sclater. She was twelve years his junior and she came from a more affluent property-owning family. Her father, William Lutley Sclater, was an Oxford graduate like James, but after his time at university he joined the ranks of the landed gentry by inheriting the estate of Basing Byfleet from his half-uncles. He married in 1821 at the age of thirty two and his first son, George, was born in London five years later. When George was three a brother, Philip Lutley, was born in Hampshire at a house named Tangier Park in Wootton St Lawrence. The family then moved to the village of Upton Grey where William was rich enough to be able to afford a grand country home, Hoddington House. This was a handsome early eighteenth century mansion which was built on raised land and which was surrounded by fifty acres of grounds and meadows and two hundred acres of woodland.

William's daughter, Dora was born in Upton Gray and on 5 October 1835 she was baptised in St Mary's Church. Her childhood was spent in comfortable surroundings and she must have been brought up to a life of Christian good works which led her in her twenties to embroider a small flag for the First Hants Volunteer Battalion in Basingstoke. Her family seems to have been a tight-knit one and she apparently remained close to her two older brothers as she grew older. Whilst there was no question of Dora earning her own living, her eldest brother, George, trained as a barrister before becoming a Conservative Member of Parliament and representing his constituency (first North Hampshire and then Basingstoke) for thirty years. Philip Lutley also became a barrister, but his real passion was the natural world and he developed into an eminent zoologist with a particular interest in birds. Eventually he built up a huge ornithological collection and established a considerable reputation in this field which led to him having several birds named in his honour including the Ecuadorian Cacique called *Cacicus sclateri*. Almost certainly it was these two brothers who introduced their nephew, Christopher, to an understanding of both legal matters (with which he would frequently become entangled) and scientific ideas. It might well have been Philip who first encouraged Christopher to take an interest in birds. Although he never developed his uncle's expertise, he always noticed birds and later assiduously fed them in his London garden. It could also have been through George and Philip that Christopher first became aware of London itself - the city in which he spent much of his life. Both the brothers regularly visited the metropolis and they were members of the Zoological Society there. Significantly this was an organisation which attracted many contemporary intellectuals - including some with rather radical ideas. Notably these included a gay man called George Cecil Ives, who became a good friend of Oscar Wilde's, and who campaigned not only on prison reform but on the reform of the laws relating to gay sexual activity. However George and Philip seem to have been considerably more conservative in their outlook and both no doubt approved when their sister, Dora, became engaged to the mature and reliable James Millard. She married him at Upton Grey (in the church where she had been baptised) on Thursday 5 April 1866.

Dora settled down quickly to life in the Basingstoke rectory and became pregnant within a few weeks of her wedding. The Millards' first child, a daughter, was born on 5 March 1867 and she was christened Magdalen in commemoration of her father's alma mater. Before the end of the year Dora was pregnant again and this time she gave birth on 16 July 1868 to a son. He was baptised George Michael with 'Michael' marking his father's association with the church in Basingstoke. The next child was a second daughter, Theodora Elwin, who was baptised on 15 March 1870 and given the 'Elwin' name from her paternal grandmother, Philippa Frances Elwin. Unfortunately Dora and James' third child was a weak baby and she died when she was just a few months old. However Dora was soon expecting again and she gave birth to Philippa Sibyl, on 30 May 1871. Then Christopher followed eighteen months later when James was already forty nine. Their relationship would prove to be a difficult one and some of the problems that arose between them probably stemmed from this considerable age gap which meant that by the time Christopher reached his teenage years his father was already an old man, set in his ways, and perhaps with little understanding of the younger generation. In his turn young Christopher would be eager to distance himself from his father's views on many subjects including both politics and religion.

On 23 November 1873, a couple of weeks after Christopher's first birthday, his sister Dorothy Virtue was born. Christopher had received the Sclater family name as his second name and his sister's middle name also came from one of their ancestors. Two years after Dorothy's birth, Dora gave birth to a boy, James Lawrence, on 1 July 1875. But, like Theodora, he failed to thrive and he died soon after his first birthday. By then Dora was already pregnant with her eighth child who was born on 8 September 1876 and was baptised Paul Elwin in a second attempt to commemorate James' mother's maiden name. Finally seven years later, when Dora was already forty eight, she gave birth to one last child named Baldwin, who was given the middle name of 'Salter' after his grandfather, the naval midshipman.

The rectory grounds at Basingstoke

Christopher Sclater Millard's story begins in the large Georgian rectory in Basingstoke where he grew up with his three brothers and three sisters in comfortable circumstances. The house ran smoothly with the help of a cook, a housemaid, a nurse, a scullery maid and a footman all supervised by Christopher's mother and no doubt it was a typically Victorian home cosily crammed with furniture, with a combined library and study that was mainly James' preserve. From the windows at the front Christopher would often have seen a pony and trap drawing up outside bringing a visitor or waiting to take James around his parish. Beyond he would have looked out over the main lawn of the rectory grounds which was enclosed by a fence. On the other side of this was a little stone bench by the side of the Loddon whose two streams joined as they flowed across the rectory land. In an earlier century this very watercourse had inspired the son of a previous incumbent to write a sonnet, but by Christopher's time it was no longer very appealing as it was polluted by sewage. Nevertheless Christopher might have spent time sitting on the bench reading or thinking, though he probably enjoyed romping in the garden with his brothers and sisters too. As befitted a cleric's son, he also regularly walked the short distance across the rectory grounds and over the little footbridge that crossed the stream to reach the parish church. Attendance at St Michael's with his family was undoubtedly an important part of young Christopher's life and he quickly became familiar with Anglican services and with the regular pattern of the church year as he listened to his father preach from the pulpit and joined in with the hymns which provided his first experiences of communal singing. He enjoyed such shared music-making for the rest of his life - though he ended up singing rather different songs.

St Michael's Church, Basingstoke

Probably from an early age Christopher developed a keen interest in history. This was undoubtedly encouraged by his father, and it must have been at least partly fostered by the rich history of St Michael's Church itself. The oldest part of the building was its chancel, which was over four hundred years old, and the nave, aisles and porch were early sixteenth century. There were a number of impressive church monuments commemorating previous Basingstoke residents including the merchant Sir James Lancaster. He had been one of the founders of the East India Company and he left money to fund a teacher at the Petty School next to the church.

Although naturally much of Christopher's time was spent at home there were occasional trips away from Basingstoke and it is possible that he accompanied his father and his eight year old sister, Magdalen, in October 1875 when they travelled to Sandown on the Isle of Wight. It was during this family holiday that James and Magdalen were introduced to the author and academic, Charles Dodgson, who wrote as Lewis Carroll. Two months later Charles visited the Millards at the Basingstoke rectory and a few days afterwards on 15 December he wrote Christopher's sister an amusing letter in which he apologised, "I was sorry to miss you but you see I had so many conversations on the way." He had been detained by various people in the street including 'me' and 'myself' and he recounted their imaginary conversation: "I said, 'Do you remember when we all met at Sandown?' and myself said, 'It was very jolly there; there was a child called Magdalen,' and me said, 'I used to like her a little; not much you know—only a little.'" The three fictional characters, 'I', 'myself' and 'me', then headed for the station where they met "two very dear friends of mine" who signed themselves 'Lewis Carroll' and 'C. L. Dodgson'.

Such contacts demonstrate that the Millards' life at Basingstoke rectory was far from an isolated one. Christopher's father had connections with both the ecclesiastical world and the academic one which meant that from a young age Christopher was brought up in an environment where clerics discussed ecclesiastical matters and academics from Oxford discussed intellectual ones. His home was also a place where books and the ideas they contained were highly valued. No doubt this was the reason that Christopher grew up to be such an avid collector of books. In that he closely resembled his father who, over the years, acquired a wide range of books, some of which were quite valuable. They included about ninety volumes written by old boys of Magdalen College School and seventy one early printed books. He also amassed historical manuscripts and autograph letters.

The rectory was also where Christopher and the other young Millard children received their early education. Their father must have been fully involved in their instruction and the three girls almost certainly received all their education from him or their mother. However all four boys were sent away to school once they were considered old enough. When Christopher was nearly eight, his older brother, George Michael, departed for a preparatory school called Wingfield House. This was located by the coast in Dover about a hundred miles away from Basingstoke and it was run by a clerical headmaster called Henry Jolly. After two years George transferred to a school in Oxford. This was closer to home but still forty miles away which meant that he spent his four years there as a boarder. Perhaps unexpectedly he did not attend his father's old school but instead he joined a rival school, St Edward's, which had been founded in 1863 and was affectionately known as 'Teddies'. By the time George became one of its pupils, it had moved to a site to the north of the city centre in Woodstock Road where the buildings set around a quadrangle lay on one side of the road and opposite lay the school playing fields.

In May 1884 when Christopher was eleven and a half he, too, left home, though he did not join his elder brother at St Edward's - even though both his younger brothers would shortly go there. However Christopher's father held a perpetual curacy at the little village of Bradfield by the river Pang, not far from the Thames, and no doubt he had heard favourable reports of the recently appointed headmaster at Bradfield College, Herbert Branston Gray, who was making sweeping reforms there. Herbert was a man of great physical energy and attention to detail, as well as an eloquent preacher and innovative teacher. He tightened up discipline at his school and introduced many new activities for the pupils. He had considerable enthusiasm for the classics and he introduced the tradition of producing plays in the original Greek beginning (just before Christopher's time) with *Alcestis* by Euripides. James and Dora must have believed that their second son would benefit from this classical education and it is true that he remembered the school's Greek plays many years later. But he did not complete his education at Bradfield. When he left at the end of the summer term of 1886 he never went back. Instead at the beginning of the following term, shortly before his fourteenth birthday, he transferred to Queen Mary's Grammar School back in Basingstoke.

So what prompted this change of school? There are various possible reasons. Firstly there had been substantial changes in Christopher's family by this time. His grandfather, William Sclater, had died during the previous academic year and as Dora continued to grieve she might have wanted the son who bore the Sclater name back at home with her. Equally significant was the fact that Christopher's older brother had just made a momentous decision. George had grown into an adventurous young man who was keen to broaden his horizons. Perhaps he had come to resemble the fictional Hilary in his father's book, *The Island Choir*, who is described as "a sturdy boy, with a ruddy face, and a proud lip, and an eye that seldom ceased to laugh". Aged just eighteen, he boarded the *Lydian Monarch* and set off the United States. He never lived in England again but instead spent the next eight years in Orlando in Florida before moving to Texas. Two years later he took American citizenship and he worked his way up from peace officer through deputy sheriff, mounted patrolman and deputy marshal eventually becoming state ranger. He married in America and his children were American by birth. Back in September 1886, his departure clearly left a gap in the Millard family and it quickly seems to have become evident that Christopher was now expected to fill the position of eldest son. Gradually he could well have come to resent his older brother, who had escaped the family's clutches and successfully rejected the conventional lifestyle that had no doubt been expected of him. George had been able to put the kind of distance between himself and his relatives that Christopher himself often sought, but never managed to achieve. However that might not have been George's own intention. True, he does not seem to have been particularly close to Christopher, but he apparently had a good relationship with his youngest brother, Baldwin, even though the latter was only three years old when George emigrated. They continued to correspond and Baldwin travelled several times to the United States to visit George. Even after George's death both Baldwin and his sister, Philippa, continued to take an interest in their American niece and nephew.

The combination of William Sclater's death and George's departure might well be enough to explain James and Dora's decision to remove Christopher from Bradfield although there might also have been further reasons. Perhaps they thought he would be happier living at home and attending school as a day boy especially if he had shown some signs of homesickness. However this would have been rather ironic in the light of his later desire to spend as little time with his family as possible. Then the fact that neither of his younger brothers was sent to Bradfield might suggest that Christopher's parents were unhappy with the school for some reason. Perhaps the change was forced upon them though, if Christopher was asked to leave Bradfield, possibly because of some sexual misdemeanour. There is no real evidence for this apart from his later claim that nearly every boy was involved in gay sexual activity at school. If, as seems probable, he based this remark on personal experiences, it was much more likely that these dated from the period when he was boarding at Bradfield than from the time when he was living at home and going to school in Basingstoke.

But perhaps the real reason for the change of school was simply that although Bradfield had provided a good preparatory education for Christopher (as Wingfield House had done for his brother) his parents thought that Queen Mary's was a better choice for his years as a senior pupil. Certainly it had a good reputation and it was a long established school which dated back to the sixteenth century. It had at least one renowned past pupil – the naturalist Gilbert White, who had been educated there in the mid eighteenth century. And if the teaching was true to the school motto of *Spiritum nolite extinguere* ('Never extinguish the spirit') it would surely have suited Christopher.

It was a tall rather gangly boy who entered the schoolroom in Worting Road for the first time in the early autumn of 1886 and he was directed to join his fellow pupils seated on one of the hard wooden benches. There were then about fifty boys at Queen Mary's. Some of them, like Christopher, lived locally and attended daily, but there were others who were boarders and who came from various parts of the country including Devon, Newcastle and London. The senior boys were mainly taught by the headmaster, Reverend Arthur Forster Rutty, who stood magisterially above them on a raised platform and over the next few years Christopher spent many hours studying in the stone floored schoolroom with its whitewashed brick walls and timbered roof. Each year, as the days grew colder, a metal stove was lit to keep the room warm.

Christopher was still at Queen Mary's when his mother heard the news that her brother, George, had been created Lord Basing. This must have shed a reflected glory on the whole family and no doubt Dora was delighted. However her brother was actually not highly regarded by most of his contemporaries who considered him a rather dull and pompous man, and he had already been caricatured in *Vanity Fair* as *The Safe Man*.

Still the Sclater family name clearly counted for something – as did its wealth – and that would prove useful to Christopher on at least one future occasion.

As Christopher moved up through the school, there must have been some family discussion about his future. There seems to have been no serious suggestion that Christopher might follow his Sclater uncles into the legal profession and it is likely that he was already being prepared for an ecclesiastical career during his time at Queen Mary's. His father must have been keen to see his scholarly second son follow him into the Church, particularly because his eldest son had already chosen a very different path, and Christopher seems to have been happy at this stage to go along with his father's wishes. So his name was duly put forward for a university place in Oxford, not at his father's old college, but at Keble. This had only been founded in 1870 and it was a college after James Millard's own heart – a High Church Victorian establishment which had been established to provide an academic education for prospective Anglican clergymen. There was already a family connection with the college because Christopher's cousin, William Lutley Sclater, had recently studied there and had qualified as Master of Arts.

Keble College, Oxford

Christopher prepared to take up his place at Keble towards the end of 1890 and by this time his father was already sixty seven years old. His health was deteriorating and he was forced, perhaps reluctantly, into retirement. He must have been missed by many of the people of Basingstoke when he left "a parish that had been a good deal neglected, in a state of thorough organisation". James was obviously both hard-working and adept at arranging parish affairs and he seems to have passed his organised and methodical approach on to Christopher. It was already standing him in good stead in his studies and later he would apply it effectively to his research and his writing.

When James retired he, Dora, and the five younger children moved to Oxford, a city which held many fond memories for James and which Christopher, in his turn, grew to love. The family settled into a large house at 157 Woodstock Road close to 'Teddies' where Paul Elwin was already at school. As in Basingstoke the Millards employed several domestic servants - a cook, a parlour maid and a house maid – to carry out everyday chores and almost certainly a man was employed to help Christopher's father. James, who in his youth had been a vigorous gymnast, swimmer and runner, was now crippled by rheumatism and the only way he could get out and about was to be drawn around Oxford in an invalid chair. But he was probably consoled by the fact that his second son was about to embark on the studies which would prepare him to continue James' work in the church. The reality, however, was that Christopher was gradually moving beyond his father's control. Oxford gave him the opportunity to broaden his horizons and to start to make his own independent decisions.

CHAPTER THREE

OXFORD

"Oxford was, no doubt, lovely as ever" - Christopher in a letter to R. of 9 July 1918

The Michaelmas term of 1890 began on Friday 10 October so it was a few weeks before his eighteenth birthday that Christopher, now a tall handsome young man with wavy brown hair and dark eyes that twinkled between strongly-marked eyebrows, walked through the main gate of Keble to join his fellow students. He held his books in the long, delicate fingers which he had inherited from his father as he walked beneath the tower, past the porter's lodge, and into the Liddon Quad where no doubt he paused to orientate himself.

He was there to read theology and was one of about fifty male undergraduates who began their studies at Keble that term. Most of them went on to take holy orders after completing their degrees and embarked on clerical careers. Others became teachers, including John Shortridge Cuming, who taught at Hereford Cathedral School, and Thomas George Ligertwood, who went to South Africa and became an inspector of schools in Johannesburg. Nothing is known of Christopher's friendships at Keble but perhaps he was drawn to the less conventional students who took more unexpected paths. One of these was Archibald Williams who began as a teacher but who went on to write over twenty five books many of which were aimed at young people. He was fascinated by science and engineering and wrote about *The Romance of Modern Invention* and *Victories of the Engineer*. Another of Christopher's fellow students, Charles Augustine Castleford Jeffcock, adopted a more Bohemian lifestyle running a café in Brighton, whilst working as a watercolour artist painting landscapes and sea creatures.

At Keble, like Archibald and Charles and the other students, Christopher was required to attend both the lectures, which were held in rooms in the tower, and the seminars with individual tutors. He was also expected to undertake extensive independent reading. He looked in detail at books from both the Old and New Testaments including Isaiah and historical books, such as Kings, as well as the synoptic gospels, St John's Gospel and the epistles and analysed them thoroughly. He might well have enjoyed this careful examination for its own sake, but at the same time it helped him to master an approach which would stand him in good stead in his later bibliographical work. Christopher studied biblical archaeology too and looked at the historical evidence that lay behind the biblical texts. This focus on history had largely been fostered by Dr Edward Bouverie Pusey, a member of the Oxford Movement who had considerably influenced the teaching of theology at Oxford, and who had also decided that students should examine ecclesiastical history and the development of the early church. In other lectures and seminars Christopher and his fellow students explored church liturgies, the articles of Christian faith and the doctrines of the church, as well as the symbolism used to represent Christian concepts.

The college was a close-knit community and like all its members – including both students and staff – Christopher was required to eat his meals communally in the large gas-lit dining hall which lay across the lawned quad. Dinners were formal affairs at which the wearing of academic gowns was compulsory and Christopher ate at one of the large tables with his fellow students, whilst the Fellows who taught them ate together at the raised high table. The room next to the dining hall was the library – an impressive room with a lofty roof – but Christopher probably spent little time there as it was mainly intended for the use of the senior members of the college rather than the undergraduates. So for the first two years of his time at Keble he possibly never saw Holman Hunt's famous painting *The Light of the World* which then hung in the library. However when in 1892 it was transferred to the chapel, Christopher could then have regularly appreciated its detail, its symbolism, and its rich colours.

Unsurprisingly attendance at the chapel was compulsory and Christopher spent many hours in the magnificent building full of colour and pattern, which appealed both to the senses and to the soul. There were bright tiles, colourful stained glass windows and sparkling mosaics full of Christian iconography including the depiction of Christ in Judgement above the altar. The services in the chapel with their High Church emphasis on the beautiful and sensual aspects of worship must have caught Christopher's imagination. In fact a similar emphasis could be found in the aesthetic movement which had developed beyond Keble's walls and which Christopher would come to find so fascinating. Part of this beauty came from music and the Keble chapel's acoustics were perfect both for the singing of the choir and congregation and for the organ. No doubt Christopher fully appreciated this music and joined in enthusiastically with the singing.

He spent four years at Keble before receiving his Bachelor of Arts degree during the Michaelmas term of 1894. He had gained not just academic skills and knowledge during his time there but also something of a reputation. He was known for his impulsive nature and he had been something of a rebel, sometimes ignoring college rules and taking part in various acts of what were described as "noisy folly." It has been claimed that, whilst at Keble, Christopher began publicly flaunting "his friendships with telegraph-boys" and the implication was not only that he was spending time with those who were regarded as his social inferiors but that at least some of these friendships were sexual relationships. He had also become an enthusiastic and dedicated Jacobite. For the rest of his life he would always be a man of strong convictions and apparently this was the first cause to really attract him. Jacobitism offered him the opportunity (which he always relished) of challenging conventional views and he remained committed to the movement for many years. Such dedication was central to his character and it would re-emerge each time he found a new cause to endorse. If the cause was an unpopular one so much the better.

He did have Jacobite allies in Oxford though and historically the city had long been a centre of support for the movement which sought to restore the heirs of the Stuart king, James II, to the throne. He had been a Catholic monarch, who had tried to introduce religious tolerance to his country, but he had been deposed in 1688. He was then sent into exile and was replaced on the throne by his daughter and her Protestant husband. In the late nineteenth century there was a brief revival of political Jacobitism and it was at this time that Christopher became involved. He attended meetings at which the removal of James II was declared to have been illegal and which affirmed that the king's direct descendant, Prince Rupert of Bavaria, was their rightful ruler. A number of Jacobite societies were created at this time including the Order of the White Rose and the Legitimist Jacobite League of Great Britain and Ireland. It was the latter organisation which Christopher joined along with a friend, Alexander Teixeira de Mattos.

Christopher's life was never lived in isolation of course and his story is constantly interwoven with the stories of other lives. To understand him more fully it is important to give something of the flavour of those lives which intersected with his own. Alexander's was the first of these and he was almost certainly an important influence in Christopher's developing interest in the Stuart cause. Jacobitism was closely associated in the late nineteenth century with Catholicism and as Alexander was also a Catholic he probably contributed to Christopher's growing interest in this religion. He was seven years older than Christopher which was old enough for him to have acquired more of an air of worldly wisdom without seeming to be too remote and he probably had a certain glamour because he had spent the first nine years of his life abroad. Physically he was an imposing man, tall and broad-shouldered. And he enjoyed good food and wine so perhaps he introduced Christopher to its pleasures. Christopher stayed in touch with Alexander for some time and they remained in contact after Alexander moved to London where he worked as a journalist, drama critic and translator. In 1900 he married Lily, the widow of Oscar Wilde's older brother, and he thus got to know various members of Oscar's circle - including two of Oscar's former lovers, John Gray and Robbie Ross. Alexander could well have been instrumental in introducing Christopher to Robbie, amongst others, and this was to prove pivotal because from then on Robbie would play a central role in Christopher's life.

Both Alexander and Christopher remained committed Jacobites for years and Christopher demonstrated his dedication in several ways. When he began to publish his work, he adopted the pseudonym of 'Stuart Mason' to show his loyalty to the Stuart kings and every year on 19 November he faithfully laid a white rose at the foot of the statue of King Charles I to mark the ill-fated king's birthday. He kept this custom up for the rest of his life. Furthermore after Oxford he became increasingly active in the Legitimist Jacobite League. In June 1902 he became its honorary secretary and then from April 1903 until June 1904 (when it folded) he edited its monthly pamphlet, *The Jacobite*. In addition he contributed pieces to other Jacobite publications including *The Fiery Cross*.

In this commitment to the Stuart cause, Christopher was probably influenced not only by Alexander and other friends he made at Oxford, but, more unexpectedly, by his father. James Millard's own considerable sympathy for Charles I and the royalist side in the Civil War became evident during his time as headmaster at Magdalen College School when he clashed with one of his pupils - the future historian, John Richard

Green. John had already managed to annoy James with various antics, but when he submitted a prize essay, which concluded that Charles I's opponents in Parliament had been correct to challenge him and to defend English liberties, James became incensed and he had John expelled. James might also have felt sympathetic towards John Paulet, the Catholic owner of Basing House which lay in ruins near Basingstoke and perhaps he gave his children an account of its capture which caught Christopher's imagination at a young age. During the Civil War John Paulet remained loyal to the king which led to Parliamentary troops besieging his house. James would not have felt any more favourable towards these troops when he learned that they had stabled their horses in St Michael's Church. Eventually the troops captured and demolished Basing House and John was taken prisoner. He was first held in the cellars of the Bell Inn in Basingstoke and then sent to the Tower of London. His estates were confiscated and his sons were taken away to be brought up as Protestants. When Charles II was restored to the throne John was reinstated, but his Protestant heir later supported the removal of James II. For Christopher this story remembered from childhood, might well have strengthened his commitment to both the Royalist cause and indeed to the Catholic one, though whilst at Keble, he remained a member of the Church of England.

Another factor in Christopher's attitude towards both Jacobitism and Catholicism was his developing awareness of his own attraction towards other men. He was no doubt alert to the late nineteenth century tendency to define Royalist Catholicism in opposition to Puritanical Protestantism and to associate the latter with chastity and bourgeois morality, and the former with a sympathetic attitude towards sexual expression in general, and in particular with an acceptance of more diverse sexualities.

Christopher did not occupy all his time at university with studying or with politics. Nor did he spend all of it developing his friendships with telegraph-boys! Almost certainly he also first began to enjoy messing about in boats at this time by rowing on the Thames (which is known as the Isis where it flows through Oxford.) Rowing was a popular pastime for many undergraduates who enjoyed it both as a leisure activity and as a sport and Christopher's college had its own boat club (though it did not attract many top-class rowers). Christopher's enthusiasm for boats lasted for the rest of his life and after university he was introduced to sailing: "I used to do a little coasting with a friend in a 10 ton yawl some years ago". He did protest that he was "not a very good sailor", but eventually he became something of an expert, particularly in navigating his way through the Essex creeks, and he enjoyed trips on the river right up to the time of his death.

Boats on the Isis

The years at Keble passed quickly and it was not long before it was time for Christopher to move on to the next stage of his career. Initially he continued to diligently follow the path his father had chosen for him and in order to continue his theological studies he took up a place at Salisbury Theological College amongst "the grey twilight of Gothic things". This college had been established in 1860 specifically to train students for holy orders, and it had proved popular and been expanded during the 1870s. Its architecture would already have seemed very familiar to Christopher because much of it was designed by the architect of Keble, William Butterfield. It was a smaller institution that the Oxford college however and Christopher probably soon got to know most of his fellow students. Whilst he began his studies at Salisbury, back in Oxford his brother Baldwin joined Paul Elwin at St Edward's School from where Paul would go on to their father's college, Magdalen.

But James Millard would not live to see this happen. His health had continued to deteriorate and on Thursday 20 September 1894, probably very soon after Christopher had departed for Salisbury, he died at the family home in Woodstock Road and his funeral took place shortly afterwards. His death was probably not entirely unexpected but Dora, in particular, must have found it hard to bear. However James had left his family well provided for and at least Dora was financially secure. In his will James left his "dear wife" everything and this amounted to over £7000. This substantial sum ensured Dora could support both herself and her dependent children for the rest of her life.

Within a year of James' death, Christopher decided to abandon any thoughts of a clerical career presumably because he finally felt free from the pressure of having to live up to his father's expectations for him. Now that his father was no longer around to disapprove, Christopher might also have felt more confident about exploring his sexuality and he is thought to have had at least one sexual relationship at Salisbury Theological College possibly with a young man from New Zealand named Huyshe Melhuish Cathcart Worthy.

Huyshe was a year younger than Christopher and had been born in Christchurch in New Zealand after his parents had emigrated. He was the youngest of four children and like Christopher he had an Oxford graduate, Edward Athelstan, as a father whilst his mother, Anne, was a solicitor's daughter. After his father's death in New Zealand, his mother brought Huyshe and the younger of his two sisters back to England and it was decided that Huyshe would follow in the footsteps of his paternal grandfather and become a cleric. So he, too, found his way to Salisbury joining the theological college a few months after Christopher. Their time there thus briefly overlapped and the two became close friends and could well have been lovers although the nature of their relationship, like that of Christopher's with a number of the other men that he knew over the course of his life, is inevitably a matter of speculation. He was more open about his sexuality than many of his contemporaries, and there were men who certainly were his lovers. However there were others with whom he undoubtedly had significant intellectual and emotional bonds, but whether they also had a sexual relationship cannot be known for certain.

Christopher was still at Salisbury and presumably already involved in a relationship (either with Huyshe or with another unknown man) when he heard the news that on Saturday 25 May 1895 at the Central Criminal Court, Oscar Wilde had been convicted of gross indecency and been imprisoned for two years with hard labour. No doubt Christopher had been following the case in the newspapers and the outcome made the twenty-two year old angry enough to make a public protest against the prosecution of gay men. On 29 May he posted a letter to *Reynolds'* newspaper (one of the few more sympathetic papers) in which he claimed that Oscar had been persecuted by the press and boldly argued that he had been imprisoned merely for "satisfying his natural passions". Oscar had harmed no-one and done nothing out of the ordinary. Gay sexual activity was in fact so widespread that the Crown could have prosecuted "every boy in a public or private school or half the men in the Universities" on the same charge. No doubt Christopher counted himself amongst their number and his words would prove prophetic because eleven years later he would indeed be convicted in his turn.

Christopher was not only coming to terms with his sexuality during his time at Salisbury. Whilst he was there he made another important decision when he resolved to join the Roman Catholic Church. Interestingly the same choice was made by a number of his fellow graduates from Keble and it could well have been inspired by their High Church experiences there. Another convert was Christopher's exact contemporary at Keble, Alban Henry Baverstock, who became an influential figure after adopting his new faith, founding the Catholic Literature Association and writing numerous books on aspects of Catholicism.

But Christopher's religious outlook might also have been influenced by his father and their views were closer than might be expected from a superficial assessment. Although James was always firmly committed to the Church of England, he was a High Church Anglican by the time he left university and he remained sympathetic towards the Oxford Movement, which sought to reintroduce aspects of the traditional medieval (and therefore Catholic) liturgy. During his time at Magdalen College School he gradually gathered around him a group of Oxford graduates with similar religious views. They included his good friend Robert Henry Codrington, who later ran a mission school on Norfolk Island in the Pacific Ocean and sympathetically studied the Melanesian people and their languages. The Oxford Movement, which these men supported, had a significant impact on the Church of England and led to an increased emphasis on ritual as in the celebrating of the Eucharist, which re-enacted the Last Supper with bread and wine, and the wearing of vestments. However it was a controversial movement which was frequently criticised for trying to Romanise the church. Some of its prominent members, including John Henry Newman, did indeed subsequently convert to Catholicism, and perhaps Christopher's early exposure to its ideas helped to encourage him to take this step too.

To mark his religious conversion, Christopher took the names 'Marie' and 'John' and as he was a man who paid careful attention to names, his choices were significant. 'Marie' might well have referred to the repentant sinner, Mary Magdalene, after whom his father's college and school had been named whilst he probably chose 'John', meaning 'God is gracious', in honour of John the Evangelist, 'the disciple whom Jesus loved'. This saint was popular with gay men as Jesus' love for him seemed to legitimise theirs. Christopher remained a committed Catholic to the end of his life, although his attraction to Catholicism was primarily emotional and aesthetic and apparently he never saw any contradiction between his Catholicism and his sexuality. Michael Davidson thought he was "too honest with himself to obey her [the Catholic Church's] formal commands without going the whole hog and renouncing the flesh and the devil, and he had no intention of doing that." In any case his religious views were generally unorthodox; in a letter dating from about ten years after his conversion he wrote, "I am glad you, too, do not hold the conventional ideas about heaven and hell."

Christopher's change of faith took place at a time when Catholicism was generally becoming more influential in England. This development had begun with the passing of the Catholic Emancipation Act in 1829 and it continued with the establishment of a church hierarchy during the 1850s. The Catholic Church soon began to establish a significant presence, particularly in London, and its importance increased under the influence of the convert, John Henry Newman. It was further encouraged by the rise of a Catholic intellectual elite and by the revived political influence of various old Catholic families. Interestingly the decision to convert to Catholicism from Anglicanism was taken by a sizeable number of Christopher's gay male contemporaries including both Alfred Douglas and Robbie Ross. This might seem unexpected but many wealthier gay men had a strong cultural bond with Catholic Europe and in particular with those Catholic countries (including both France and Italy) which had implemented the Napoleonic Code of 1791 that decriminalised homosexuality. And for many gay men, particularly those in artistic circles, there were close connections between their homosexuality and their Catholicism which were both regarded as 'other' and 'non-British'. Furthermore many gay men could readily identify with the image of the suffering martyr which was an important part of the religion. Catholicism undoubtedly had an aesthetic and sensuous appeal too and it could offer a form of sublimated sexuality. Its religious themes could provide artists with legitimate subjects for erotic art and Saint Sebastian, in particular, became the focus of much homoerotic imagery whilst a number of gay writers drew on the associations between Catholicism and homosexuality. The Catholic elements of John Blox(h)am's story *The Priest and the Acolyte* (about the doomed affair between a young curate and an acolyte) added to its decadence, whilst Oscar Wilde's *The Picture of Dorian Gray* highlighted the appeal of Catholic ritual describing how Dorian "loved to kneel down on the cold marble pavement and watch the priest, in his stiff flowered dalmatic, slowly and with white hands moving aside the veil of the tabernacle, or raising aloft the jewelled, lantern-shaped monstrance with that pallid wafer."

CHAPTER FOUR

TEACHING

"We teach people how to remember, we never teach them how to grow." from The Critic as Artist by Oscar Wilde

Christopher's conversion obviously meant he had to abandon any idea of a career as an Anglican cleric so instead he turned to teaching (following his father into that profession at least). Towards the end of 1895 he was appointed as assistant master at a Catholic preparatory school called Ladycross which was a new school that had been set up during the previous year by a man named Alfred Francis Roper. It was located in Bournemouth and Christopher spent the next few years teaching by the sea. He must have spent some of his free time in the town perhaps walking on the sandy beaches, strolling through the pleasure gardens or attending concerts at the Winter Gardens But he also continued his reading. As Bournemouth had its own railway station it was easy enough for him to travel back to Oxford and he probably spent many of his holidays there and enjoyed visiting its bookshops. In 1896 it was at Blackwell's bookshop in Broad Street that he bought a first edition of *A Shropshire Lad* by Alfred Edward Housman. Christopher loved this book of poems which dealt with the passing of youth and love and wrote 'that it was "the only book of poetry that I know in which literally every poem is a delight."

One of the delightful aspects of this book for Christopher (and the small number of other readers sensitive to it) was its gay subtext. Its author nursed a lifelong unrequited passion for a man he had met at Oxford and was deeply troubled by his sexuality. Most of the allusions to the subject in his poetry are covert ones and include the many references to a comradeship of "lads". But occasionally he is more direct. Poem forty four in *A Shropshire Lad* is an elegy to a gay army cadet who shot himself rather than face "long disgrace and scorn" and poem thirty speaks of being one of those who have "sweated hot and cold" whilst "through their reins in ice and fire/Fear contended with desire."

Christopher probably worked at Ladycross until the end of 1900 when he seems to have resigned. Then early in the following year he received his Master of Arts degree. As he was now a Catholic this was awarded not by his old college, but by a private hall, which might have catered primarily for Catholic monks.

Photograph of Christopher February 1901,
Robert Ross Memorial Collection MS Ross 13/1*

On Saturday 2 February 1901, to celebrate the occasion, Christopher arranged to have his photograph taken; copies of this sepia coloured image survive showing a handsome young man neatly dressed in a suit, shirt and tie with an academic cloak. There are slight creases in his trousers suggesting he had been sitting for a time earlier in the day, but now he stands in front of a backdrop painted with sky and trees. One of his hands is casually placed inside his pocket, whilst in the other he holds a mortar board. His wavy hair is neatly combed with a central parting and it is short enough to reveal quite prominent ears. And what does the still unlined face of this twenty-eight year old give away? Well he seems rather self-conscious, perhaps both slightly arrogant and rather guarded. His eyes are intelligent but their gaze doesn't quite meet that of the viewer. His mouth is a little uneven. His pose is off centre. The overall impression is of a young man who doesn't quite fit in, but doesn't think that he minds too much about not doing so.

At first Christopher almost certainly took considerable pride in his qualification, even though he later he stopped referring to it and eventually requested, "Please don't address me 'M.A.' – I never use it now that I am no longer engaged in tuition: and it's rather like hanging up your sword & Sam Browne in your best parlour after demobilisation." But for now it was a valuable acquisition because it qualified Christopher to run his own school. He was keen to get started on this and the end of March 1901 saw him duly recorded in the national census as the headmaster of a small Catholic school. He had decided to settle on the outskirts of London and had found a house called The Priory in High Elms, Woodford Wells which lay in Essex just a few miles to the north east of the metropolis. Christopher already had two pupils boarding at his school and was probably teaching other boys who attended daily. He might have temporarily employed a young teacher named Richard Woods (who was staying at The Priory in 1901) and he had found a housekeeper called Mary Connor, a widow in her fifties, to look after the school's domestic arrangements.

The school probably closed for the Easter holidays soon after the night when the census was taken and Christopher was certainly in Oxford at the end of April when he attended the wedding of his youngest sister, Dorothy Virtue, to the Manchester-born cleric, Arthur Wells Hopkinson. Christopher dutifully agreed to take on the role of elder brother and he accompanied his sister down the aisle. Dorothy looked lovely in her dress of ivory duchesse satin, trimmed with lace and pearls, and with a yoke and sleeves of tucked chiffon. Her head was covered by a tulle veil and, she carried a wreath of the traditional orange blossom. No doubt Christopher's mother and his sisters and brothers all attended the wedding too. Paul was now aiming for his own higher degree in order to become a cleric, but Baldwin had already decided not to go to university and instead had started training as an engineer.

After the wedding Christopher returned to Woodford Wells to his school (which seems originally to have been known as St Francis' College though he might well have already renamed it Priory School). For the rest of the year he probably taught there with the assistance of one or more temporary teachers. Then in 1902 he was joined by a new assistant master – a man called Alan John Alington.

Christopher already knew his new colleague well and almost certainly it was Christopher's brother, Paul Elwin, who had first introduced them. Alan, who was two years younger than Christopher, had been a pupil at St Edward's School at the same time as Paul. They seem to have got on well and Alan remained Christopher's close and loyal friend for many years. It seems likely that they were also lovers, at least at some stage.

Like Christopher, Alan came from a clerical family, and his father (Alan Marmaduke Alington) had studied in Oxford as Christopher's father had done, though he had attended Worcester College. In 1864 (the year that Christopher's father moved to Basingstoke) Alan Marmaduke became the rector in the large scattered village of Benniworth which lay above the valley of the river Bain in Lincolnshire. Two years later (again in parallel with James Elwin Millard) he married. His bride was a thirty year old vicar's daughter - Katharine Paulina Atwood – and Alan was their third son. However their first son died when he was just seventeen days old and when their second boy died at the age of twelve. Alan became the eldest surviving son and so he later inherited the Pye estate from one of his uncles. His father died when Alan was only fourteen and within a few years his widowed mother moved back to Oxford (where she had lived before her marriage) and Alan and his younger brother, Charles Winford, were sent to school there. Alan stayed at St Edward's School until the age of seventeen before spending time with a tutor in Weston Super Mare preparing for entry to his father's alma mater, Worcester. In his mid-twenties, perhaps influenced by Christopher, he converted to Catholicism which obviously ruled out a career in the Church of England so Alan, like Christopher, turned to teaching after graduation.

In 1903, the year after he joined Christopher in Woodford Wells, Alan qualified as Master of Arts and from this point onwards he seems to have run a school jointly with Christopher (rather than remaining as an assistant master). The two men continued working in Woodford Wells but they might have moved premises; their school was certainly run under a new name - Forest House School. It catered for about fifteen boys and several photographs of the school exist. These date from about 1910 and show a substantial three-storied stucco villa set back from the road behind railings with a large back garden of lawn and trees.

There are now few physical traces of Christopher's time in Woodford Wells and it seems that neither The Priory nor Forest House survives. But despite the busy road running through it today, Woodford Wells still has something of the air of the little eighteenth century hamlet which grew up along the high road leading to Newmarket when large houses were built for merchants from the city. Its medicinal springs were popular for a short period and a famous botanic garden was established there. By Christopher's time this hamlet had become a middle-class suburb with a number of schools including both smaller establishments, like St Aubyns, and larger ones, notably the well-known Bancroft's School.

The Catholic church of St Thomas of Canterbury still stands prominently by the main road - as it did in Christopher's time. Its foundation stone had been laid in 1895 (the year of Christopher's conversion) and at the same time a Franciscan community of about forty friars was established besides the church. St Thomas' could hold up to seven hundred worshippers and during their time in Woodford Wells Christopher and Alan must regularly have taken their young pupils to services there and have got to know the Franciscan friars.

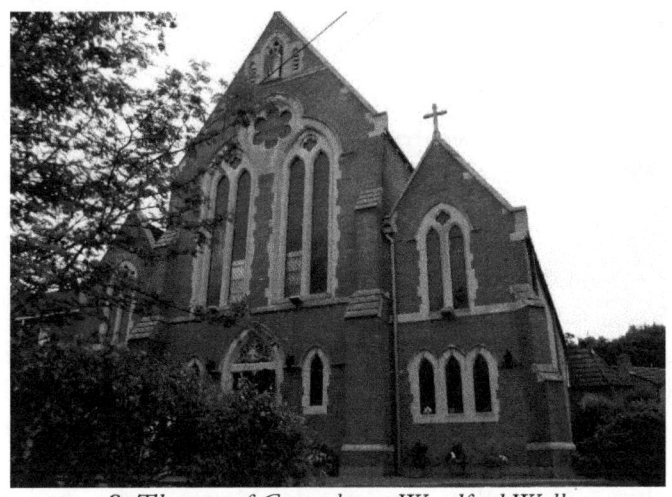

St Thomas of Canterbury, Woodford Wells

However Christopher did not remain a member of this congregation for very long because during the course of 1904 he moved away from Woodford Wells leaving Alan behind to run Forest House School alone. Christopher's first biographer, Harford Montgomery Hyde, suggested that Christopher was forced to leave the school after a scandal and speculated that this might have involved some kind of relationship with one of his pupils. It is perfectly possible that this is true, but there does not seem to be any evidence to support it. Christopher certainly remained close to Alan for the rest of his life and another possibility is that there were rumours at Woodford Wells about the nature of their relationship. But the fact that Alan stayed on at Forest School for several more years and that he then returned to Woodford Wells after the First World War makes it unlikely that he left under any cloud. Perhaps Christopher had simply decided that he no longer wanted the responsibility of running a school.

During his time at Woodford Wells, Christopher had apparently begun eagerly reading as much material by Oscar Wilde as he could find. Perhaps he had already become familiar with Oscar's writing whilst he was at Keble, though it could have been that his interest had initially been sparked by the news of Oscar's imprisonment and one reason that he was so motivated to track down his work was because he knew Oscar shared his own sexual orientation. Gradually he conceived the idea of compiling the author's definitive bibliography. This turned out to be an extremely demanding task, which eventually took him many years to complete. But he never abandoned the idea. No doubt he saw the project as a tribute to a man he very much admired.

In the summer of 1904 Christopher made his first journey abroad travelling to France with two friends on a trip that was inspired both by his fascination with Oscar and his enthusiasm for the Jacobite cause. One of his travelling companions was the forty year old American actor, Donald Bruce Wallace, who published an edition of Oscar's *The Picture of Dorian Gray* in New York in the same year. The other was the journalist and writer Robert Harborough Sherard (also in his forties) who had been Oscar's friend and was writing his biography. Both Donald and Robert were part of the network that had first formed around Oscar but which continued even after his death. It is clear that by this time Christopher had managed to gain entry to this circle and it is very likely that it was his fellow Jacobite, Alexander Teixeira de Mattos, who had made the introductions.

Together Christopher, Donald and Robert made a shared "Pilgrimage of Love" to Bagneux when they walked the mile from the tram stop at Arcueil to lay arum lilies and red and white roses in such profusion on Oscar's grave that it looked like "one nosegay". Christopher was particularly taken with Donald (who had photographed the flower-covered grave) describing him as "a most charming person" and "a beautiful personage" and saying lightly, "I quite fell in love with him in Paris." After the trip Donald returned to England before sailing back to New York on the *Etruria*.

Christopher also enjoyed spending that summer with Robert Sherard. At the time Robert (like Christopher) was not very well off and Christopher found him "very pleasant." However when he later became more successful and more pleased with himself, Christopher revised his opinion. He disliked much of Robert's work, including his books on Oscar, and eventually he declared Robert himself "unbearable with his fur coat and purse of gold."

During their time in France, the three men visited the Hotel d'Alsace to see the room in which Oscar had died. It had been carefully preserved and still contained the books and magazines he had been reading before his death. Christopher and his companions reverently examined them. There were two novels by Honore de Balzac, whom Oscar had long admired. One was *La Cousine Bette* which centres on a middle aged woman who plots with a younger unhappily married one to destroy the Hulot family. The relationship between the two women is often interpreted as a lesbian one. The other was *Eugenie Grandet* about a miserly father and his daughter whose relationships are unhappy but who eventually becomes a contended and wealthy widow. However Christopher found that much of the material in Oscar's room was about English prison life and this had clearly been one of his major preoccupations before his death.

As well as visiting places associated with Oscar, Christopher went twice to St Germain-en-laye which he was keen to visit because of its Jacobite associations. On his first trip he was accompanied by Robert, "the author of *The White Slaves of England* and other well-known books", who had a family link with Jacobitism because his ancestor "known as 'Galloping Harry Curwen' accompanied King James to France". Christopher was "allowed to place a large bunch of white roses on the monument" to

45

James II and was "pleased to notice traces of former tributes from Stuart admirers there" A few weeks later he went again, apparently alone, and in July whilst he was staying in the city of Vernon on the Seine between Paris and Rouen, he wrote an article about this second trip.

From the station at Poissy Christopher took the steam tramway up the very long hill to St Germain and the chateau where "our last legitimate sovereign lived from 1689 to 1701." The French king Louis XIV had given the palace and a generous allowance to James II, his wife and their young son when they were "driven from this country by the revolutionists." After James II's death, his son was proclaimed King James III on the palace terrace. Christopher admired the grand chateau and its grounds: "The gardens and terraces … are very fine … much more beautiful [than those of Hampton Court]" and he enjoyed the view: "Paris can be seen in the distance, the intervening space of twenty miles lessening considerably the gaunt ugliness of the Tour Eiffel, which raises its iron skeleton over the picturesque city on the Seine."

Christopher re-visited the church at St Germain with its "magnificent, though simple, marble monument to King James II" and again admired the floral tributes placed there: "Here is an example of 'things they do better in France', for, it will be remembered, that on the last occasion on which wreaths were placed on the tomb in Westminster Abbey of Mary, Queen of Scots, they were removed within a few hours 'by order of the Dean and Chapter'." Jacobitism was clearly a controversial issue in England. Christopher was impressed that, by contrast, in St Germain many of the local cafés proudly advertised 'rose blanche' [white rose] beer for sale. No doubt he enjoyed a glass or two!

He ended his article with a staunch defence of the Jacobite monarchs: "For over two hundred years have sovereigns of Britain been in exile, then as now, together with many of their subjects, the victims of iniquitous law and the oppressed of usurping and tyrannous oligarchy." No doubt this appealed to the readers of his article which subsequently appeared in the November issue of *The St Germains Magazine*, a Jacobite publication produced in London which sold for one penny.

Christopher was back in England by late summer and it was then that he moved to the outskirts of the Sussex village of Wadhurst. This had its own railway station on the line between London and Hastings and was located a few miles from the town of Tunbridge Wells. Here Christopher settled in the Beech Hotel, an old coaching inn about a mile or so from the station run by a young London-born man, Alfred Thomas Kerwin.

Beech Hotel, Wadhurst

Christopher might well have been attracted to Wadhurst because of the presence of a number of Catholic institutions in the area. There was a Rosminian monastery near the station with a chapel where Christopher could have attended mass and then just a few miles from Wadhurst was a Catholic boarding school for boys housed in buildings designed by Edward Welby Pugin.

In Sussex Christopher began coaching older pupils, possibly some of whom were from the boarding school. They were presumably young men either preparing for university or needing extra help with studying for their degrees. Nothing is known about most of his pupils, but they did include the twenty-year old Arthur Edward Joseph Noel (Viscount Campden) who came from an aristocratic Catholic family living at Exton Hall in Rutland. Perhaps Arthur was spending the Michaelmas term working towards examinations because Christopher was in Wadhurst throughout that entire period. He certainly worked hard as a tutor. He taught for five and a half days every week and only had Saturday afternoons and Sundays free. However when he was neither teaching nor reading, he must sometimes have gone walking in the local Sussex countryside and he occasionally travelled up by train to London too.

CHAPTER FIVE

OSCAR AND WALTER

"The flame of our friendship has burnt steady and bright" - *Walter Ledger in a letter to Christopher of 10 December 1924*

By this time Christopher had already begun to correspond with Robbie Ross, Oscar's former lover and it is quite likely that it was again Alexander Teixeira de Mattos, who suggested that they should get in touch. Robbie had loyally stood by Oscar throughout his trials and he had been with him when he died. Now he was working tirelessly as his literary executor in order to revive his reputation as an author and to protect his estate. Robbie would prove to be a supportive friend to Christopher too, and for the next fourteen years the two of them worked closely together.

It was Robbie who proposed that Christopher should make contact with another man called Walter Edwin Ledger, who seemed to be as keen as Christopher to produce a bibliography of Oscar's works. So on Sunday 27 November Christopher sent his first letter to Walter, and he received a reply two days later. At first he tried to persuade Walter to come down to meet him in Wadhurst: "I cannot get away very well except on a Saturday afternoon & then there is no train arriving in town till 3 pm which makes it rather late getting down to you. I suppose you would not care to accept my hospitality here for a night or two? It is only 1 ½ hours from London by a fast train."

But instead Walter invited him to his home in Wimbledon and on Thursday 8 December Christopher travelled up to meet him for the first time. Walter proudly displayed his library and Christopher was most appreciative: "Thanks so much for all your kindness yesterday. I enjoyed seeing your books immensely." Thus began a friendship that ebbed and flowed, but that lasted, despite difficulties and differences, for over twenty years.

Walter was about ten years older than Christopher and he was a kind and gentle man. He spoke knowledgeably in his distinctive high-pitched voice and he always read through a pair of steel-rimmed pince-nez. He was a cultured man interested in literature, art and music, and he was an accomplished pianist, who particularly loved playing pieces by Frederic Chopin, Like Christopher, Walter was gay, but he was much less comfortable with his sexuality and it is possible that he never actually had a sexual relationship with another man.

Although Walter was British, he had been born in the French city of Lille where he had been baptised in the British chapel on Thursday 17 July 1862. He was the son of John Ledger and the French-born Elizabeth Mary nee Bonsor whose father, James Bonsor, had been an amateur poet. Walter had a much older sister Anne Marie (Nanny), who was already fifteen when he was born, and a brother called Percy George. At first Walter was privately educated in France and his early exposure to both French and English helped him develop a facility for languages. Then after John Ledger died, Walter and his siblings moved to England with their widowed mother. At first they spent time in Leicestershire, but Walter then moved south where he began training as an architect. He was articled to a man called William Henry Crossland, who received the commission to design Royal Holloway College near Runnymede in Surrey. William Crossland involved young Walter in this project and it was later claimed that "a considerable portion" of the final design, which was based on the chateaux of the Loire valley, was "due to Mr Ledger's facile pen." However, although Walter retained an interest both in architecture and in drawing, he never practised professionally.

In his late twenties he moved to Wimbledon where he spent the rest of his life living on a private income and renting the house at 5 Wilton Road (later renamed Wilton Crescent). Unlike Christopher, he was close to his relatives and he shared Wilton Crescent with his sister for many years. They were joined there for a time by their elderly widowed aunt Clara Eugenia Lezain (their father's sister) and a loyal servant, Harriet Minnie Noble, looked after Walter and his relatives and came to be regarded as a family friend.

In his suburban villa Walter had money and leisure enough to indulge his passion for collecting books, prints and manuscripts and gradually he built up a very substantial collection. His acquisitions included a watercolour of *A Cottage Girl resting on her return from Market* by Richard Westall R.A., two watercolours of exotic birds by John Gerrard Keulemans, and a volume of prints of shipping by the artist Gerrit

Groenewergen. Of greater interest to Christopher, naturally, was Walter's extensive, and eventually almost unrivalled, collection of material by and about Oscar Wilde and his contemporaries. Walter had begun collecting this material in the 1890s and as his library grew he, like Christopher, had begun to think seriously of compiling Oscar's bibliography so he had contacted Robbie Ross in June 1902 to ask for his assistance. Gradually the two men had become friends and Robbie subsequently introduced Walter to Oscar's former lover Alfred Douglas.

Books, paintings and music were not Walter's only enthusiasms. He also loved sailing and over the years his face gained the weather-beaten look of a man who spent many days afloat. Even ashore he liked to dress as an old fashioned sailor in an open necked shirt with a blue and white collar, bell bottomed trousers, and a hat with the name of his beloved boat on its ribbon.

Furthermore Walter established not only a library at Wimbledon, but a garden, which eventually contained a magnificent collection of rare and unusual plants sent to him from many parts of the world, and through his enthusiasm for horticulture Walter made a number of friends. He had contacts both at Kew Gardens and at the John Innes Horticultural Institute in Merton, and their shared interest in plants brought him into contact with a man called Edward Augustus (Gussie) Bowles, who had a notable garden at Myddelton House in Enfield and who was an influential figure in the gardening world becoming the vice-president of the Royal Horticultural Society, writing extensively about gardening, and travelling widely to collect plant specimens. Walter soon came to regard Edward as his dear friend and later bequeathed him three keepsakes - a small oil painting of a Venetian boy by Eugen Blaas, a bronze statuette of Caesar Augustus, and a pair of candlesticks. It could well have been that through Edward, Walter became part of a small network of gay male gardeners, as he was part (if only peripherally) of a gay literary circle. There is no firm evidence about his friend Edward's sexuality, but Walter's gift to him of a painting of a Venetian boy seems suggestive because from the eighteenth century onwards Venice was home to one of the best known gay communities in Europe. Then Edward was known to have been close to another horticulturalist, Reginald Farrer (who had a garden in Clapham) and Reginald might well have been gay as his letters to his Oxford contemporary, Aubrey Herbert, provide evidence of an intense relationship between them.

Whilst Walter could share his enthusiasm for plants with Edward, he was delighted to find in Christopher someone who shared his equally strong enthusiasm for Oscar's work. Soon after they met the two men committed themselves to jointly producing the writer's full bibliography and they were quickly absorbed in researching the details of Oscar's life. Not everyone approved of this preoccupation. Robert Sherard warned Christopher, "I wish you could get your mind on other things. You cannot live for ever in the past!" though this might have been because he saw Christopher as a rival who was keen to get to the truths behind the stories Robert (and others like him) told about Oscar.

In any case Christopher ignored this advice and frequent letters began to flow between Wadhurst and Wimbledon as he exchanged information with his new friend: "I am sending you particulars of the 2nd D[aily] Chronicle letter and La Plume which I have just bought... Do you know this – Ave Imperatrix: A Dirge of Empire by Oscar Wilde ... This is a charming little book. I gave 21 shillings for mine." Christopher was soon trying to persuade Walter to publish the bibliography they were compiling: "It seems between us we have got nearly all the information obtainable. Will you write to Methuen & ask him to publish it. It would be a pity to let someone else slip in and spoil our labours."

Walter kept every letter Christopher wrote to him and carefully pasted them into five albums. At the front of each album Walter glued a copy of the bookplate which he had designed for himself and which reflected his varied interests. It shows a youthful sailor leaning back in his elegant chair, arms behind his head, looking out of the open window towards a ship sailing on the horizon. On the table in front of the window is a vase of daffodils and a book which the sailor has just laid aside. These albums now form part of the Robert Ross Memorial Collection at University College, Oxford. This largely consists of Walter's collection of more than eight hundred volumes either of, or about, Oscar's work. They are in a wide variety of languages including Russian, Finnish, Yiddish and Armenian and many are annotated by Walter. No doubt Christopher was familiar with many of these books.

Their friendship certainly developed rapidly. Within a few weeks of meeting they were already close enough to exchange Christmas presents. Appropriately enough these were items written by Oscar. Walter gave Christopher a "beautiful copy of The Harlot's House" - a handwritten transcript which Walter had decorated himself. Christopher was delighted: "It is really most good of you to take so much trouble over it for me." In return he sent "a copy of the Cornhill Booklet containing *The Ballad of Reading Gaol*" asking Walter to "accept it, trifling as it is, with my very good wishes."

Along with the booklet Christopher posted a copy of a newspaper to his new friend. This was the December edition of *Scottish Patriot* and Christopher was obviously very proud that he featured in its pages as an honorary Scot in the column called *Scots over the Border*. He was eager to share this achievement with Walter, though he requested, "When you have feasted your eyes on it long enough will you kindly forward it … as I have not another copy to spare." Above the complimentary text which discussed Christopher's Jacobite work, a recent photograph was reproduced. Signed "Yours loyally" it shows Christopher as a smartly dressed young man in a collar and tie with a neat central parting in his hair. His dark eyes gaze out, shaded under strong eyebrows. He looks calm and self-possessed. More the dapper man-about-town than the academic, it marks his gradual shift from teacher to writer and researcher.

Before the end of the year (probably at the end of the Michaelmas term) Christopher left Wadhurst to return to the Oxford area. At first he asked Walter to send letters to West Hagbourne (about ten miles south of Oxford) but by the middle of January 1905 he had moved into a little cottage called The Lawn in the village of Iffley. This was situated by a lock on the Isis a couple of miles downriver from the centre of Oxford. Despite its proximity to the busy university city, which was only about half an hour's walk away, Iffley was still a rural village with an old corn mill, a manor house and a Norman church. Here Christopher did continue to coach some students, but teaching was no longer his main occupation.

Soon after the move to Iffley, Christopher spent time away in Norfolk where he stayed at River House in Wroxham on the Broads. This was the home of the Catholic chaplain to Wroxham Hall, a position then occupied by a priest called Henry Stanley who might have played some role in Christopher's spiritual life. But Christopher's visit to Norfolk was only a brief one and by mid-February he was back at The Lawn.

CHAPTER SIX

THE ROAD TO PRISON

"He may keep the law and yet be worthless. He may break the law and yet be fine." from The Soul of Man under Socialism by Oscar Wilde

Soon after his return, Christopher received news that must have upset him though he made only a brief reference to it in his letter to Walter: "The Curate of Gillingham who died over a gas jet Tuesday night was a great friend of mine." Huyshe Worthy, his friend from Salisbury, had killed himself. He was thirty two years old.

Whilst Christopher had abandoned his ecclesiastical career, Huyshe had continued with his. After two years at the theological college where he had met Christopher, Huyshe moved to London to continue his studies at a college in Southwark. At the same time he began working as a curate at Christ Church in Clapham, a church which served poor parishioners most of whom lived in slum housing. He spent two years in Clapham and then he left London to take up another curacy at St Mary's in Strood in the county of Kent where he was soon joined by his mother and sister. After another two years he moved again and this time he was appointed as curate in Gillingham (also in Kent) where he worked alongside the incumbent at the church of St Mary Magdalene. His mother and sister moved into Gillingham House with him. However Huyshe was unwell during his time at St Mary Magdalene and in 1904 he was transferred to a curacy in Epsom in Surrey where it was hoped that his health would improve. His mother and sister remained behind in Gillingham, and Huyshe came back from time to time to visit them there.

He made the last of these visits on Tuesday 14 February 1905. He seemed well when he arrived at Gillingham House and his mother and sister noticed nothing wrong with him. He spent the evening of that Valentine's Day apparently contentedly "reading a novel in the drawing room prior to retiring." At about eleven o'clock he went to bed. Forty five minutes later his mother "noticed a bad smell of gas, and with the idea of calling her son to find out the cause went to his door, which he always locked, and knocked. She got no answer, and therefore concluded he was asleep, tired out after his long journey."

But next morning Huyshe did not get up. "Mrs Worthy, getting anxious, went to his bedroom and again knocked. Still she could get no reply, and thereupon called her daughter, who also failed." They couldn't get the door open so they called a neighbour, Mr Jackson, to help them break in. When they eventually managed to get inside they found Huyshe dead "lying on the hearthrug in front of the fireplace. He was wrapped in a blanket, which not only enveloped his head but also covered a gas tap where there had once been a gas-fire. The tap was found to be full on. The window was closed, and the register of the grate pulled down." Huyshe had used his cassock to completely block the grate which had ensured that the room had rapidly filled with gas.

In his letter to Walter, Christopher commented wryly that Huyshe "was always mad!" Perhaps all he meant by the word 'mad' was that his friend was mentally disturbed. Both Huyshe's sister and his doctor described him as an eccentric and excitable man and he could have been suffering from a mental illness during the year before his death. The verdict at the inquest was that Huyshe had been temporarily insane when he had committed suicide. However perhaps there was another meaning intended by Christopher's use of the term 'mad'. He had previously used it several times in his letters to Walter to refer to himself writing, for example, "I, too, am mad sometimes!" or signing his letter: "Madly as ever." Here this reads as though it might be a coded reference to his sexuality. In that case his use of the same word to describe his friend might have been intended both to communicate Huyshe's sexuality to Walter and to imply that this might have been a factor in his suicide. Christopher never seems to have referred to Huyshe again, but the brief comments in his letter to Walter almost certainly concealed strong emotions of shock, grief and anger.

A few days later another, rather different, event occurred, which also unleashed powerful emotions because on Thursday 23 February a version of Oscar's prison letter to Alfred Douglas (edited by Robbie Ross) was published under the title *De Profundis*. At this stage there was no indication that the letter was addressed to Alfred, and Robbie had removed several sections both to protect Alfred's feelings and to avoid provoking him. Initially this seemed to have worked and Alfred wrote an "excellent review" of the book in *The Motorist and Traveller* of 1 March.

Nevertheless the publication eventually contributed to a major rift between Robbie and Alfred as they fought for control over Oscar long after his death. The resulting feud dragged Christopher, amongst others, along in its wake.

Both Walter and Christopher were amongst the early readers of *De Profundis*, though Christopher apparently had to wait a few days for his copy of the book to be sent on to him. He was at his mother's at Wintney House, a substantial house of thirteen rooms in the Hampshire village of Hartley Wintney (about ten miles north east of Basingstoke) where she lived with Christopher's two unmarried sisters, Magdalen and Philippa, and employed a cook and a housemaid.

Christopher was pleased that *De Profundis* was generally well-received, though he actually thought that the work should have been published in its entirety. He avidly read the reviews and was pleased that "So far the *D. Chronicle* is the only one which writes unkindly or rather flippantly. *The Standard* & *The Morning Post* have so far had no notices. Perhaps they think the author is not quite 'respectable'." In fact members of the 'British Public' showed considerable hypocrisy towards Oscar's work as despite criticising his morals they were happy to profit financially from his writing. This annoyed Christopher: "What humbugs the B.P. are. As soon as it is a question of £.s.d. they are no longer shocked at the wonderfully wicked life led by the great reprobate." Nevertheless *De Profundis* did appeal to more open-minded clergymen and later that year when Christopher visited the Clarendon Hotel on the Cornmarket in Oxford he found "an old parson friend of mine" there, reading out excerpts from the work to the "bar-'lady.'"

Restless at his mother's in Hartley Wintney, Christopher was keen to return to The Lawn: "I return to Iffley on Wednesday. Deo Gratias. I so much prefer living alone: my relations are <u>so</u> tedious." He was back at Iffley by the beginning of March when he ordered six copies of the magazine in which Alfred's review of *De Profundis* appeared and continued to spend "more than I ought" on books by and about Oscar, which he confessed had an "immense fascination" for him. He added these to the growing collection at his cottage. Although he said that he liked living alone, Christopher was keen for his friends to visit him there. He invited Walter to come for a few days: "I can put you up with pleasure if you don't mind the discomforts of a really small cottage to which yours is a palace."

Later that same month Christopher met Edward Carpenter in Oxford. Edward had been considerably influenced by the poetry of Walt Whitman and become an adherent of socialist politics, a supporter of education for the working-class, and an advocate for women's suffrage. He believed strongly that gay love could undermine class boundaries and he had himself fallen in love with a working class man, George Merrill. They spent the rest of their lives together. It seems highly likely that Christopher was influenced not only by Edward's positive attitude towards his sexuality but by his socialism and he, too, committed himself to the idea of treating working class men as friends and equals. He sent Walter a copy of the advertisement for Edward's *Prisons, Police and Punishment*, which discussed the causes of crime and challenged society's responses to it. Presumably he read the book himself and a few years later no doubt both he and Walter were enthusiastic readers of Edward's *The Intermediate Sex*, the first widely available book in English to depict gay sexuality in a positive way.

During April Christopher had "a delightful week in Surrey--- the scene I can imagine of [Robert] Hichens' *Surrey Week* in the *Green Carnation*." His reference was to a satirical novel on the Aesthetic movement (published the year before Oscar's conviction) in which several Londoners spend a week at a country estate. The group includes two witty dandies antagonistic to conventional Victorian morality - Esme Amarinth, based on Oscar and Lord Reginald Hastings based on Alfred Douglas, and perhaps Christopher saw himself playing a similar role.

He continued to try to persuade Walter to collaborate on Oscar's bibliography and was eager to learn of his latest findings. When Walter tracked down Oscar's pieces in the literary magazine *Court and Society Review*, Christopher warmly congratulated him: "Bravo! You have indeed done well." The two men got as far as discussing how their names would appear on the cover of the bibliography: "No, my name will appear as STUART MASON and I shall not put M.A. so I think yours had better be Walter E. Ledger, or Walter Ledger, or W.E. Ledger, as you like."

Christopher now spent most of his days busy writing and Saturday 10 June was no exception though it would turn out to be a significant date. As usual he had a break for lunch when he visited a local public house for a pint or two of beer and he sent a letter to his friend and fellow Catholic, George Augustine Graham, who was shortly to pay a visit to

The Lawn. George was in his fifties and after studying in Bruges, he had been ordained as a Catholic priest. He was currently in charge of the church of Our Lady and St Thomas of Canterbury in Roxborough Park, Harrow on the Hill.

Then after finishing work for the day, Christopher set off to walk towards central Oxford as far as the Empire Theatre in Cowley Road which was well known for its variety acts. At around nine o'clock near the theatre he met a youth called Harry Tinson. Harry was a labourer who was employed by the Tramway Company and he lived nearby with his parents. He was accompanied by a friend – Cecil Henry Ferris Bryan - who lived and worked in his father's saddlery business in the High Street not far away. Harry and Cecil regularly met up to go to the Empire together and it seems likely that Christopher had seen them around before.

On that particular Saturday he invited them both for a drink and they accompanied him to a local public house -the Elm Tree. After spending about an hour there, they took a short walk to another public house - the Fir Tree on the Iffley Road – where Christopher paid for more rounds of beer. At about eleven o'clock all three left together. They crossed Iffley Road and headed not back towards the busier streets where Cecil and Harry lived, but down towards the river along Jackdaw Lane. At this time of night this was an unlit and secluded track and as they walked along in the dark Christopher made some overtures towards Harry. In fact it is difficult to avoid the conclusion that all three had deliberately chosen this quiet lane because of its possibilities for sexual activity.

On the following Saturday Christopher breakfasted at ten thirty. Later he went down to the river to bale out his punt and despite the showery weather he was out on the water from about one o'clock. He bathed at Long Bridges, which lay about a mile from Iffley on a quiet backwater close to Donnington Bridge, and ate his lunch by the river. He was back at The Lawn for tea at six o'clock and two hours later four of his friends turned up – Anderson, Bert, Arthur and another man. They did not stay very long and when they left Christopher walked back towards Oxford with them. They parted when they were in the vicinity of the Empire and Christopher headed for one of his regular drinking spots – probably the Elm Tree. On the way he bumped into Harry and Cecil again and invited them for another drink. They readily agreed and all three spent the next couple of hours drinking beer (again mostly bought by Christopher) first at the Elm Tree and then at the Fir Tree. Here they met up with some other youths who seem to have been well known to Christopher and who were described in his diary as the 'gang'. Harry and Cecil were probably part of this group and it seems that Christopher was in the habit of treating these young men to drinks and of chatting and flirting with some of them. They were joined by Christopher's friend George Augustine Graham, who was staying with him at The Lawn. Christopher bought drinks all round - lemonade for Walter Earle and beer for everyone else - and the entire 'gang' stayed perhaps right up until closing time.

All the young men then walked along with Christopher and George towards Iffley following the road for about twenty minutes as far as the bend known as Iffley Turn. Here most of the youths set off for home, but Christopher invited Harry and Cecil back to The Lawn. The walk took them about a quarter of an hour and it was around eleven thirty by the time they arrived. Christopher showed them into his front sitting room which was soon filled with a pleasant scent as Christopher burnt incense in the bowl which hung from the ceiling. The fragrance enhanced the general air of decadent luxury as the four men sat eating strawberries and biscuits, smoking cigars, and drinking wine and whisky. And after a while Christopher led Harry off into the bedroom and closed the door behind them. Back in the sitting room George allegedly began to caress Cecil and removed his jacket.

When Christopher and Harry re-emerged from the bedroom, everyone drank and smoked into the early hours of Sunday morning. Christopher then produced his little birthday book and asked Cecil and Harry to add their names to it, something which he seems to have regarded as a symbolic act of friendship. The two young men then departed but George offered to accompany them for part of the way into Oxford and as they walked along he asked them whether they would like to come on holiday with him. Cecil and Harry might have considered the idea seriously, though Cecil admitted that his father would not let him have a holiday. Soon after this exchange George took his leave and retraced his steps to The Lawn.

Neither Cecil nor Harry seemed unhappy with the evening's events at the time and it is likely that they were both willing participants in any sexual activity that took place - even though they later denied this. Harry claimed that he had told his mother about what had happened but Cecil did not mention any of it to anyone. He saw George a few months later when he was on his way to the fair at Botley, but they did not speak to each other. Almost certainly none of the four men gave the events of that June evening much further thought. But they would resurface later with a vengeance.

In his little cottage, Christopher continued working hard on his first book about Oscar. This was his translation from French of Andre Gide's essay on Oscar's last days. The account was quite a negative one, but it was an important early piece on Oscar and it did allude to sex between men. Christopher added notes to the text and attached an appendix which contained a list of Oscar's published writings. It formed Christopher's first step towards a complete bibliography. He asked Walter if he would be "sweet enough to run through it" and on the final page of the book he drew attention to the fact that he and Walter were preparing a full bibliography. By mid-summer the proofs of his translation were ready to go to Andre Gide who made some "quaint" suggestions and Christopher took a break of "a week on the river between here and Cricklade" returning "just before the weather broke".

On 16 September Christopher's short letter about *De Profundis* was published in the periodical *Notes and Queries* under the name 'Stuart Mason'. It clarified the fact that Robbie had edited the Methuen version using his discretion in deciding which passages to omit. The letter also drew the reader's attention to the fact that Christopher's forthcoming book would contain a list of Oscar's published writings and that a full bibliography was "in course of preparation". In October 1905 *Oscar Wilde: A Study from the French of Andre Gide with introduction, notes and bibliography by Stuart Mason* was duly published in Oxford by Holywell Press. 500 copies went on sale at 3s 6d along with 50 signed copies on handmade paper priced at 10s 6d. Christopher had dedicated this book to his American friend, Donald Bruce Wallace in memory of their visit to Bagneux the previous year. He sent copies to both Walter ("'with the author's love'") and Robbie, and he was pleased with his work. He was far from disheartened when *The Oxford Magazine* described it as "dull and uninteresting" merely retorting that the magazine itself was "run by a set of old dons – the quintessence of dullness and uninterestingness!"

He was also happy with the way Holywell Press handled the publication of his book and probably relieved too, because during the previous year he had had problems with another publisher. He had shared two photographs of Oscar and Alfred with a company called Wright and Jones (based at 350 Fulham Road in West London) which had offered to publish some of his own work. But Robbie was unhappy about this perhaps because the publisher was producing pirate editions of Oscar's work and he asked Christopher to retrieve the photographs. However Wright and Jones had already made copies to sell and refused to relinquish them. Christopher was annoyed: "If I can get up to town I shall call and give him a piece of my mind," he warned.

Christopher had not only been working on his translation that year. He was trying his hand at writing his own poetry and he sent one of his pieces to a competition in the periodical *Truth* (best known for its investigative journalism) which required contestants to produce a rhyme to 'chrysanthemum'. Christopher's entry (which did not win) reads: "It is full autumn! Drearier the sound/Of forest tempest-rock'd is than the hum/Of bees that, not alighting, hover round/Thy florets, many-hued Chrysanthemum!" Christopher was not a very talented versifier, but might well have liked to imagine himself as a poet following in Oscar's footsteps. At the same time he keenly read the work of members of Oscar's circle and was pleased when a young friend, who worked at James Tregaskis' London bookshop, agreed to secretly copy a sonnet by Alfred Douglas.

Christopher was unable to buy all the poetry books he wanted because money was an on-going problem (despite the publication of his first book). Soon he was even considering selling items from his much loved library: "I am not keen on parting with any of my Wilde books except duplicates, but as I cannot live on love and roses the dreadful prospect of being compelled to do so looms large and savagely on the horizon." He was not averse to trying to get money from his relatives when he was short of funds: "I am trying to negotiate with a rich young cousin of mine to help me pay my debts (£200) on the strength of some money due to me on the death of a relative. But relatives know not how to live or when to die." Nevertheless although he needed money he continued to avoid his relatives as far as possible. "I am not going to the Isle of Wight after all. It is too full of my relations, and I prefer solitude and independence, even with poverty as a handmaid, to being interfered with and badgered." Although he seems to have disliked most of the members of his extended family, they certainly had traits in common and his cousin, Charles Killick Millard, shared his willingness to champion unpopular causes. Charles Killick's particular interest was in medical matters and he argued forcefully both for vaccination and against the isolation of patients with scarlet fever. Even more controversially he was in favour of voluntary euthanasia.

With no money forthcoming from his family, Christopher's lack of funds eventually put paid to a plan he had conceived of producing covers for some of his books. He had asked Walter for some designs knowing his friend had a talent for drawing. "You are so clever at it," he cajoled. Walter was flattered and produced several drawings in response. Christopher was very pleased with them: "Your designs are really delightful, especially the shamrock one" but had to concede, "I fear the expense would be too heavy."

Despite his money problems, Christopher was growing in confidence in both his political and his literary activities and he seemed to be increasingly assured about his sexuality too. A new flirtatious note emerged in his letters to Walter over the course of 1905. He ended them with more affectionate phrases: "Ex corde", "Yours with accumulating affection", "Toujours a toi", "Ever to thee" and was increasingly open about his interest in gay sexuality sending Walter a newspaper cutting: "Fancy two Lesbian and Sapphic lovers in our prosaic XIX or XX century! The husband, curiously enough, is charged with immorality with boys. So wags the world along." He alluded to Oscar's sexual activity saying of John Moray Stuart-Young's recent book *Osrac*, "He is very insistent on repeating that he was not corrupted by Oscar. I am not surprised, though I fear at times O. did go rather low," and he exchanged photographs with Walter sending: "Countless tas for your letter and all your pretty sayings. If I am really so nebulous in your vision perhaps the accompanying counterfeit presentment of myself will recall me to your memory. I have your features firmly in mind, but, still, if you have a photograph to spare I shall delight in it."

Walter seemed to respond to Christopher's overtures. He asked ingenuously what Christopher meant by 'Ex corde', though he must have known the Latin. Christopher replied in the same strain, "I have never thought of digging very deeply into the meaning of 'Ex corde' and suppose it is simply 'From my heart'." In October the usually strait-laced Walter even seems to have opened up about his own (presumably solitary) sexual activities to an extent that Christopher had possibly not anticipated. Nevertheless he responded immediately. "Your last letter shows you in rather a new light! I, too, am mad sometimes! What is a 'love-vibration' and is 'twice a week' enough?" He continued to refer to his own sexuality and on 2 November he wrote with some sense of pride, "I am browsing through Max Nordau's *Degeneration* again. I seem to have in myself several of the symptoms which he attributes to the Degenerate."

Max Nordau's book is an extended attack on over-emotional, immoral and self-absorbed 'Degenerates' and on many aspects of modern culture. It criticises many major contemporary figures including John Ruskin, Paul Verlaine, Friedrich Nietzsche, Emile Zola, and Henrik Ibsen who is condemned for favouring anarchy and attacking marriage. Oscar Wilde himself is described as an antisocial egomaniac, who wanted to create a sensation, courted contradiction, and admired immorality. Other causes close to Christopher's heart are seen as symptomatic of psychological disorders thus Max Nordau claims that those attracted to Jacobitism suffer from excessive self-esteem and a desire for dogmatic argument, as well as an unfocused discontent and an inability to adapt.

Where Max Nordau considers sexual matters his main concern is with heterosexuality. However towards the end of his book he includes a passage which attacks those who dress in ways that challenge gendered conventions: "men [who] clothe themselves in a costume which recalls, by colour and cut, feminine apparel. Women who wish to please men of this kind wear men's dress, an eyeglass, boots with spurs and riding-whip." He goes on to claim that "The demands of persons with the 'contrary' sexual sentiment that persons of the same sex can conclude a legal marriage has obtained satisfactions, seeing they have been numerous enough to elect a majority of deputies having the same tendency."

Christopher is unlikely to have taken *Degeneration* very seriously and, if anything, it would have reinforced his commitment to the causes he believed in. But more difficult to deal with was the fact that he could not discuss the things that were closest to his heart with any of his relatives. Nevertheless he felt obliged to spend Christmas 1905 at his mother's. "As for my relations with my relations I want to offend them but they won't be offended. I want to quarrel with them but they won't be quarrelled with, and write me letters begging me to go home for Christmas. But I loath the festive season and politics and religion have fixed a big gulph[sic] twixt them and me." In spite of this he was pleased to receive a Christmas present from Walter - a copy of Walter's own article on his local church.

Soon after Christmas, Christopher became actively involved in the Labour campaign for the forthcoming general election: "The delirious delights of electioneering have knocked all things literary out of my mind." His own money problems must have helped him to become aware of the hardships of poverty and this, combined with his strong desire for justice, led him to develop an interest in socialist politics, which no doubt his contact with Edward Carpenter had fostered. It was a commitment which he retained for the rest of his life. In the event the Labour Representation Committee (which became the Labour Party after the election and which was a coalition of socialists and trade unionists) gained 29 seats in the 1906 election whilst the Liberals secured a large majority. Both benefitted at the expense of the Conservative party and the result seemed to mark a significant turning point in domestic politics. The new government was a progressive one and it introduced a number of the changes for which Christopher's party had campaigned including the introduction of state pensions and of unemployment and sick pay.

Christopher began suffering from a bad cold at the start of January 1906 and he acquired a sore throat which he could not shake off. Perhaps he had tonsillitis. When his friend George Augustine Graham heard about his illness he invited him to visit him in the seaside resort of Ilfracombe in North Devon where he was now living. Christopher gratefully accepted and spent several weeks with George at The Presbytery in Runnacleave Road, which was attached to the church of Our Lady, Star of the Sea. He enjoyed the break and on his way back to Iffley he stopped for a night either at Bristol or at Bath in order to "go the round of the bookshops."

He was pleased to be back at The Lawn though where he continued his research on Oscar at the Bodleian Library and elsewhere. He investigated Oscar's life in considerable detail, for example checking the information on his baptismal certificate by ordering a copy from Dublin. Walter was always keen to hear the results of his investigations and Christopher knew this and tantalised him by teasing, "However, possess your soul in patience and I will try and find out more on the morrow."

By now Christopher had become an integral part of the circle of Oscar's friends and followers and was writing to various people who had known Oscar personally. One of his regular correspondents during this period was John Moray Stuart-Young, the author of *Osrac*, who was then living

64

in Nigeria and who had relationships with both men and women. But members of Oscar's circle did not always get on well. Robbie did not like John and regarded him as "a dreadful person" who was "simply an ex male prostitute." Eventually Christopher fell out with him too, after the publication of John's next book *An Urning's Love*. This "GHASTLY production" made him "disgusted" with its author and he determined to "chuck correspondence with him. Not that there is a word of impropriety in it -- far from it – it is deadly dull."

In March Christopher went to stay with Walter and his sister again: "I will come down to Wimbledon in the evening and we might go up to town together on Saturday morning." Presumably Walter and Christopher spent an enjoyable day browsing in the bookshops together. The two men had gradually grown closer and their letters reveal their increasing intimacy. Whether their relationship would have continued to develop is impossible to say. Things were about to go badly wrong for Christopher, and his life would never really be the same again.

But for now he was unaware of what lay ahead. He was always happier in the "sunshine of Spring and Summer" and that April Christopher enjoyed walking in the countryside around Iffley and spending time on the river. On Tuesday 3 April he sent Robbie some flowers he had picked whilst walking in the local meadows and a week later on Wednesday 11 April he had a long country walk to Nuneham Woods which reminded him of Oscar's poem, *Ravenna*, as they were one mass of "the primrose, pale for love uncomforted". The next day was "a glorious day" and Christopher spent the afternoon on the river.

Meanwhile his friend, Walter, spent much of that spring and summer aboard the three-ton *Shrimp*, a boat which he owned for twenty years. He usually sailed her alone and he undertook some extended journeys which included sailing the little cutter all the way by river and canal from the Thames to the Severn and back. His continued enthusiasm for life afloat led him to support several naval charities particularly The Royal Sailors Orphans Girls School and Home in Hampstead and the Mercury Training Ship for Boys which was based on the Hamble near Southampton.

Walter was still involved in Oscar's bibliography and Christopher certainly remained committed to the idea of publication. Robbie had arranged for the book to be produced by Methuen and had agreed to pay half of the costs involved. Christopher was also helping Robbie edit Oscar's complete works and his research included a letter to *Notes and Queries* requesting information about Oscar's poem *Roses and Rue*, which had appeared in a journal called *Society* that was not held at the British Museum. Although Christopher had advertised, he had "not succeeded in procuring a copy" which he wanted for the volume of poems for "Messr Methuen's forthcoming uniform edition of Oscar Wilde's works." In his letter (published in the issue of 5 May) Christopher made sure he promoted this book by promising it would include "at least one unpublished poem of exquisite beauty".

But both the bibliography and the collected edition were still works in progress. Christopher's second publication, which appeared that April, was a shorter work - an edition of Oscar's *Impressions of America* for which Christopher had written an introduction. The book, priced at 2s 6d, was published by Keystone Press (based in Sunderland) and Christopher dedicated it, "To Walter Ledger: Pignus Amicitiae" as a token of their friendship. Possibly on the strength of this latest book Christopher ordered some new clothes from a firm of Oxford outfitters. In addition to the cheaper copies, fifty numbered and signed books went on sale at five shillings each and doubtless one went to Walter.

On Easter Saturday (14 April) Christopher left The Lawn for a short break in Hassocks in the South Downs, where he stayed at the Downs Hotel, and afterwards he spent a day in London to visit Robbie, who was busy moving house. He then returned to Iffley and over the course of the following week two things happened which would lead to his arrest.

On the morning of Friday 20 April Christopher asked a local young man, a baker's son named Sidney Jackman, to get him some 'snakes-heads' - presumably the flowers known as snake's head fritillaries which grew in profusion in the ancient Iffley Meadows. Sidney duly gathered some bunches and took them round to Christopher's house soon after noon. Christopher asked him inside and then noticed Sidney's friend, Percival (Percy) Arthur Ludlow waiting at the gate and asked him to join them in the front room.

Percy was the son of a local boat builder and his family lived for a time at The Prince of Wales public house by the river at Iffley. He had known Christopher for about a year (though it is unclear whether he was part of the 'gang') and he willingly enough went inside. In the front room

Christopher produced his birthday book and (as he had requested Harry and Cecil to do the previous year) he asked Sidney and Percy to write their names and birthdays inside. Percy, who had just had his birthday, duly wrote his name on the page for April 10. Christopher then caught hold of him and fondled him briefly though he soon released him, possibly when Percy protested. Percy then walked out into the street but Sidney remained inside with Christopher for several minutes and, although he could have been remonstrating with Christopher over his behaviour, it seems more likely that he was engaging, probably not for the first time, in some kind of sexual activity with him.

Then Christopher spent the evening of Monday 23 April drinking with a friend and he didn't begin walking home until the early hours of Tuesday morning. As he neared The Lawn he passed the pumping station at Iffley and it was there that he encountered another young man, Thomas Bradbury, whom he had seen more than once before around the village. Thomas lived at home with his parents in Cowley and his background was rather a poor one. His father was a bricklayer's labourer and his mother worked as a charwoman. Thomas himself was employed as a labourer by the drainage contractors, Davies, Ball and Co. and was spending that particular night pumping water at intervals from a trench. In the gaps between pumping he walked back to the warmth of the watch-box about a hundred yards away, where the watchman, Frank Hall, sat by the fire and baked potatoes.

As Christopher passed the watch-box on his way home, Frank noticed him. He knew him well enough to invite him to join them by the fire. Christopher sat down and thankfully accepted a potato to eat. Keen to be sociable he then asked whether Frank and Thomas would like a beer and offered to fetch some from his house. But Frank already had beer in the watch-box and perhaps they all had a drink together before it was time for Thomas to go out into the cold to pump out the trench again. Christopher was keen to accompany him. Initially he challenged Thomas to race him to the pump but once they began to run he admitted that he was too tired (or perhaps too drunk) to keep going. Instead he walked alongside the young man and slid an arm around his shoulder.

The river at Iffley

Thomas told him not to come across to the pump as the ground was muddy but Christopher continued to follow and then he began to caress Thomas who apparently did not resist, at least at first, and did not call out to Frank for help, though later he said that he had been too frightened to protest and that might have been true. In any case things did not go very far because Thomas moved away to climb the fence around the trench. He warned Christopher that it was too dangerous for him to come down because the joints were off the pipes and Thomas then crept along the trench until he was out of sight. As Christopher waited he began working the pump himself for a short time before whistling and calling out to Thomas to encourage him to return. However he did not appear. Christopher tried again and then went back to the watch-box to fetch Frank. The watchman brought a lantern and helped him to search for Thomas. But they couldn't find him and concluded that he must have gone home.

At that point Christopher abandoned the search and headed off towards The Lawn. Once Thomas had seen him leave, he felt it was safe to climb up out of the trench and he walked back to the watch-box where he complained to Frank about Christopher's behaviour. When Frank heard

Thomas' story, he set off after Christopher, but he did not follow him very far before giving up and returning to the watch-box. Thomas remained with him until six in the morning, continuing to pump out the trench as necessary, and he then went home. But when he got there he did not say anything to his mother about what had happened, nor did he say anything to his father when he came home from work that evening.

However Christopher was feeling anxious. He went back to see Frank on the following evening. Frank questioned him about what had happened with Thomas, but Christopher said he had been too drunk to remember anything. He left Frank a shilling to treat Thomas to a bottle of beer and he no doubt hoped that this would be enough to smooth things over.

But an official complaint must have been made because at about 4.30 pm on Friday 27 April two policemen arrived at The Lawn with a warrant for Christopher's arrest. They met him coming out of his front gate and ordered him back into his house. In the sitting room where he enjoyed entertaining his friends, he now found himself facing Inspector Timms who cautioned him and then read out the warrant. Initially Christopher seems to have misunderstood the charge as one of assault rather than gross indecency and he protested, "I know absolutely nothing about it. I was drunk at the time and did not remember anything about it until the next morning. I found my boots very muddy. I must have been helping him do the pumping."

During the late nineteenth century The Offences Against the Person Act and the Criminal Law Amendment Act had both been implemented. These had not only reinforced pre-existing restrictions on gay sexual activity but had stressed that not only anal sex (which had long been the focus of hostility) but all forms of sexual activity between men were prohibited. Twenty years before Oscar had felt the effect of this homophobic legislation. Now it was Christopher's turn.

He was charged with gross indecency with Thomas Bradbury - a term which covered any sexual activity between men apart from anal sex and which carried a maximum penalty of two years imprisonment with hard labour. He was then remanded in custody in Oxford Prison to await his hearing. Because he needed assistance he was forced to turn to his relatives and no doubt he did so reluctantly, particularly because he had to reveal the details of the charges he faced, to his mother amongst others. Almost certainly she was very shocked but nevertheless she asked her nephew, George Sclater-Booth, to organise legal representation. Although his Sclater relatives did provide practical support, Christopher must have hoped for greater sympathy when he wired to Robbie expecting that, as a fellow gay man, he would be more understanding. Robbie responded by travelling to Oxford to see Christopher in prison. Initially Christopher was optimistic about the outcome. He protested his innocence and declared, "I am in strong hopes of being acquitted at the Assizes."

But before this he faced the initial hearing on Saturday 5 May at the Bullingdon Petty Sessions which were held at the County Hall next to the prison and where Christopher was represented by Harry Turrell. Robbie attended to demonstrate his support though he only stayed for part of the hearing as he found the evidence distressing. Both Thomas and Frank were in court to give their versions of events, but Christopher's representative argued that there was little evidence to support the charge and suggested that Thomas had not been an unwilling participant.

By this stage, though, a second more serious charge had been made. This concerned the events of the previous summer involving Harry Tinson. It was alleged that Christopher had indecently assaulted Harry and tried to "commit and perpetrate the abominable crime of buggery." If he had been found guilty of having had anal sex, Christopher would have spent at least ten years in prison. Eventually, however, this charge was abandoned; indeed it was often a very difficult charge to prove.

Christopher was refused bail and was remanded in custody for a further seven days reappearing at the Bullingdon Petty Sessions on Saturday 12 May. This time it was Harry Tinson (then living in Hertford Street) who appeared as a witness. By now yet a third charge had been brought against Christopher that "being a male person" he "unlawfully did commit a certain act of gross indecency with another male person" - Percival Arthur Ludlow.

Additionally a second arrest had been made. Inspector Timms had travelled to Ilfracombe with a warrant for the arrest of Christopher's friend, George Augustine Graham, which he issued on Monday 7 May. George was brought to Oxford on the 1.35 pm train from Ilfracombe and he too appeared at the Bullingdon Petty Sessions on 12 May. He was accused of committing an act of gross indecency with Cecil Bryan, who was summoned to the hearing from Salisbury Plain where he was training with the Berkshire Militia. The magistrates decided that both George and Christopher should be sent for trial at the Oxford Assizes. George was released on bail, but Christopher remained in custody and was probably still in prison when on 20 June Robert Harborough Sherard's book *The Life of Oscar Wilde* was published which contained a sixteen page list of Oscar's works that Christopher had prepared before his arrest.

The Oxford Assizes opened on the following day - Thursday 21 June - at eleven o'clock in the morning and were presided over by Sir John Compton Lawrence. The fifth case heard that day was that against George Graham for gross indecency. George was defended by Charles Frederick Gill who drew attention to the inconsistencies in Cecil Bryan's evidence. When the judge gave his final address to the jury, he emphasised that Cecil had been very drunk on the evening in question and that he had not spoken about the incident until about a year later. The jury retired to consider their verdict and took twenty five minutes to find George not guilty.

By late afternoon it was Christopher's turn to face three separate charges to each of which he pleaded not guilty. Christopher's cousin (George Sclater-Booth) had engaged a leading barrister, Charles Willie Matthews, as Christopher's defence counsel (assisted by Harry Turrell). It was Charles who in 1895 had represented Oscar when he unsuccessfully sued Alfred Douglas' father for libel. He was instructed in Christopher's case by Arthur Newton, possibly the solicitor who helped Lord Arthur Somerset avoid prosecution when the police discovered a male brothel in London's Cleveland Street in 1889.

The prosecution, led by Hugh Sturges, began by setting out the evidence against Christopher related to the charges involving Percival Ludlow and Thomas Bradbury. By the time this was done it was already five o'clock and the court was adjourned for the day. Christopher was released on bail putting up £1000 in his own name with his brother Paul Elwin putting up a similar amount. Neither of them had that much money so presumably it had been supplied either by their mother or by other relatives.

That night Charles Matthews arranged a meeting with Christopher. His message cannot have been a particularly welcome one. After having heard the evidence so far and having weighed up his client's chances he told him bluntly that he did not think that he could persuade a jury that

Christopher was entirely innocent of all the charges. Eventually Christopher agreed to follow his advice and when the court resumed at ten thirty the following morning Charles informed the judge that his client had decided to plead guilty to the charges involving Thomas Bradbury and Percy Ludlow. In his turn Hugh Sturges agreed not to offer any evidence on the charges involving Harry Tinson and the jury was instructed to find Christopher not guilty of these.

Having got the more serious charges out of the way Charles Matthews felt able to ask the judge to show leniency in sentencing saying that Christopher's reputation had previously been good and that there were men in court who were willing to speak for him. He argued that Christopher's actions in April should be seen as due to "some sudden obsession, confined to a very limited period of time" an argument which only worked because the charges relating to the previous year had been dismissed. The judge apparently accepted this when he sentenced Christopher to three months with hard labour telling him that he had brought disgrace upon himself and that part of his punishment would be his loss of character. Christopher rapidly found himself back in Oxford Prison. Ironically this has now been converted into a hotel and some of its cells (perhaps even the one Christopher occupied) are now guest bedrooms. The time he spent within its walls did not deter him from continuing to have sexual relationships with men. But it did scar him. For many years afterwards he had nightmares in which he imagined that he was back in prison and when the writer Osbert Burdett met him he immediately saw that "the shadow of calamity had dimmed him."

Harder to bear than the conditions in prison was the sense of betrayal he felt. This was uppermost in his mind when he confessed to Walter: "One of my friends tells me I am become 'hard and cynical'". He had thought of the young working class men in the 'gang' as friends and he felt they had turned against him. The 'evidence' against him was "all the result of blackmail and 'revolting malice'" and his trust had been betrayed: "It will be a lesson to me in future not to carry the principle of my 'social democracy' to the length of making friends with the lower classes and trying to treat them as equals….all my schemes of 'elevating the masses' & ignoring social distinctions have received a rude shock!"

The working class youths themselves no doubt saw things differently. Cecil, Harry and Sidney do seem to have willingly engaged in gay sexual activity but they might nevertheless have considered that Christopher and

George, who were both middle-class men, were fair targets for blackmail. Perhaps they felt too that they had been exploited by men who were considerably older than themselves. However their relative youth does not necessarily mean they were naïve about sexual matters and it seems more likely that their main concern was to protect themselves from imprisonment by refuting any suggestion that they had consented to sex.

Christopher's overtures towards both Thomas and Percy make more uncomfortable reading, though here too it is difficult to be sure exactly what happened. Once such encounters became the subject of a court case it was in the interest of all the participants to lie about their involvement. In fact the law did not protect gay men either from blackmail or from sexual exploitation. Of course the temptation as a biographer is to exonerate Christopher from any suggestion of sexual coercion. However it must be acknowledged that Thomas doesn't seem to have been part of the 'gang' and Percy was at most a peripheral member. This makes it more likely to have been true that neither had wanted to take part in any sexual activity. But this is still far from certain because men in their position almost invariably described themselves as innocent victims of unwanted advances regardless of the truth of the matter.

Probably at worst Christopher was guilty of misreading the signals. When gay sexual desire was so ruthlessly suppressed and could only be expressed covertly, misunderstandings were almost inevitable. As a gay man Christopher took a risk every time he approached someone for sex and he could only try to minimise that risk. He could wrongly have assumed that Percy's association with Sidney meant that he, too, would be a willing partner if Christopher made the first move. When, as in the case of Thomas, he met someone by chance and so was less sure of his ground, he began by making tentative advances to see how the other man responded. If he did not seem to protest, Christopher then assumed he could go further.

No doubt he had time in his prison cell to brood on his errors of judgment and to nurse his resentments. In addition he was anxious about all the books he had left behind at The Lawn. He thought Walter would help so he used up one of the limited number of letters he was allowed to ask his friend if he could "manage to come up to Oxford one day and go through my books and remove all the ones which I have collected for the Bibliography. I can think of no one else who will be able to pick them

out … I do not want to have to part with them if I can possibly help it."
He even hoped that Walter would be sympathetic enough to agree to
visit him in prison: "You can also call and see me here if you like and we
can have a ½ of an hour's chat."

But Walter had been deeply troubled by Christopher's imprisonment and
by the events that had led up to it. He was keen to distance himself from
the whole affair and refused to come to Oxford. He made no contact
with Christopher for the next four and a half months.

CHAPTER SEVEN

CHARLES SCOTT MONCRIEFF

"Mind of my intimate mind, I may claim thee lover" from a poem by *Charles Kenneth Scott Moncrieff addressed to Philip Bainbridge and published in the introduction to Charles' translation of La Chanson of Roland*

When Christopher was released from prison in late summer he had to find somewhere to live as he could not return to The Lawn. His books had probably been retrieved from Iffley by Robbie, who had taken them to his house in London. But it was Christopher's brother, Paul Elwin, who offered Christopher himself a place to stay.

Unlike Christopher, Paul Elwin followed closely in their father James' footsteps. He studied for his degree at James' college (Magdalen) and then worked towards his ordination by studying at Cuddesdon Theological College (a few miles south east of Oxford). At the age of twenty three he was sent as a curate to Forest Gate which lay to the east of London. Here he began working at the church of St Edmund, King and Martyr which had opened just a few years previously. Worship followed a ritualistic High Church tradition which appealed to Paul Elwin (as it had to his father). As a young curate he was given lodgings at the vicarage next door to the church and it was here that Christopher joined him. (The church has now been replaced by flats, but the large vicarage, where Christopher stayed with his brother, remains - though converted into a multi-use centre. There is a figure of *Christ Triumphant* from the church mounted high on a side wall, whilst some of the church fittings and glass were re-used inside the chapel which forms part of the centre.)

St Edmund's Vicarage, Forest Gate

At least Christopher had a roof over his head as he prepared to face the future. His major concern was his precarious financial position: "I must sell most of my collection as I shall not be able to afford to add to it. The costs of my trial amounted to so many hundreds of pounds that it makes the luxury of book collecting impossible." Because of his prison record, he found it difficult to get work and again he approached Robbie for assistance. Robbie proved very helpful and organised a position for Christopher at the *Burlington Magazine*, an arts magazine based at 17 Old Burlington Street. It was edited by Lionel Cust and Roger Fry with the assistance of Robbie's old friend, William More Adey. Christopher might well have found William sympathetic because he too, had studied at Keble and subsequently become a Catholic convert. Robbie also offered Christopher secretarial work for which he paid him generously. This mainly involved continuing to help with the editing of the volumes of Oscar's complete works, which were being prepared for Methuen.

There were other friends, who were sympathetic towards Christopher as well, though it was apparently only Robbie who combined compassion with practical assistance. Christopher had fallen out with Robert Sherard before his imprisonment, for example, but heard that he "wrote sympathetically to a friend of mine during my troubles." In late September Christopher also tentatively renewed contact with Walter, though he was unsure of the reception he would receive: "Only just a line to tell you where I am in case you care to write. After what has happened, of course I leave it entirely to you."

Despite his reservations, Walter did reply. He kept the draft of his own letter which he had clearly found difficult to write. "I have had," he began. Then he started again, "You, my poor friend". He must have thought this sounded patronising and he crossed out "my poor friend." He tried again for the third time. "You have been a good deal in my thoughts, and I was pleased to hear from you. I hope you never thought I was lacking in charity in the time of your trouble." He tried to justify not having written before: "My silence was due in good measure to inability to be of any use to you."

No doubt it was true that he hadn't known what to say. But although he felt sorry for Christopher, he was adamant that he no longer wanted to be involved in the publication of a joint bibliography. He was desperate to prevent his own sexuality from coming under scrutiny and unwilling to upset his relatives: "We are none of us able to act with perfect freedom & situated as I am I fear it will not be possible to renew our former collaboration." In fact he had already expressed reservations about the project even before Christopher's arrest. He enjoyed the research involved, but did not want the pressure of publication. "I have no idea of turning this hobby into a harassing drudgery for months to come." But he must have been wary of publicly associating his name with that of Oscar Wilde, and his fears must have multiplied after Christopher's imprisonment.

He did assure Christopher that, "my collection of O.W books is always at your service," although he was no longer comfortable about inviting Christopher to Wimbledon: "If ever you want to see any I can send them to you." Christopher realised how uneasy Walter felt and he did not push for a meeting. Later he explained, "I would have asked you over to Forest Gate … only I had a feeling that after what took place last year you might not care to come."

During the autumn Christopher spent several weeks "by the sea in Norfolk" before returning to Forest Gate where he continued to try to come to a decision about the bibliography. At times he thought of abandoning the project writing to Walter, "I do not think I can ever do it independently of you and it would hardly be fair to publish it under my name alone, though I fully understand, of course, that you do not wish your name to appear in collaboration with mine after what has occurred." Thanks to Robbie, Christopher was at least earning some money, but it was not enough to prevent him being forced to put his collection up for sale: "It nearly breaks my heart to part with them all." He did continue to look for more items to help him with his research: "I am on the track of several unpublished poems in MSS at present in Philadelphia, in the collection of a millionaire. I shall be quite content if I can get a copy". But he could no longer envisage owning original material and the enforced sale of his books continued to rankle: "I bitterly groan at times over my lost collection of O.W. but it was inevitable, I suppose."

Still Robbie was generous towards him both financially and socially and Christopher was always very appreciative. By now Robbie had introduced him to Frederick Stanley Smith (Freddie) who was Robbie's lover and, at the time, was employed as his secretary. When Freddie later relinquished this role, Christopher took it on. Robbie acknowledged Christopher's dedication and hard work, but there were also times when he rather unkindly disparaged his "trivial little works" behind his back and he never regarded him as particularly original or creative.

As the end of 1906 approached, Christopher had occasional breaks from the routine of work. He went to Ealing "to see *The Importance of Being Earnest* ...by an amateur society calling themselves 'The Hypocrites'" and just before Christmas he had a few days in Warwick, which he described as a "delightful old town." More delightful still was the fact that Robbie introduced him to a handsome young Scot named Charles Kenneth Scott Moncrieff, who was then seventeen. Charles was at Winchester College as Alfred Douglas, Oscar's great love, had been twenty years before. Christopher was immediately attracted to this striking young man with strong features, dark blue eyes and a clear but gentle voice, who could be by turns both charming and moody. It was not long before they embarked on a relationship in which intellectual and erotic pleasures both played a part. The relationship with Charles was an important one for Christopher. As fellow gay men, who moved in the same social circles, their lives remained entwined from this point onwards. They stayed in contact for the rest of their lives and Charles was to write warmly of Christopher after his death.

Charles had been born on 25 September 1889 in Stirlingshire. He was the third son of a lawyer and was related not only to a wealthy merchant, but to an undersecretary of Scotland and a senior army engineer. He had two older brothers Colin and John who were already away at school when he was born so he spent long periods of time playing alone or reading. He quickly developed a great love for words and began making up poems. He rapidly learned a second language, French, from a nurse who spent a year with his family.

When he was seven, his family moved north to the little town of Inverness where he attended a small day school and at the age of nine he began boarding first at Inverness College and then at a preparatory school by the sea at Nairn where he enjoyed acting in the school plays. He won a scholarship to Winchester College when he came top in the Latin and Greek translation entrance examinations and joined the school in early September 1903 just before his fourteenth birthday. There he spent much of his time in the Moberley Library continuing to read voraciously. Mainly he read poetry and nineteenth century novels such as *Edwin Drood, Jane Eyre,* and *The Return of the Native* though in 1904 he acquired a copy of *The Challoners* by Edward Frederic Benson soon after its publication and probably identified with Helen Challoner who appears smoking and reading *The Mill on the Floss* in the lyrically described opening scene. Charles filled notebooks with extracts from his reading and continued to write his own poetry. He was renowned for his skill at parody, but he also carefully observed the natural world watching as the sun set in "lines of grey and lemon" and the colour "changed from orange to a dried blood tint."

At the age of fifteen he went to London to stay with his brother Colin. There he dined at his father's club, had tea at Lyons' and visited Madam Tussaud's. A few months later he spent a month with his family in Belgium first by the sea at Heyst-sur-Mer enjoying the celebrations to mark the feast of the Assumption, and then in Brussels. In the summer of 1906 (which Christopher spent in prison) Charles travelled to Switzerland to spend time by the lake at Lucerne.

So by the time he met Christopher at the end of that same year, Charles was already well-read, well-traveled, witty, and in love with both language and art. No doubt he had already been emotionally and sexually involved with some of his fellow pupils at Winchester (as his predecessor Alfred Douglas had been) and now he was confident enough to begin a relationship with the older, more experienced Christopher, who was a member of a social and literary circle which Charles was keen to join.

Quite how much Christopher and Charles thought of themselves as replaying the Oscar-Alfred relationship is a moot point. But it would have been surprising if the parallels had not occurred to them as they took on the respective roles of the older Oxford graduate, who was part of London's literary circle, and the younger, charming, occasionally petulant Wykehamist. Doubtless they also saw such a romantic attachment between an older 'teacher' and a younger 'student' as an embodiment of the Platonic ideal espoused in Ancient Greece. However the parallels with Oscar and Alfred would not be exact. Neither Charles nor Christopher became as notorious as their predecessors had been – though Christopher did have something of a reputation. In the long term their relationship was certainly a less stormy one and they remained good friends for the rest of their lives even after their sexual relationship ended. And undoubtedly it was the younger of the two who possessed the greater literary talent.

At Winchester, even before he met Christopher, Charles had begun employing this talent to express his sexual orientation. He edited a school literary magazine called the *New Field* and contributed poems both to this magazine and to others. These poems were apparently uncontroversial, because they were couched in classical terms. But through them Charles was exploring gay themes - most obviously in his *Hylas* which appeared in June 1906 when he was just sixteen. Here he uses Greek mythology (as other gay authors were doing) to legitimise love between men and to associate such love not with effeminacy but with the ideal of the warrior. In selecting this particular subject he might have deliberately intended to associate his sonnet with those works by Oscar which refer to the same Greek myth in which Hercules loves the beautiful Hylas and they are inseparable. One day when Hylas goes to fetch water from a stream he is seduced by the water-nymphs and vanishes without trace. In some versions of the myth he drowns whilst in others he goes to live with the nymphs in an underwater cave. But in each case although Hercules frantically searches for him he never finds him. Charles' octet emphasises Hercules' despair and ends with his cry of "Hylas come!" whilst the sestet opens with that cry unanswered – "Yet he came not" - and considers Hylas' fate. The poem clearly sympathises with the gay lovers and represents the heterosexual seduction as destructive: "Perchance he is not dead/ But rules their region and is fancied free;/ While lank-stemmed lilies, wreathed about his head,/ Rise to the air and plead for liberty."

Although he was fascinated by this captivating young man who was writing so confidently about gay subject matter, Christopher had to accept their time together was limited. They corresponded when they were apart but meetings had to be planned around Charles' school terms and Christopher's work commitments. In many ways things were becoming increasingly difficult for Christopher during the spring of 1907. Although he was enjoying his new relationship with Charles and was continuing to correspond with various people on matters relating to Oscar – his letter about *The Rise of Historical Criticism* was published in *Notes and Queries* on 5 January and his letter about *The Sphinx* appeared in the *Academy* on 23 February - he was feeling trapped in Forest Gate and wanted to get away. He complained that "These spring winds are dreadful and I wish I could get away to green fields etc", but the real issue was that he was well aware that he would continue to fall in love with men and to have sexual relationships with them, but he knew what the consequences were likely to be. He was convinced that his relationships were being scrutinised by the authorities and his fears were apparently well founded. It is thought that he was subject to intermittent police surveillance for years.

So, like a considerable number of other gay men, Christopher made the decision to move to France, primarily because of the country's more tolerant attitude towards homosexuality. "I have not been happy or comfortable in England since last year and I am sure it is for the best."

CHAPTER EIGHT

EXILE AND RETURN

"The things people say of a man do not alter a man." from The Soul of Man under Socialism by Oscar Wilde

As Oscar had done ten years before, Christopher took the boat train across the Channel to the seaside town of Dieppe, where in the summer, holiday-makers bathed in the water or strolled along the beach dressed in sailor suits and straw hats. However it was still too early in the year for the crowds and Christopher found it "a quiet little place out of the season." He was not entirely alone in Dieppe; there was a friend of Robbie's there, though he was "about the only man I know." Later Reginald (Reggie) Turner, another gay writer in Robbie's circle, came for two nights from Paris and Christopher saw something of Harold Mellor, who had known Oscar. But Walter declined to come over in his boat, pleading a mishap, but perhaps still uncomfortable around his friend.

Christopher settled at 47 Faubourg de la Barre about ten minutes from the sea front and on the whole he liked "being here better than Forest Gate, though it is quite as dull as the average English town, and I am rather bored at times." He did feel "rather out of the way of hearing of things" but "for many reasons", including the less hostile attitude towards his sexuality, he liked "French life much the best." He borrowed a bicycle and cycled the five miles along the coast to Berneval to see the "old landlord of the hotel where O.W. lived" – the Hotel de la Plage - as well as the Chalet Bourgeat - "the villa where he was for some time". Back in Dieppe he worked on the final details of his first bibliography (which dealt only with Oscar's poetry) but found this difficult because he had to correct the proofs without having any of the original texts available.

Whilst he was in France, most of his collection of Wildean material was auctioned by Puttick and Simpson and at least he was reasonably pleased with the prices realised. He had reluctantly accepted that he could not afford to keep the collection up to date and in any case he no longer had a permanent base for it; he anticipated leading a nomadic existence for some time to come. But he confessed, "It nearly breaks my heart to part with them all." However he hoped that either Walter or Robbie would purchase at least some of the lots as he knew they would appreciate them. He urged Walter to consider buying the volumes of newspaper cuttings such as that in lot 410, which contained *De Profundis* press cuttings nicely bound on hand-made paper. He also encouraged him to buy the Russian books, several photographs, and a Polish *Dorian Gray* "translated by a very charming countess whom I met in Oxford two years ago and gave a very grand tea party to, with cigarettes and countless varieties of liqueurs." His fondness for the items in his collection and the associations they had for him is obvious, and long after the auction was over he continued to regret having had to sell. "I bitterly groan at times over my lost collection … but it was inevitable, I suppose."

Despite the loss of his books, he still wanted to produce a full bibliography of Oscar's works. He raised the issue with Walter yet again. "I hear from Ross today that Grant Richards 'is very excited to get hold of the bibliography' and that he has a publisher in America who will bring it out there. I know you have always been rather against publication but I do hope you will re-consider it. I am quite willing that my name should not appear, if that has any weight with you. It seems to me that this year with Methuen's new edition coming out will be the time to do it, and we may not find it always easy to find a publisher." But Walter was adamant and Christopher again seemed ready to give up: "My own collection was so very much smaller than yours that I can do nothing alone." He did ask once more though, "I suppose you will not change your mind. If you do, I would return to London and do whatever I could to relieve you of all the clerical work of the bibliography."

This comment is revealing as it indicates that within a few weeks of his arrival at Dieppe he was already contemplating a return to London. In May he did come back briefly, primarily to see the revival of Oscar's *A Woman of No Importance* at His Majesty's Theatre. The house was crowded but Christopher thought Herbert Beerbohm Tree's performance as Lord Illingworth "horrid" and considered that "Oscar's plays are always spoilt in the acting." Christopher spent a few days in London staying at the Grand Hotel in Trafalgar Square and then travelled to Hampshire to see his relatives before returning to Dieppe.

His Majesty's Theatre

He still felt happier in France and soon after his return he moved the few miles west from Dieppe to nearby Pourville "which I like immensely." But life across the Channel was not cheap: "I have had a most enjoyable time here and have made scores of new friends, but it is a fearfully expensive life and I am nearly at the end of my resources." In the end he could not afford to stay any longer: "I … fear I shall have to return to England and seek some sort of drudgery by September."

And indeed by mid-September 1907 he was back for good. He found "a humble lodgement" in London at 44 Hallam Street off Portland Place, a house which had been divided up into bedsits. In the room he rented on the ground floor Christopher tidily arranged his remaining books and it was here that Osbert Burdett first visited him and was fascinated by the skill with which he prepared their tea and toast: "The speed and deftness with which Millard made hot buttered toast in front of his gas-fire was really astonishing. With the expertness of a trained servant and with the ease of an aristocrat, the thing was done. Not a crumb was burnt. Not a speck of butter escaped. There was no mess, no flurry, and the toast was piping hot, drenched with butter, while, most marvellous of all, the easy conversation, now begun, was not for an instant interrupted by this difficult activity. ... Millard not only fetched hot water from the gas-jet on the stove, but filled the kettle, and put it back, and made hot toast the while, and never spilt anything, or stumbled, while talking, without any seeming interruption, in utter and unconscious ease."

Christopher began working at Jacobs' a booksellers and publishers at 149 Edgware Road, where he planned to learn more about the bookselling trade. He had a small desk inside the dimly lit shop where he spent long hours for low pay. From Monday to Friday he was there from nine till seven (with an hour for lunch between two and three) though on Saturdays the shop closed at two so he had the afternoon free. And in some respects Jacobs' shop was a good place of work for Christopher. Its proprietor, Mr Jacobs, was a sympathetic man who had travelled to meet Christopher in Oxford in 1905 to discuss publishing a book about Oscar Wilde's trials and Christopher liked him: "He is rather a good sort personally, but not much of a business man I fancy." His shop would have particularly appealed to Christopher because it specialised in Oscar's work along with that of the artists Aubrey Beardsley and James Whistler (as well as in Anglo-Judaica). And it was located in the cosmopolitan Edgware Road, which had something of a reputation as a gay locale.

As Christopher learned about bookselling at Jacobs', his lover Charles Scott Moncrieff began his final year at Winchester College, where he was soon to publish a highly controversial piece in the *New Field*. This was his short story *Evensong and Morwe Song* which features two boys at a public school, Carruthers and Maurice, who are involved in a sexual relationship. Carruthers, the elder boy, who is depicted as the nonchalant seducer of the younger one, later becomes the headmaster of another school. The story mainly attacks his hypocrisy when he himself deals with a "painful incident" at his own school and expels one of the boys (who turns out to be Maurice's son).

The Winchester College authorities responded by suppressing the magazine, although Charles was apparently not expelled for writing the story (although it is often claimed that he was.) Indeed, although the story acknowledges the existence of gay sexual activity at public schools it does not particularly celebrate this. Although it is much cited as a brave depiction of gay sexuality and certainly its condemnation of hypocrisy is unambivalent, the work does strongly suggest the younger boy is corrupted by the elder. Nevertheless it was courageous for a young writer even to refer to such sexual activity and no doubt Christopher was impressed by Charles' willingness to court controversy. (The story was re-published privately in 1923 primarily for circulation amongst gay literary circles.)

That October Christopher and Walter met, possibly for the first time since Christopher's imprisonment, at a performance of Oscar's *The Florentine Tragedy* at the Cripplegate Institute. Christopher bought the tickets beforehand and posted one of them to Walter along with a programme and a note saying, "I shall be so glad to see you there". In the event both men were disappointed with the play, which had been "dreadfully mauled", but they were delighted to see Oscar's son, Vyvyan Holland, in the audience.

Then in November Christopher's *A Bibliography of the Poems of Oscar Wilde* finally appeared in an edition of 475 copies, with twenty five of those being numbered copies printed on handmade paper. The book had been published by E. Grant Richards (of 7 Carlton Street) and was intended to complement Methuen's forthcoming volume of poems which was eventually released in early 1908. It is full of Christopher's careful research into the publication of each of Oscar's poems including details of every edition and information about translations, pirate editions and even the parodies of Oscar's work which were written by others. The book, priced at six shillings, included photographs of Magdalen College and of the hotel in Berneval, and largely consisted of factual descriptions of papers and wrappers, although there were occasional comments which reveal something of its author's views. For example Christopher first notes that *On the Massacre of the Christians in Bulgaria* (dealing with events of May 1876) was not an entirely successful poem and that it was thought to have been written when Oscar was an undergraduate. But quickly he allows his own political opinions to emerge: "The atrocious massacres committed without provocation by the Turkish irregular troops in Bulgaria provoked a strong outburst of feeling in the humane portion of the English people."

He acknowledged the significance of his relationship with Charles Scott Moncrieff by dedicating this first bibliography to "S.M. amico desideratissimo S. M." addressing Charles (as 'Scott Moncrieff') as "the most desired friend" of 'Sclater Millard' (or 'Stuart Mason'). The phrase he chose - 'amico desideratissimo' - was one which resonated for gay men and thus it was used two years later by another gay writer, Frederick William Rolfe (Baron Corvo), as the dedication for his book *Don Renato*.

Now that *A Bibliography of the Poems of Oscar Wilde* was finally on sale, Robbie encouraged Christopher to spend his evenings working on a complete bibliography for Methuen. This was to include all the English editions of Oscar's books as well as all the pieces published in magazines and Christopher was soon hard at work on the project. He was also involved in the decision to reprint the short story *The Priest and the Acolyte* (which had first appeared in the *Chameleon* magazine and which was now to be included in an unauthorised American edition of Oscar's collected works). He wrote an introduction to the work which protested that it should never have been attributed to Oscar as it had been written by an undergraduate at Exeter College, Oxford whose name - John Francis Blox(h)am – was an open secret. The story had been the subject of questioning at Oscar's trial when an extract had been read out in court and Oscar had responded by declaring it badly written and improper, but not blasphemous. Christopher might have had two distinct reasons for being involved in the reprinting *The Priest and the Acolyte*. Primarily he wanted it to be made clear that the story was not by Oscar. But in addition he might have felt some satisfaction in overseeing the publication of a work that deals with a gay relationship and includes a robust defence of gay love: "There is no sin for which I should feel shame … God gave me my love for him."

Over the winter Christopher suffered from various illnesses (including chilblains) and spent Christmas at Forest Gate with his brother. In the New Year he arranged to rent a room near Marble Arch in Connaught House (owned by the Connaught Club). He continued to spend his days working in Jacobs' bookshop and to occupy much of the rest of his time in writing, but he also led a busy social life and one of the first invitations he received in 1908 was to a Twelfth Night party organised by Robbie's lover, Freddie Smith.

Connaught House

On Thursday 13 February Methuen issued six volumes of the first edition of Oscar's collected works, which Christopher had helped Robbie to edit. Only eighty copies of each volume were issued and they were printed on Japanese vellum and had a design by Charles Ricketts on the cover. Five more volumes followed on Friday 13 March and Christopher's notes on Oscar's sonnets, which he had originally prepared in 1906, presumably found their way into volume nine – *The Poems of Oscar Wilde*. It was probably following a review of this book that Christopher was prompted to write to *The Sunday Times* to defend the poem, *Ravenna*. In his letter published on 5 April he drew attention to its relationship to later poems by Oscar. The twelfth volume of the collected works, *The Picture of Dorian Gray*, appeared just over a week later on Thursday 16 April, though it was published not in London but in Paris by Charles Carrington. Christopher, like Robbie, must have been gratified by the impact of these volumes which renewed interest in Oscar's writing and were widely reviewed in the press.

However the review in *The Athenaeum* provoked Christopher into writing a letter to the journal, which he composed when visiting Oxford, possibly for the first time since his imprisonment. Extracts from his letter were published on Saturday 23 May: "They have inserted but a mutilated portion of it: still I am glad it is in as I have always wanted an opportunity of thrusting that point home to the B.P. [British Public]."

The extracts appeared under the heading *Oscar Wilde's Letters on Prison Reform*: "In your long and interesting review of *The Works of Oscar Wilde* you state that the 'two terrible, unforgettable letters' on the cruelties of prison life were 'no doubt useless.'" But Christopher challenged this assumption: "I am sure that you will be the first to rejoice to know that, so far from them being 'useless', there is scarcely a single reform suggested in them by Wilde that has not been carried out more or less as he proposed.... It is related on undeniable authority that the Commissioners appointed to inquire into the question of Prison Reform in the years 1897 and 1898 spent three days considering the suggestions made in Wilde's letters, with what good results may very briefly be stated as follows: - At the end of the first month's imprisonment a prisoner is allowed to write a letter or to receive a visit, and to read a book, instead of waiting three months as formerly; the sanitary arrangements have been improved; the food weighed out each day is somewhat less scanty and more varied; the plank bed is insisted on for the first fourteen days only, instead of a month; and though little children are still committed to most of the horrors of prison life, much has been done of late years in the way of extending the Borstal system." Christopher was drawing on his own experience in this letter because he had benefitted from these improvements during his own spell in prison.

By late June Christopher had completed another piece of work for Robbie - *Mr Stuart Mason's memorandum of the authorised editions which may be sold in the United Kingdom* – which Robbie released in July along with a circular for the book trade that was intended to control unauthorised reprints of Oscar's work. With the *memorandum* finished, Christopher was able to take a short break from work: "I had a week up river above Oxford (Bablock Hythe, Buscot, Kelmscott, Lechlade) last week & am ever so much better for the holiday." He then spent a few days "rusticating ... at a little place on the Berkshire downs." But despite the payment he received from Robbie, money continued to be a problem. Christopher wanted to subscribe to the *Publishers' Circular* (and advised Walter to do so) but explained, "I cannot do it myself just now as it might bring all my creditors (and their name is legion) down upon me."

That autumn Charles Scott Moncrieff went up to Edinburgh University where he was soon busy studying and making new friends. But he wrote lively and racy letters to Christopher (as well as to Robbie) about literary and other matters and they continued to meet at intervals. Perhaps their sexual relationship continued for a time too.

Back in London things were changing for Christopher. He had decided to leave Jacobs' bookshop to concentrate on his writing in a move that seems to have been partly funded by Robbie. Nevertheless in September it was Jacobs' who published the book *Oscar Wilde, Art and Morality: A Defence of The Picture of Dorian Gray*, which Christopher had edited. Christopher was particularly fascinated by Oscar's sole novel and in his introduction he describes *Dorian Gray*'s "strangeness of colour and its passionate suggestion flickering like lightning through the gloom of the subject." After giving details of the publication of *Dorian Gray* and of its various editions and translations (amounting to over 140 volumes almost all of which Christopher owned) he reproduces reviews of the novel from a range of publications including *St James's Gazette*, *The Daily Chronicle* and *Punch*. Alongside these he places Oscar's published replies in which the author argues for example that the artist should not "be troubled by the shrill clamour of criticism".

In his introduction Christopher observes that "The Puritans and the Philistines, who scented veiled improprieties in its paradoxes, were shocked" by *Dorian Gray* but it "delighted the connoisseur and the artist". So in the main part of the book he includes several sympathetic reviews of the novel including one by Walter Pater as well as two from *Lippincott's Monthly Magazine* - in which *Dorian Gray* first appeared in its original form. Anne H. Wharton, an American author from Pennsylvania describes the novel as the work "of an artist and apostle of the beautiful" and admires the "air of probability with which he has endowed the absolutely impossible evidences the artistic and dramatic power of the writer." She describes Lord Henry as "Wilde's Mephistopheles" who is an entertaining character "debonair, witty, learned", and true to himself. She also hints at the homoerotic current in the work in her reference to Dorian Gray as an "Antinous-like" young man (Antinous being the lover of the Roman Emperor Hadrian who had him deified after his death). Similarly Julian Hawthorne, admires the book as a "salutary departure from the ordinary English novel" and calls Oscar "original and audacious." However more typical of the reviews which the novel received on its release is that from *The Athenaeum* which calls the book "unmanly, sickening, vicious (though not exactly what is called 'improper') and tedious."

In 1895 *The Picture of Dorian Gray* had featured prominently in Oscar's trials and Christopher's book ends with an account of the references made in court to this work and in particular to its homosexual aspects.

There had been allegations that the book "was intended to be understood by the readers to describe the relations, intimacies and passions of certain persons guilty of unnatural practices" and the section which described the meeting of Dorian Gray and Basil had been read out. Much had been made of phrases which referred to the feelings of one man towards another such as "I adored you madly" and "I was jealous of every one to whom you spoke." In court Oscar had been challenged to say whether he himself had any such sentiments and had been forced to argue, disingenuously, that they related to art and not to the body.

Christopher appreciated the opportunity to re-read *The Picture of Dorian Gray* as he compiled *Oscar Wilde, Art and Morality*. However at around the same time he read an issue of *The Children's Encyclopaedia* which he found much less enjoyable. Indeed he rather resented having spent 7d on it protesting, "What an awful, appalling production it is to put into the hands of young or old." This illustrated encyclopaedia was published in fortnightly parts between March 1908 and February 1910. It was full of facts and stories and the intention was not only to make learning interesting but to develop the character of young people by teaching them about great lives and golden deeds. Its writers took pride in the British Empire and in a sense of British superiority, and it was doubtless this jingoistic attitude that Christopher particularly disliked. Despite his reservations though, the work was extremely popular and sold in large numbers.

Oscar Wilde, Art and Morality was not Christopher's only publication that autumn. On Tuesday 6 October he took the first step towards his comprehensive bibliography when his *Bibliography of Oscar Wilde* was privately printed in Edinburgh by T. & A. Constable. This was a preliminary edition of just eleven numbered copies and it was basically a list of all Oscar's printed works – both books and articles – which included the articles in *Court and Society Review* that Walter had tracked down for his friend. Christopher kept one copy of this work for himself and sent others to the British Museum and to the libraries in Oxford, Cambridge, Dublin and Edinburgh.

Copy number two was given to Robbie whilst Christopher presented copy number four to his lover Charles Scott Moncrieff. This book, with the inscription which Christopher dated 7 October, is now in the British Library.

The handwritten inscription reads:

"Stuart Mason

     f   c

  me   e   it

    d   d

Carolo Scott Moncrieff"

The Latin 'Me fecit' is the standard form for 'I made it' found on architecture, sculpture and paintings and 'd d' presumably stands for 'donum dedit' which means 'he gave the gift'. Christopher deliberately arranged this inscription in a form that must have had some personal significance. Perhaps it was intended to evoke the shape of the Stuart white rose.

By now Christopher was gradually rebuilding his friendship with Walter and he invited him to visit "the remnants of myself and my belongings". It was probably on this occasion that he presented copy number three of his *Bibliography* to Walter and soon he was reminding him "It is four years ago yesterday since I first visited you at Wimbledon!" Walter was working on his own bibliographical work at this time which involved compiling a list of the various translations of *Salome*.

The final two volumes in the first collected edition of Oscar's works appeared on Thursday 15 October. As far back as early 1906 Christopher had begun editing a book originally known as *Views and Reviews: The Uncollected Prose Writings and Letters of Oscar Wilde* and it seems this was eventually divided into these two separate volumes. Volume thirteen contained Oscar's reviews whilst volume fourteen was titled *Miscellanies*. Robbie dedicated this to Walter and it includes various pieces such as the poem *Rome Unvisited* that was praised by Cardinal Newman. There are notes on Oscar's university career too and on his reception into the Catholic Church. The book also includes a bibliography which contained the same text as Christopher's privately printed book. There are four pages listing authorised English editions of Oscar's work, another page itemising editions that had been privately printed for Oscar, and then a list of his miscellaneous contributions to magazines.

A few weeks later Christopher was amongst the nearly two hundred guests invited to a public dinner at the Ritz in Robbie's honour. This was held on Tuesday 1 December and marked the winding-up of Oscar's estate as well as the issuing of his complete works. The speakers included the writers Herbert George Wells and Frank Harris and the guests included many notable members of London's literary and artistic circles. Both of Oscar's sons were there as were Walter, Robert Sherard and Osbert Burdett (who sat next to Christopher). Robbie's relatives were invited and so was his secretary and lover Freddie Smith. Reggie Turner had written to ask Alfred Douglas to attend but he had refused. It was a sign of his increasing hostility towards Robbie.

Christopher no doubt enjoyed the occasion and must have been particularly gratified by Robbie's acceptance speech in which he acknowledged the role "Mr Stuart Mason" had played in reviving Oscar's reputation. Unfortunately afterwards Christopher was unwell and had to stay in bed with "one of my periodical 'throats'" which meant "it hurts intensely to swallow." Nevertheless he sent a letter to *The New Age* (a weekly paper of "Christian culture, social service and literary life") to challenge an article full of errors about Oscar's life. He was always annoyed when myths and legends were published instead of facts and was keen to ensure that the truth about Oscar emerged – even on minor points.

At the beginning of 1909 Christopher moved out of Connaught House, which he was finding too expensive, and into a room at 5 Bramerton Street in Chelsea "more suited to the narrow limits of my purse". In March he might have visited Keble College because he wrote to *Notes and Queries* on college notepaper with a request for information about the original publication date of Oscar's *The Birthday of the Infanta*. He wrote again to this periodical in June to correct an assertion that *The Ballad of Reading Gaol* was written in prison. Perhaps shortly after sending this second letter he set off on a trip to Ireland primarily to visit sites associated with Oscar. It must have been funded by Robbie and it lasted several weeks.

Christopher's itinerary is largely unknown, but he might first have travelled to the west of Ireland perhaps going as far as Connemara whose wild beauty was known to Oscar. To reach Dublin from there, Christopher would then have returned eastwards. Certainly on 25 June he was in Lismany and unimpressed with what he found: "I am in a very dull and unpicturesque part of the Emerald Isle – six miles from the town of Ballinasloe (an achievement to have reached it: a triumph to have survived it!) and the weather has so far been most disappointing." If he was familiar with Lismany's history, this would not have endeared it to him either, as it had been forcibly cleared of its Catholic tenants by the Scottish shipping agent, Allan Pollok, who wanted it for his exclusive use. Fortunately Christopher had a more enjoyable time in Dublin where he went to see several places connected with Oscar – his birthplace at 21 Westland Row, 1 Merrion Square where he grew up, and Trinity College where he studied.

Afterwards Christopher travelled back to London. His British Museum reader's ticket had finally arrived and he was eager to carry out his research in its collection. On 20 July Oscar's remains were transferred to the Pere Lachaise cemetery in Paris under Robbie's supervision, and it is possible that Christopher attended the ceremony, though there is no firm evidence that he was present. He would no doubt have approved of the inscription chosen for the memorial. Robbie had selected a verse from *The Ballad of Reading Gaol* which would long resonate with gay men: "And alien tears will fill for him/Pity's long-broken urn/For his mourners will be outcast men/And outcasts always mourn."

Christopher spent the August "Bank 'Oliday" by himself "as I hate going out these days" though at some point he probably had a trip on the river above Oxford with some friends. Meanwhile Walter was not only sharing his horticultural knowledge with the director of Kew Gardens (sending him specimens of two unusual succulent climbing plants - *Ceropegia brownii* and *Ceropegia rendallii*) but finalising his bibliography of *Salome* for Methuen in which he describes the various editions of this work including translations and reprints. Christopher helped him track down material for this and during August he "found another Yiddish translation of *Salome*" and followed this up with a visit to the address given by the publisher, who was named Friedman. When he called at 81 Berwick Street he "found a Hebrew baker who says Friedman used to occupy his cellar. He translated the title page for me but was rather afraid that I had come from the CENSOR!"

Although Walter was certainly very knowledgeable about Oscar's work, it was Christopher, rather than his more retiring friend, who was increasingly widely known as an acknowledged expert on Wildean matters. Consequently he was frequently contacted for information. One of those who got in touch with him at this time was Desda Cornish, who wanted to borrow the programmes for the original productions of Oscar's plays. Desda was American – a minor literary figure who was involved with the United Arts Club at 10 St James Street. She wrote for *The New Age* and had written a supportive account for a Boston paper about the dinner given in Robbie's honour.

On 2 September the first volume in the second collected edition of Oscar's works was issued by Methuen. Again Christopher had assisted Robbie in preparing this edition – which was intended to be a less expensive, popular alternative to the limited first edition. Further volumes followed at fortnightly intervals. The volume containing Walter's eighteen page bibliography of *Salome* (as well as the play itself in addition to *La Sainte Courtisane* and *A Florentine Tragedy*) appeared on 11 November and no doubt he was gratified to see his research in print at long last.

By the time that volume went on sale, Christopher had moved home again. Chelsea was not close enough to the centre of his social and literary life and it seems that he was now able to afford something more convenient. So on 27 September 1909 he moved back to the Edgware Road area where he had found an apartment in Molyneux House at 10 Molyneux Street. He was to spend several years here in flat number six, which had three rooms, and for which he paid about £36 a year.

Molyneaux House

Entrance to Molyneaux House

CHAPTER NINE

ALFRED DOUGLAS

"When people agree with me I always feel that I must be wrong." from The Critic as Artist *by Oscar Wilde*

Within a few months of Christopher's move to Molyneux House, he heard the news that Alfred Douglas was due to appear in court. It was one of the first of many such appearances. Alfred was now the editor of the *Academy* (a journal Robbie had previously written for) and he had appointed a man called Thomas Hodgson Crosland as his sub-editor. Alfred had known him for several years and contributed poems to the *English Review*, which Thomas edited.

Thomas was a man who (rather like Christopher) enjoyed controversy. He grew up in Leeds where he suffered from poor health, but he developed into a talented artist, and a poet. He worked briefly as a schoolteacher (which he disliked) then set off for London where he found work as a journalist and began to develop his career. His articles and reviews became increasingly polemical and he was always keen to express his views on morality and to condemn work which he regarded as pornographic. He proved to be a powerful, if unreliable, ally who encouraged Alfred's worst traits. Alfred had grown jealous and resentful of his former friends, quick to take offence, and increasingly homophobic. In collusion with Thomas he was to do a great deal of harm to Robbie and to those around him. Christopher was particularly badly affected by their actions.

During 1909 Alfred had tried (with Thomas' encouragement) to get money from Frederick Walpole Manners-Sutton, who was a partner in the publishing firm Cope and Fenwick. Alfred needed the money because of the *Academy*'s financial difficulties, but Frederick refused to give him any. In retaliation the *Academy* printed an article that suggested Frederick was publishing "dubious stories of a highly spiced nature." Frederick responded by accusing Thomas of criminal libel and the case went to the Central Criminal Court. It was heard during February 1910.

Christopher went to watch Alfred's cross-examination: "He floored [Edward] Marshall Hall all along and must have done a good deal to win the case." When Frederick's counsel tried to bring in Alfred's connection with Oscar to undermine his evidence, the attempt backfired. But this was only because Alfred denied there had ever been any sexual relationship between them and presented himself as Oscar's noble friend, who deeply disapproved of his 'sins'. Robbie was furious at what he saw as Alfred's betrayal of Oscar, but the tactic was undoubtedly effective. The jury cleared Thomas and decided that the libel was true and published in the public interest. Alfred was delighted with the outcome. He was soon involved in another libel case in which he successfully sued a nonconformist minister who accused him of using the *Academy* to promote Catholicism.

Walter probably discussed Alfred's tactics on one of his regular visits to Molyneux House where Christopher was always pleased to see him: "I am nearly always in at four o'clock, so I hope you will look in one day" ... "I want to see you about several things, so if you come up ... you might come back here to tea." Christopher's friendship with Oscar's son, Vyvyan, was developing too and he introduced him to Walter.

During the summer Christopher no doubt also met up with Charles Scott Moncrieff (who spent the vacation in London) and heard about his life at university. Charles was frequently the centre of attention at Edinburgh and flamboyantly posed at one fancy dress ball as a faun draped in a leopard skin and with vine leaves in his hair. He was falling for a succession of young men including a handsome student called Guy Lawrence and two fellow poets - Philip Gillespie Bainbridge (Bainbrigge) and Ian H. T. McKenzie – who probably both became his lovers. Charles introduced Christopher to Philip, who was both scholarly and witty and who wrote amusing verses full of gay sexual innuendo notably *Achilles in Scyros* with its preface in which Eros plays "his boy's games" with "his toy ... that nestles warm between/ His dainty rosy thighs." The poem is based on an episode in the life of the Greek hero, Achilles, when he is sent to Scyros disguised as a young woman. In Philip's version Achilles is a gay man exiled as a punishment for his sexual relationship with his tutor, Patroclus, and the poem plays with notions of gender identity, though all ends happily for the reunited male lovers. Although the poem was never published during Philip's lifetime, it seems likely that Christopher was allowed to read it. He could also have read Ian's poem, *Desire* (which later appeared in a war-time collection called *More Songs by the Fighting Men*). If he did, he no doubt picked up on the poem's strongly erotic undercurrent.

As far as work was concerned, Christopher was mainly occupied with research. He was tracking down more material for his bibliography as well as locating pirated editions of Oscar's work. Robbie was keen to control these in order to protect Oscar's estate and Christopher's discoveries helped him to trace the source of a 6d pirate edition of *De Profundis* which led to a successful prosecution at the Old Bailey in July. Christopher was also preparing a book for the Bloomsbury publisher, Frank Palmer, based in Red Lion Court. It was to be called *The Oscar Wilde Calendar* and was to have a quotation by Oscar for each day of the year. For the frontispiece Christopher chose a portrait by Harper Pennington showing a young confident Oscar with a cane and for November 7, his own birthday, Christopher selected a rather poignant quotation: "It is not the perfect but the imperfect who have need of love." The book appeared in November. (A second revised edition appeared in March 1911 and a third in 1914.)

1910 also saw the first steps towards a much more controversial work when the publisher Martin Secker commissioned a young writer named Arthur Ransome to write a critical study of Oscar. Arthur was soon introduced to Robbie, who was keen to support what he hoped would be a more serious and trustworthy account than previous books by the likes of Robert Sherard, and the young author had already begun the first steps towards his book when Richard Strauss' opera *Salome* had its London premiere on 8 December at Covent Garden conducted by Thomas Beecham. The opera was based on Oscar's play and contained the notorious Dance of the Seven Veils. Christopher wrote to Walter beforehand, "I fear it is difficult to get tickets. And in any case my dress suit is in pawn." But nevertheless he might have attended if the ever-generous Robbie paid for his ticket.

Royal Opera House

Christopher's writing did not absorb all his time that year. His political activity continued, although he despaired of influencing the conservatively minded Walter. "I suppose it is useless to attempt to persuade you to refrain from voting for that aged pauper (with a £1200 a year pension) Henry Chaplin! In any case such a thoroughly respectable neighbourhood as Wimbledon is not likely to elect a Liberal." The wealthy landowner, Henry Chaplin, had been returned as member for Wimbledon at the by-election in May 1907 and was indeed to hold the seat until 1916. Although Walter seems to have been reasonably content with this state of affairs, Christopher found it frustrating. He remained strongly committed to socialism (despite the comments he had made after his arrest) and retained his sympathy for the down-trodden.

But he was not particularly active over the winter as he became unwell following a cold spell: "My throat is much better but I am still something of a wreck." He sent no Christmas cards that year, "it is a custom I have long since given up" but he wrote to thank Walter "for your Christmas card and good wishes ... I like being remembered by others."

Christopher and Walter continued to correspond about books during 1911. Christopher told Walter that Aleister Crowley had a copy of Oscar's *The Ballad of Reading Gaol*, which he was willing to sell, but that "this is in strict confidence as he does not want it known that he is selling his books." Aleister (born Edward Alexander) was a notorious figure who was fascinated by the occult. He had numerous relationships with both women and men including Herbert Charles Pollitt, whom he met at Cambridge, and Oscar's friend Ada Leverson.

But although Christopher urged Walter to buy Aleister's *Ballad* he warned him against a new book - "an appalling production" - by the American singer and writer Anna Comtesse de Bremont nee Dunphy called *Oscar Wilde and His Mother*. "It out Sherards Sherard." His comparison with Robert Sherard's 1906 *The Life of Oscar Wilde* was an apt one as both books use flowery hyperbole and offer amateurish attempts at psychoanalysis. Robert Sherard describes Oscar before the trial as close to megalomania and his talent as "peculiar genius" and suggests that Oscar was suffering from mental illness when he wrote the "silly" novel *Dorian Gray*. He also recounts an unbelievable story of Oscar knocking on his brother's door and pleading, "Willy give me shelter." *Oscar Wilde and His Mother* repeats this story and depicts Oscar as having a "feminine soul… a suffering prisoner in the wrong brain-house." It was this that gave him both "the lust for forbidden pleasures" and "the supreme love and appreciation of beauty."

Another writer, who was more genuinely sympathetic towards Oscar, was now in London. Dalhousie James Young (better known as a composer and pianist) had met Oscar in France and later published *Apologia Pro Oscar Wilde* which challenges the notion that Oscar's writing was immoral and seditious. Despite this Robbie didn't like him and Christopher, who could be influenced by Robbie's opinions, might have avoided him. However around this time Christopher did become friendly with someone else - a young gay man called Aylmer Gustavus Clerk, then in his mid-twenties and working as a solicitor. He soon became part of a group of young men with whom Christopher socialised.

There was not much time for socialising though. Christopher had already been working for some time on his latest book on Oscar - *Oscar Wilde: Three Times Tried*. By late May he had "just passed the final proofs" and took time out to go to Sotheby's for a private view of a collection of newspaper cuttings which Walter subsequently bought. He lent it to Christopher so that he could take notes and copy out the *Court and Society* articles for Robbie. Christopher was still writing for the *Burlington Magazine* too and was extremely busy there: "I have been rather rushed about at the *Burlington*." … "Saturday is my only free day now: with

101

Wednesday afternoon occasionally." As at Jacobs' the hours were long and the pay not very good and Christopher struggled to work in the sultry weather, which made him "indolent". He envied Walter, who was sailing as usual: "On the water I suppose you do not mind the heat. I never used to care how hot it was in the days when I cruised round the coast." By now Walter had replaced his *Shrimp* with the larger *Blue Bird*, a six-ton cutter, in which he cruised about the East and South coasts.

One of Christopher's tasks at the *Burlington* during the hot summer was to review *Forgotten Shrines* by Dom Bede Camm (which included a chapter on Oxford) and his appreciative piece appeared in September under his initials (CSM.) He considered that "There is always something fascinating in the history of ancient houses" and thought that the book, which dealt with Catholic families, would nevertheless be of interest to others "including those readers with no faith at all."

Not long afterwards, on 14 October, he went to see a performance of *Lady Windermere's Fan*, which he described as "quite good" but he was now mainly preoccupied in revising the edition of *Salome* which Alfred Douglas had translated. Christopher was scathing about Alfred's English: "It was crowded with mistakes of all kinds." His derisive remark was symptomatic of the widening rift between Alfred and members of Robbie's circle. Reggie Turner, who was wintering abroad, was one of those who tried to remain friends with both men and Christopher corresponded with him from time to time mainly about books. Reggie was cautious about parting with those he owned but he proved willing to sell his copy of *Vera* to Walter for £12: "You need have no scruples about asking R. T. for *Vera*: he is quite prepared to sell it to you, but would not care to part with it to a stranger."

Walter continued to expand his book collection, but he was also intent on completing his account of his recent voyage on the *Blue Bird*. This rather irritated Christopher because it was at the expense of work on Wildean matters. But he wrote generously enough to thank Walter for his Christmas present of "the really interesting account of your tour. I shall value it specially as being a presentation copy of a very limited edition." Walter's accounts of his cruises were originally published in the *Royal Cruising Club Journal* and show his evident pleasure in his trips. The *Blue Bird* must have been a cosy boat to sail in with its cushions and bunks covered with "cretonne of an old design of exotic flowers and bluebirds" that gave the cabin "a very bright and cheerful appearance, particularly when lighted up at night."

CHAPTER TEN

ADMIRING OSCAR

"From the filthy web of lies" - Christopher in Oscar Wilde: Three Times Tried

From Christmas onwards Christopher was "rather rushed" because of the imminent publication of *Oscar Wilde: Three Times Tried* which appeared in January 1912. Like *The Oscar Wilde Calendar*, it was published by Frank Palmer. It had Robbie's full approval and was (as Christopher claimed) "very different" from the "absurd volume" called *The Trial of Oscar Wilde* which had been edited by Charles Grolleau and privately printed by Charles Carrington in Paris six years previously. However Christopher admitted "it is far from being as complete or as accurate as I could have wished."

His preface set out his intention which was to clear Oscar "from the filthy web of lies" surrounding him "in comparison with which the bald truth – ugly as it is – seems almost clean." Here Christopher appears to accept social disapproval of Oscar in the language he uses, though doubtless this was only to please the wider audience he was aiming at. He does refer to "repulsive" truths and "sins", but at the same time mocks "virtuous hatred", society's "ecstatic horror" and the "mud of the moralists" which had buried Oscar's personality.

He wants Oscar's genius to be acknowledged, and his work examined, not "from between our fingers" but with appreciation. In order to ensure this happened, Christopher felt it was important to offer a full account of the three trials in which Oscar was involved. He claims that his book was the first attempt to "give a fair picture" of the events and he draws on inside information (from Robbie amongst others) to describe the court proceedings and recounts the evidence, apparently unflinchingly and in an even-handed way, including that given by the various young men who were supposed to have had sex with Oscar. His book ends with the conclusion of the final trial at which the judge told Oscar, "You must be dead to all sense of shame" and handed down the maximum sentence possible which he declared "totally inadequate." It was at this point in the book that Christopher finally expresses his anger at society's treatment of Oscar as he vividly describes a scene outside the court where "harlots lifted their skirts and danced with delight to the vociferous cheers of the ever-virtuous British public." Oscar had been convicted by a jury satisfied with the "evidence of two blackmailers and some hysterical servant girls. The charges he had faced "even the Judge ... stigmatised as unfair." The state prosecutor was vindictive and intended to "hound a man to his ruin" and the prosecution used means "which did not square with an Englishman's notion of justice and fair play."

Christopher regarded *Oscar Wilde: Three Times Tried* as an important contribution to the process of raising Oscar's profile and recovering his reputation. His next step would be the production of a complete bibliography of the writer he so admired. Thomas Werner Laurie was now interested in publishing one, and Christopher wrote yet again to Walter on the subject. "Will you collaborate with me?" he pleaded, "I cannot attempt the translations." But Walter continued to be reluctant. "I don't want to disappoint you very much, but I don't see my way to joining in it. I have been working at my own ponderous opus lately (in spite of a cold & a family bereavement which has upset us a good deal) but I find that when I try to put on steam my old machinery creaks & warns me I can't do it. So I've no idea when I shall get through with it." He assured Christopher, "If you undertake a Bibliography off your own bat for Werner Laurie remember that you have in me, not a jealous rival, but a friend who will be pleased to help you if he can."

Christopher was disappointed with Walter's response, although pleased with his generous gift of several of the books which Christopher had previously been forced to sell. "I am delighted to have them so unexpectedly restored to me," he quoted from *The Importance of Being Earnest*, "It has been a great inconvenience being without them so long, as Miss Prism would have said." However he sometimes felt overwhelmed by the task of tackling the bibliography alone: "I have so little spare time except in the evenings now with my *Burlington* work all day." He continued to share his finds with Walter though. They included his acquisition of a copy of one of Oscar's books which was inscribed to Ada Leverson: "To the Sphinx of Pleasure." Then in February he shared the worrying news that Oscar's son, Vyvyan, had been taken ill: "Poor

Vyvyan is lying very seriously ill in hospital (La Fonda Italiana, Calle Real, Algeciras) of enteric. I believe there is rather better news to-day, but last week it was thought he could not recover." Fortunately Christopher soon learned that Vyvyan had regained his health.

Gradually Christopher reluctantly accepted that he would have to complete Oscar's bibliography alone if it was ever to appear. His book on *Dorian Gray* proved popular enough to be reissued confirming there was a demand for material about Oscar so he continued to work on his research and to correspond with those who had useful information. He gathered many interesting snippets and was particularly delighted to learn that "Germany has produced tins of DORIAN GRAY CIGARETTES!" When he discovered a new piece by Oscar in *Macmillan's Magazine* he wrote excitedly, "NOW CONTROL YOURSELF, MY DEAR WALTER EDWIN LEDGER. And go on to the next page of this letter. !!" There seemed always to be new discoveries even at this stage. "I wonder how much more there is still to find?" And Christopher was so absorbed in his research that he even dreamed about it: "The *Athenaeum* turned out, as I feared, to contain only a reference to O W in a review… It kept me awake most of the night, and when I did sleep I dreamed that I saw the article signed 'O W'!"

Christopher knew Walter would be an appreciative audience for such snippets: "I hope you won't be bored by my perpetual writing to you, but when I think of anything or make a discovery my only way is to get it off my mind at once." In continuing to share information about the gay author they both admired, they cemented the bonds between them. Christopher had kept Walter's letters to him (as Walter had kept his) and he was now rereading them: "I have been filing all your letters from 1904. It is very interesting to look back and see how we knew nothing of what now seems so obvious!" He was already starting to think about illustrations for his bibliography and he commissioned a printing block of the painting by Violet Gurney (nee Troubridge) which was supposed to have inspired Oscar's sonnet *Wasted Days* about "A fair slim boy not made for this world's pain." He shared the news with Walter hoping archly that his friend would admire "the 'fair slim boy'!"

Christopher discussed the bibliography with the artist and writer, Charles de Soury Ricketts, too. He was a good friend of Robbie's, who lived with his partner and fellow artist, Charles Hazelwood Shannon. Oscar had known them both well, and they were jointly the inspiration for the character of Basil in *The Picture of Dorian Gray*. They formed the centre of an artistic circle and were avid collectors of art and antiques which they displayed in a series of beautifully decorated houses. Christopher was particularly keen to find out more about the illustrations which Charles Ricketts had made for Oscar's *Mr W. H.* and *The Sphinx*. Charles himself regarded his spare and vigorous illustrations for *The Sphinx* as his best works and thought they perfectly matched Oscar's poem. "I am going to see him one day soon," wrote Christopher, "And will let you know if I can get any information out of him." However he thought it more than likely that he and Walter knew more about Charles' drawings "than he knows himself!"

Despite Oscar's gradually recovering reputation, his work was still not free from censorship and this continued to anger Christopher. On 20 February it led him to make a protest at the Prince of Wales' Theatre. As the performance of the comedy, *Dear Old Charley*, by Charles Hallam Elton Brookfield drew to a close, Christopher shouted out loudly from the gallery that it was "a filthy play!" *Dear Old Charley* featured a philanderer (played in this revival by the actor Charles Hawtrey) and indeed it was thought to be slightly scandalous. Christopher's quarrel, though, was with the play's author on two counts. Firstly Charles Brookfield was now the official censor of plays and Christopher was annoyed at the censorship Oscar's *Salome* had suffered over the years. Secondly there was a rumour that Charles had helped to gather evidence against Oscar in 1895 because he had been very jealous of Oscar's success.

In March Arthur Ransome's book, *Oscar Wilde: A Critical Study*, appeared and Christopher received a copy with a handwritten inscription by the author. Arthur had dedicated the work to Robbie - apparently without asking his permission – and the book drew heavily on material he had supplied, including a copy of *De Profundis* which contained the sections omitted from the published version. These were highly critical of Alfred Douglas (as well as of Alfred's father) and made it clear that *De Profundis* was addressed not to Robbie, but to a friend who had caused Oscar much unhappiness. *Oscar Wilde: A Critical Study* suggested that the friendship had been disastrous for Oscar and, although it did not actually name Alfred, his identity would have been obvious to those who knew something of the history of the matter. Understandably Alfred was furious. Thomas Crosland urged him to issue writs against Arthur Ransome as well as against the publisher, the printer, and The Times

Book Club (which was distributing the book). Alfred needed little persuasion particularly because he saw Robbie's hand behind the book and was keen to take action against him. Robbie in his turn supported Arthur Ransome and offered to pay his legal costs. Always on Robbie's side in any dispute with Alfred, Christopher no doubt approved of his stance.

During the summer Christopher managed to spend several weekends out of London first in "Buckinghamshire and the neighbouring counties" and then in Norfolk. But he was troubled by the continued public hostility towards Oscar, which emerged in various forms. There was criticism of the Jacob Epstein sculpture for his memorial in Paris and its unveiling was postponed. More upsetting was Thomas Crosland's parody of *De Profundis* which he published that autumn. *The First Stone* was a scathing attack on Oscar's letter. Christopher bought a copy of the "filthy book" from Thomas himself at 14 Conduit Street. It describes Oscar as a "scented posturer" and "canting knave." It paraphrases and mocks *De Profundis* and derides Oscar's admirers who, like Christopher, "make swift trips to Dieppe,/ When they think the police/ May call…" The poem ended with an epitaph to Oscar "Whose soul was all a sin,/ Whose heart was all a lust,/ Whose brain was all a lie." Christopher was so furious when he read it that he refused to return to buy another copy for Walter. Christopher was also considerably affected by Alfred's increasing hostility towards Robbie, which manifested itself in several letters accusing him of sodomy. These were intended both to frighten him and to goad him into suing for libel. A very public scene followed at a party on 29 November when Alfred accused Robbie of being a "bugger and a blackmailer."

At Christmas Christopher was at least able to take a break from work: "I hope to have a holiday all next week and until the New Year." Walter sent him a copy of *Sebastian Melmoth* as a Christmas gift. This had been published in 1904 by Arthur Lee Humphreys and included Oscar's epigrams and *The Soul of Man under Socialism*. Christopher might have been particularly interested in this volume because he had recently finished making another selection of quotes for a book called *Great Thoughts from Oscar Wilde* which was published by Dodge in New York. He was unsure what to give Walter in return. "My intended Christmas present to you was to have been the *Irish Birthday Book* but you forestalled me! Now I don't know what I shall be able to find you." The present he had planned was an 1884 selection from the speeches and writings of Irish men and women arranged by 'Melusine'. It includes a number of quotes from

Oscar's mother and two from Oscar himself one of which (for 7 November) expressed his pleasure in Irish appreciation of his mother's efforts in "Ireland's cause" and acknowledged the negative impact of the English on Irish art.

Christopher added Walter's gift to his collection of books which was growing again. Most had been acquired to help him with compiling the bibliography and there were enough of them to make it worthwhile taking Walter's advice and having glass doors added to his bookshelves. He organised this for January 1913 inviting Walter to "come and see them in a few weeks' time." Otherwise he was extremely busy: "I don't seem to have had a moment these last few days to write a letter. I often wonder how busy people get through their work and rest and sleep in the 24 hours. I cannot afford to pay others to help me more than is absolutely necessary, and I think I sell my labour too cheaply – though I don't know where I should find any one willing to buy my services at an enhanced price."

He was working regularly for Robbie (who was occupied both at Somerset House and elsewhere) and was keen to be supportive to him, particularly because he could see first-hand the impact Alfred's actions were having on his friend's life. Robbie's erstwhile lover and secretary, Frederick Stanley Smith, was increasingly absent, partly because Robbie's private life was under increasing scrutiny. For Christopher's this meant "A great deal of my spare time now is occupied in acting as R R 's secretary while Freddie Smith is away. But then R always pays me very liberally and it is of course a privilege to be allowed to do any thing for him." In March, with a sense of relief, Christopher "chucked the *Burlington* at last." From then on his secretarial work for Robbie became his main source of income and it included proof reading for which he received around five guineas per volume.

On 17 April the trial of Arthur Ransome for libelling Alfred Douglas opened before Justice Darling. Christopher was immediately caught up in Robbie's anxiety about the case and regularly attended the hearings at Marlborough Street to follow proceedings. Cecil Hayes presented Alfred's side of the case and tried hard to distance him from Oscar's sexual activities. However he was unable to prevent the unpublished parts of *De Profundis* being read out. Christopher wrote, "The reading of *De Profundis* was most impressive and 'sensational' (as a journalist would say)." It made public Oscar's resentment towards Alfred and his criticism of the "ill-fated and lamentable" friendship between them. These were, of course, the emotions of a despondent man locked in his prison cell and they did not express all of Oscar's feelings about Alfred. But they were part of the truth as he saw it at the time. Robbie must have been relieved that he was not called to give evidence during the trial, although his friend William More Adey did appear and spoke critically of Alfred and his influence on Oscar.

On the surface the outcome was positive for Robbie and his allies. On 23 April, when the court case was over, Christopher sent Walter copies of a newspaper which had printed pictures of the trial. "Two of the jury held out for an hour and ¾ and wanted to give a ¼ d damages!" he exclaimed. (If this had happened Alfred might have been awarded costs.) But finally the jury agreed that although the disputed sections of *Oscar Wilde: A Critical Study* could be considered libellous, they were true and both Arthur Ransome and The Times Book Club were cleared. Christopher wrote delightedly, "Darling's summing-up was an admirable speech for the defence." He took considerable pleasure in seeing Alfred squirming: "Douglas is up to-morrow at the Old Bailey for libelling Col. Custance [his father-in-law], so he has got his hands pretty full, hasn't he?" He was happy for Robbie that the court case was over, but realised that it would take him some time to recover from the considerable strain he had been under.

However, in some respects, the outcome was worrying for gay men. Robbie and his allies had adopted a dangerous strategy in undermining Alfred's case by exposing his relationship with Oscar and then exploiting the popular prejudice against gay activity in order to discredit him. The verdict itself enraged Alfred as did his inability to pay the costs involved. Both fuelled his determination to bring Robbie down and he began plotting new schemes with Thomas Crosland's support. He threatened to lodge an appeal against the verdict and even though he decided against this, he severed his long standing friendship with William More Adey regarding his testimony in court as a betrayal. More sinisterly, he employed a private detective to secretly watch both Robbie and Freddie Smith in order to collect evidence about their relationship.

As tensions mounted Christopher was keen to get away from London for a while and at Whitsuntide he went to Ramsgate passing Rochester en route – which reminded him of Walter and his boat. Christopher might have been visiting friends in Ramsgate – possibly members of either the

110

Falcy or the Pugin families. He stayed at the late eighteenth century Castle Hotel in Harbour Parade (which is now an arts centre) and found the harbour "so pretty" and thought the town was "a jolly little place – only it's too near Margate!" However he dismissed Kent on the whole as "a dull, flat and uninteresting country." After his trip to Ramsgate he spent a couple of days at his mother's and then on Friday 6 June he took the night train to Edinburgh. He spent the weekend with Charles, who by then had begun studying Anglo-Saxon for his higher degree. They had a busy weekend, presumably mostly socialising with Charles' friends, and they did not have "much time for all the bookshops" though no doubt Christopher would have enjoyed exploring them.

In July Christopher met up with Michael Lykiardopolos (Lyki) who lived in Moscow but who was spending that summer in Montague Street in Bloomsbury. They had first met during the previous year and Lyki had many contacts amongst European literary circles. He had translated Oscar's *Salome* and *The Florentine Tragedy* into Russian. Christopher considered him "rather nice" and thought he "talks English charmingly." Lyki was indeed both kind and loyal and the British agent, Robert Hamilton Bruce Lockhart) described him as "a strange lovable creature; one third Greek, one third Russian, and one third English" who had "real literary flair, an excellent Russian prose style, and a quite remarkable knowledge of eight or nine European languages." After spending a few weeks in London Lyki returned to Moscow (where he was the secretary of the Moscow Art Theatre and the ballet critic for one of the leading newspapers) but before leaving he arranged that Robbie would visit Moscow during the autumn to attend the premiere of *Salome*. There were plans in London, too, for performances of some of Oscar's works. Lou Tellegen (Sarah Bernhardt's husband) was rehearsing an adaptation of *Dorian Gray* in which he was both actor and director and intended to open this at the Vaudeville Theatre on August 28. He was also hoping to produce the *Duchess of Padua* in the West End. Christopher was not hopeful about either production: "Both will be pretty bad, I expect."

However his friend, Robbie, soon had greater concerns than the quality of the forthcoming theatrical productions. On 16 August he learned that Alfred was taking further steps against him. A twenty-six year old medical student from Ealing, Norman Ernest Farr, had been offered a bribe by a lawyer working for Alfred to say that he had had sex with Robbie. Norman refused to cooperate and felt obliged to warn Robbie of Alfred's plan. But he was worried about getting dragged into controversy himself

111

and declined to make any written statement about the matter. However it was a worrying move, which indicated how far Alfred was prepared to go in his vendetta.

CHAPTER ELEVEN

CHARLEY GARRATT

"a beauty" to "arouse his passion" - Christopher quoted in Metropolitan Police report of 26 January 1915 in MEPO 3/240 at The National Archives

Christopher was probably unaware of this latest development when he made his way through the streets of the West End on the evening of Tuesday 19 August. Shortly after ten o'clock he was at the lower end of Shaftesbury Avenue when a well-dressed fresh-faced young man caught his attention. Christopher went over to him and struck up a conversation by commenting on the Women's Social and Political Union badge that the youth was wearing.

Lower end of Shaftesbury Avenue

The W.S.P.U. was a militant, mainly middle-class, suffragette organisation, which had been founded in Manchester. It was now led by Christabel Pankhurst and its campaign of "Deeds, not words" had intensified. Members were smashing windows, setting fire to buildings, and sending letter bombs. They also targeted letters in pillar-boxes, with one of the most active members in this part of the campaign being May Billinghurst who had recently been sentenced to eight months in Holloway and subjected to force-feeding. Meanwhile on 4 June, two months before Christopher's foray into the West End, another W.S.P.U. member, Emily Wilding Davison, had been killed in a high-profile protest at the Epsom Derby. Though the majority of men were hostile towards the idea of women's suffrage, there were some who supported it. In 1907 a number of left-wing male intellectuals had formed the Men's League for Women's Suffrage (and later the Men's Political Union for Women's Enfranchisement), which was supportive both of the W.S.P.U. and the Women's Freedom League and some men became actively involved in the campaign to damage property.

Christopher was curious to learn more about this attractive young man who was sympathetic towards the suffragettes and to keep him talking he told him that he knew Mrs Pankhurst's son. If that was true Christopher must have been referring to Christabel's dead brother, Henry (Harry) Francis, who had been born in the same year as Charles Scott Moncrieff. He had been a frail youth but his mother apprenticed him to a builder in Glasgow even though he struggled with the physical demands of the job. When the builder went bankrupt, Harry came south to stay with his other sister, Sylvia, in London where she was active both in the W.S.P.U. and in the Independent Labour Party. This was the happiest time of Harry's life and it must have been at this stage that Christopher met him. Harry was in love (with a teacher called Helen Craggs) and was enjoying shorthand and typing classes at a polytechnic and using his reader's ticket at the British Museum. But before long his mother intervened and sent him to a smallholding in Mayland in Essex. He became seriously ill there and was diagnosed with polio. He died at the age of twenty.

The young man in Shaftesbury Avenue was interested in what Christopher had to say about Harry. In his turn he told his new acquaintance that both he and his mother were actively involved with the suffragettes and in order to impress Christopher, he claimed that his mother was a leading member of the movement. The claim was untrue, but he was a young man who had a tendency (according to his mother) "to appear bigger than he really was" and to hide the truth about his humble background. He introduced himself as Charles Nehemiah Garratt explaining that he was usually known as Charley, that he was seventeen years old, and that he had travelled down to London from Leicestershire.

Charley had been born in the middle of 1895 (around the time of Oscar's conviction) and his birthplace was Countesthorpe, a small settlement south west of Leicester. His father, William, was an agricultural labourer who had married a much younger woman and he died when Charley was only five leaving his thirty-three year old widow, Elizabeth, to bring up their six children alone. She struggled financially. She had had only a limited education and she was only able to read large print and that not very well. She earned just seven or eight shillings a week working as a charwoman and she used nearly two shillings of this to rent a four-roomed cottage for herself and her children in Peatling End where they seem to have just scraped by. Charley had two older brothers - Henry William and Arthur - and an older sister, Fanny. Arthur and Fanny both became factory hands and were employed at one of the hosiery factories whose steam-powered knitting machines had made Leicester into a boom city. It seems likely that Fanny worked making up and finishing items, whilst Arthur was employed to look after the machines. Both worked long hours and their pay was not high, but they were soon earning more than their mother.

However when he left school Charley did not want to join Fanny and Arthur in the factory. He was a clever young man - "the smartest in the family" – but his employment opportunities were limited. At first he worked as an assistant groom and gardener. He seems to have had the idea of studying at Kingston Agricultural College in Derbyshire, which had been founded in the year of his birth and which was partly funded by Leicester County Council. However this ambition might have remained unfulfilled. Instead Charley found work "at a fried fish shop at Leicester" though at least this got him out of his village and into the nearby town. It must have been whilst he was working at the shop that Charley found out about the activities of the local suffragettes.

The Leicester section of the W.S.P.U. was formed in 1907 and began recruiting by holding open-air meetings in factories, market squares and village greens. An office was established at 14 Bowling Green Street and various activities were organised for W.S.P.U. members. They travelled down to the mass rally in Hyde Park in June 1908 and then in the following year they heckled Winston Churchill when he spoke at the Palace Theatre in Leicester. In 1910 a local branch of the Men's Political Union for Women's Enfranchisement was established and Charley joined after attending a meeting at which he heard Emmeline Pankhurst speak.

He began working for the suffragettes under the assumed names of Carl Tuke and Alfred Richardson. His aliases were no doubt inspired by the names of well-known members of the movement. Mabel Kate Tuke played a major role in the W.S.P.U. and Mary Richardson was another prominent member (who famously slashed a painting at the National Gallery in 1914). Charley travelled down to London with the suffragettes several times (without telling his mother) and he helped organise political activities, sold papers in Piccadilly and even spoke in Hyde Park. These trips to London must have opened his eyes to a very different world. His mother later claimed that Charley "lived a decent life while with me" and there had been few opportunities to do otherwise. But London was different and one of its attractions must have been that it offered the young man the opportunity for sex with other men.

Most of his time was still spent in Leicestershire though. Towards the end of 1912 his sister, Fanny, married a local gardener, Edward Flude, and at around the same time Charley began working at the George Hotel on the Haymarket in Leicester. He was employed there as "third boots" with his work supervised by the "head boots" Arthur Williams. When not at the hotel, Charley continued "following the women who carried sandwich boards up and down the street."

The final week of January 1913 was one of sustained suffragette activity. In London there were several nights of rioting, marching and window smashing. On the evening of Wednesday 29 January corrosive fluid was poured into the box at Coventry's central post office. On Thursday night a pillar-box was damaged by acid in Liverpool and six boxes were set alight in Birmingham. There was a W.S.P.U. meeting on the same night in London at which Annie Kenny urged people to continue to target pillar-boxes. There must have been a meeting that week in Leicester too because Charley heard the suffragettes "talking about" attacking pillar-boxes and he became "interested, and went and did it." At the George Hotel he had access to the commercial and writing rooms and he helped himself to some of the hotel stationery. He tore off the flaps of the envelopes to remove the hotel's name and went to the hotel stables to get a bottle of 'Battle's disinfectant' which was kept in a drum there. His first "pillar-box outrage" took place on the evening of Wednesday 29 January when he poured disinfectant into an envelope and tipped it into the pillar-box in the High Street before it was emptied at about 9.45 pm. The liquid washed the penny stamp off one of the letters inside. On the following evening at about 8.30 pm he took a letter from the hotel hall letter-box and posted it in the pillar-box in Eastgates along with some more envelopes containing disinfectant.

The damage to the letters was immediately reported to the police and they soon tracked Charley down. At 11.45 am on the following Monday Inspector North appeared at the George and accused Charley "of putting some fluid into letter-boxes, and thereby damaging letters" and showed him four stained envelopes. Charley admitted to the attacks and was taken to the police station to be charged with damaging the property of the Postmaster General "to the amount of one penny." The next day (Tuesday 4 February) he pleaded guilty at the Leicester Borough Police Court. The Magistrates' Clerk asked him whether he had damaged any other pillar-boxes: "You might as well make a clean breast of it." But Charley replied, "No, sir. I only did these." The Chairman declared that this was "diabolical mischief" and "it must be put a stop to." He bound Charley over under the Probation of Offenders Act to "the care of Mr Ellwood" and sent him to the Church Army Home for one month.

Charley probably divulged something of this escapade to Christopher as they stood talking in Shaftesbury Avenue and as Christopher was keen to prolong the conversation he invited Charley for a drink. They met up with another man named Pat and Christopher then asked them both back to Molyneux House. There Charley consumed several whiskies and was persuaded to stay the night. He probably had sex with both Christopher and Pat, although he later refused to say "whether Millard and Pat kissed me and messed me about or whether they got into bed with me and behaved immorally."

A few days after this first encounter, Charley spent a week or so in Folkestone. He returned to London during the second week of September and Christopher spotted him "from a taxi near the Hippodrome" in Leicester Square. He greeted him affectionately and they dined together at a restaurant along with some friends. At about ten o'clock they went back to Molyneux House - presumably to have sex again - and Charley left at about midnight. They met up on the following evening and this time Christopher treated Charley to dinner at Stone's in Panton Street and then took him to see the adaptation of *Dorian Gray* at the Vaudeville Theatre in the Strand. He was clearly keen to share Oscar's work with his new companion. The play had been dramatized in three acts (with a prologue) by Grace Constant Lounsbery. It opened on 28 August and ran at the Vaudeville until 26 September. It was not particularly successful. The review in *The Times* on 29 August declared that it was "a mistake to dramatise Dorian Gray". Oscar's "characteristic wit … intellectual curiosity… aesthetic criticism … cannot be transferred to the stage". Lou Tellegen who played Dorian was no "perfect beauty" and his costume was "eccentric" whilst Franklin Dyall, who played Lord Henry Wootton did "murmur" cynical Wildean remarks but his part was "ineffective" and "absurd".

Vaudeville Theatre

Lou Tellegen might have been no great beauty but Christopher found his own young companion extremely attractive and was keen to continue their relationship. He soon confessed to a friend that he considered the young man "a beauty" who "arouse[d] his passion." Charley was apparently as eager as Christopher to continue the liaison. They met frequently and spent a number of evenings at Molyneux House. Christopher introduced Charley to some of his friends (although probably not to Walter) and Charley was soon a regular at the Café Royal, which was notorious for its "young men wearing tight suits and nail varnish … sipping crème de menthe", and at The Avenue, the public house located at 134 Shaftesbury Avenue. Mainly through his relationship with Christopher, Charley became part of a network of young men, most of whom were gay and who included a young academic named Charles Leopold Boulenger. He became particularly friendly with Aylmer Clerk and with Frank Hughes, who worked in the theatre and who was usually known as 'Fluffy'. Almost certainly these two men were lovers and they occasionally seem to have gone out with Charley and Christopher as a foursome.

Another member of the circle was Cecil Howard Turner. Charley soon realised Cecil was "effeminate" too and one evening at Molyneux House he "threw himself on the sofa" where Cecil was sitting and "endeavoured to embrace him". Cecil later denied that he was gay declaring that he "knew nothing of this sort of thing" and that he "nearly strangled 'Fluffy' when he made a suggestion to him." Nevertheless Cecil accompanied Charley, Frank and Charles Leopold when they went drinking first at the New Inn at the bottom of Edgware Road near Marble Arch and then at The Avenue. He allowed Charley to flirt with him, walking arm in arm with him and talking about him to the barmaid. And Christopher was comfortable about confiding in Cecil too, telling him on one occasion that the only thing he was interested in "was sodomy" and at other times speaking "quite openly to him about improper conduct with different boys."

Whilst Christopher's evenings were often spent with Charley and his other friends, his days were still filled with work. Robbie was planning to have the entire text of Oscar's *De Profundis* printed in New York (by Paul R. Reynolds) so Christopher spent time getting the typescript ready. (A small number of copies were duly issued on 22 September and one was given to Christopher.)

On Thursday 4 September Robbie left London for Moscow travelling at Lyki's invitation. First though he spent ten days in Paris and it was from there that he wrote to Christopher to confide his problems with his lover Freddie. Freddie was now spending very little time at Robbie's apartment and something (or more likely someone) had apparently "quite turned" his head. Robbie resented the sacrifices he had made for Freddie, who was showing him "neither affection nor regard nor sensitivity," and who seemed unsympathetic towards Robbie's plight in the face of Alfred's campaign. In fact Freddie might well have been frightened by Alfred's actions and one possible explanation for his frequent absences is that he was trying to make himself scarce to avoid becoming caught up in the feud.

Whilst Robbie was away, Christopher, accompanied by Charley, arranged to spend a weekend out of London with Aylmer and Frank. However all he told Walter about the trip was that he spent "a very jolly week-end at Westcliff, walking on Sunday via Leigh-on-sea to Benfleet which is quaint and old-fashioned." Christopher and Charley travelled out by train with Aylmer on Saturday 13 September. They had lunch in the Queen's Hotel near Westcliff railway station where they met up with Frank, who was working that week as the stage manager for a production at the New Palace Theatre. It was later suggested that Frank greeted them all warmly with kisses (though Aylmer denied this). At about five o'clock they all had tea together at Frank's lodgings at 7 Windsor Road (which were run by Mrs Susan Elizabeth Humer) and where Frank had both a bedroom and a sitting room.

After dinner Charley went with Frank to the theatre to see the last night of *The Little Damozel*. This was a recent play by the Irish writer Monckton Hoffe about a naval captain who paid one of his crew to get married, and it was performed by a company led by a young actor, Alick Northcote Chumley. Meanwhile Christopher and Aylmer went out on the town. At the end of the evening all four men went back to Windsor Road and had a late supper of oysters. Quite what the sleeping arrangements were that night is a little hazy. Aylmer later admitted sharing a room with Frank but said he slept on a camp bed. He denied that he and Frank had sex, although it seems likely that they did. He also said that Charley and Christopher had separate rooms and that Christopher's main motivation for taking Charley out of town was merely to stop him going to a suffragette meeting to "kick up a row and do damage to property". But as Aylmer said all of this whilst he was being questioned by the police, it is highly likely that he was covering up what had really happened. The landlady at 7 Windsor Road didn't remember Aylmer being there at all when she was interviewed by the police on 23 July 1914, but she did recall that Charley and Christopher had shared a double bed, though she was "positive there was nothing on the bedclothes. I saw no stains or indications of anything." However presumably with a bit of ingenuity there were ways this could be avoided!

On Sunday after breakfast Frank set off early and caught the train back to London, but Christopher, Charley and Aylmer decided to walk the six miles along the coast to the station at Benfleet. When they eventually got back Charley went to Aylmer's flat and soon afterwards Christopher joined them there. They went out to The Globe, an eighteenth century public house in Marylebone Road, where Frank met them. The evening seems to have ended with a lovers' tiff between Frank and Aylmer. Frank walked out upset, but the two men had made things up by the following evening when they both went to Molyneaux House for drinks.

It was not long after this trip to the seaside that Christopher received another letter from Robbie who was feeling rather isolated in Moscow. He admitted to Christopher that he was depressed by the lack of evidence of any "purple people or any who avowed they were or looked in the least like it." But although London did have at least a semi-visible gay community it was still a city in which life was problematic for gay men as Christopher's lover, Charley, was about to discover.

On the night of Wednesday 17 September (a few days after their weekend in Westcliff) Christopher invited Charley to dine with two friends. One might have been Frank (though the man was described as an actor rather than a stage manager). The other was "a student at Edinburgh" who was presumably Charles Scott Moncrieff. The four men met at eight o'clock and ate at a restaurant in Soho before going back to Christopher's flat. Here they later claimed to have played charades and drunk champagne – though more could have gone on as well! Charley apparently had taken "more champagne than was good for him" before he left Molyneux House shortly before midnight. Christopher thought he was going straight home to his lodgings which were at 45 Torrington Square nearby. But instead some time before one o'clock on the following morning, Charley was arrested in Piccadilly (close to where Christopher had first met him a few weeks before) and he was taken to Vine Street Police Station where he was charged with acting in a disorderly manner: "Police officers stated that they saw the prisoner with his face and lips rouged, his face also powdered, and he was smelling very strongly of scent." He "acted in an effeminate way and smiled up into the face of gentlemen." In their view Charley was a male prostitute walking the West End streets looking for clients.

This arrest and its aftermath would prove to be a disaster not only for Charley, but for Christopher and, through him, for Robbie too. Christopher first became aware of what had happened when a telegraph message arrived. It had been sent from Vine Street at 4.45 am and read, "Please inform Mr Millard, 6 Molyneux House, Molyneux Street, that Cecil Garratt is in custody at this station and will be at Marlborough Street Police Court at 10 am the 18th inst.

Anxious to help his lover, but perhaps also worried about what he might reveal about events at Molyneux House when questioned, Christopher was in court for the hearing five hours later and had agreed he would speak on Charley's behalf. When he was called, he tried to make a good impression on the magistrate by describing himself as an Oxford graduate and as the secretary to a well-known literary gentleman. He agreed that he should not have let Charley drink so much but claimed that he thought that he was not intoxicated when he left Molyneaux House but "merely excited", and he was not wearing rouge or powder at the time either. After the hearing Christopher wrote to Charley's mother telling her of her son's arrest although he did not mention the reason for it and left her to assume it was a result of Charley's suffragette activities.

By the time Charley's hearing resumed on the following Thursday (25 September) Christopher's own past had been unearthed and his intervention on Charley's behalf now rebounded on him. He was recalled and asked, "Was there any unpleasant episode while you were at Oxford?" Christopher replied, "Not at Oxford, sir", but was forced to admit his conviction for the events at Iffley seven years before. The magistrate switched his focus from Charley to Christopher, who must have suddenly felt that he was on trial again. He was warned "not to lead lads like this to that sort of ruin." He protested, "I have tried to keep the boy out of trouble." But the magistrate did not waver: "But why do you have anything to do with the boy? Why is he in your hands at all?" In the magistrate's view, Christopher was a corrupting influence on Charley and was in fact largely responsible for what had happened: "I shall not give him the sentence I should otherwise do, because I feel that the lad has fallen because of coming under the influence of you and men like you."

So Charley was sentenced to three months in prison with hard labour - an identical sentence to the one Christopher had served – but shorter than it might have been. However this can have been of little consolation to him and Charley left the court in tears. He served his time in Pentonville Prison where Christopher, who continued to feel a sense of loyalty towards him, visited him, possibly more than once, and continued to write to his mother.

To protest against his conviction Charley, influenced by the suffragettes, soon began to threaten to go on hunger strike. However Christopher was keen to dissuade him. He was sure that the authorities would be even less sympathetic towards him than they were towards the suffragettes. Indeed

Christopher seemed increasingly out of sympathy with the suffragettes himself and it might have been that his original interest in Charley's W.S.P.U. activities was largely feigned in order to strike up a conversation with a young man who had caught his eye. In one of his letters to Charley's mother he wrote dismissively (and misleadingly) "I fear your son has been led away by being left alone in London and by being mixed up with the ridiculous Votes for Women movement".

He said nothing about Charley in any of his letters to Walter. Perhaps he was wary of committing anything to paper. Early in October (soon after Charley's conviction) he did spend an afternoon with Walter and he might have told him something about what had happened when they talked face-to-face. Equally, though, he might have decided that Walter would not approve of this latest liaison and so kept quiet. However he probably confided in Robbie whom he felt he could trust. In fact even if he had said nothing, Robbie would not have stayed ignorant for long because Alfred Douglas, scenting a new opportunity to attack Robbie, posted a copy of a newspaper cutting which reported the events at the police court to Robbie's solicitor, George Lewis, along with another derogatory letter about Robbie himself.

In his turn Robbie revealed that he had decided that his relationship with Freddie was over. He did not want Freddie to know when he was due back and had planned his return so he could avoid him: "I have especially arranged to arrive on Sunday when he will be away in the natural course of events." He was unable to deal with the thought of seeing him: "His presence would moreover upset me and his artificial enthusiasm would annoy me." No doubt Christopher willingly kept the secret of Robbie's arrival on 5 October and he was flattered that he had been taken into his friend's confidence.

Later in October, whilst Charley was still in Pentonville Prison, Christopher spent some time with his old friend Alan Alington, who had arranged to visit London and Christopher might have gone to Waterloo Station to meet him off the train. Alan was still teaching, although he had left Woodford Wells and was probably then based in Christchurch in Hampshire, staying with his mother and his uncle, Francis John Atwood. Christopher and Alan had remained close and Christopher had already introduced Alan to Walter expecting that they would get on well as they were both enthusiastic sailors. They did subsequently arrange to spend time together on the river Frome in Dorset where they sailed up and down between Wareham and Poole.

Although Christopher might have talked to Alan about Charley, he would have said nothing about his lover to his relatives if, as seems likely, he was summoned to the wedding of his brother, Baldwin, which took place at the end of October in Bocking, a village on the river Blackwater near Braintree in Essex. Christopher's youngest brother had chosen well in deciding to train as an engineer and it turned out that he had a real aptitude for the work. He loved the adrenalin rush that came from racing cars and he was keen on boats too. He was an innovative man who was not fully satisfied with the performance of the propellers on ships so put his mind to designing improvements which he subsequently patented. Although there seems to have been little love lost between Christopher and Baldwin, they did at least share a common interest in sailing (which Baldwin nurtured by joining the Royal Thames Yacht Club and the Royal Motor Yacht Club) and both also took pleasure in acquiring practical skills.

But there were always tensions in their relationship. It seems likely that Christopher's sexuality was one of the issues dividing them and almost certainly this had already driven a wedge between them. However there might have been more to the disagreement and other members of the family could have been involved. It might have been that Christopher was not the only sibling to be more idealistic and less worldly than his youngest brother. In this respect Magdalen, Philippa, and Paul might have resembled Christopher more than they did Baldwin (who apparently got on better with George and Dorothy). In fact Baldwin seems to have been the most ambitious of all the siblings and the one most determined to achieve social and financial success which could have created its own tensions within the family circle. Baldwin had probably met his future wife, Phyllis Mary Tetley, when he was sailing on the Blackwater and her background seemed very suitable as she was the daughter of a silk manufacturer who had moved his successful business from Bradford to Bocking. Phyllis and Baldwin, who had two children, were keen travellers and (unlike Christopher who never went further than France) they visited many parts of the world travelling not only to the United States but to South Africa, Argentina, Egypt and Japan. Indeed Baldwin rarely spent a whole year in England, becoming restless if too long elapsed between his international voyages.

Christopher probably went to Bocking just for the day of the wedding before returning to London where he continued to provide a sympathetic ear for Robbie who was anxious about what Alfred would do next and particularly worried about what Alfred might include in his book of memoirs, *Oscar Wilde and Myself*, which was due out any day. Fortunately Robbie was not without support though because he had the backing of some influential friends including Margot Asquith, who was married to the Prime Minister (and who possibly had lesbian affairs herself).

For Christopher, books provided a useful distraction from these anxieties during what was proving to be a difficult autumn. He had no money to buy expensive items but he rather liked "collecting little out-of-the-way things." In addition he was buying books in order to re-sell them as well as selling them on behalf of other people. That December he offered an autographed *Happy Prince* owned by a woman whose recent divorce had left her very hard-up. Christopher seemed sympathetic to her plight and was keen to get as much as possible for the book, hoping for fifteen or twenty pounds.

He was pleased to meet up with "a weird American friend", Daniel Connell, from Chicago who was interested in Oscar's work and excited to learn that there had been an American edition of Oscar's poems, although at first he wasn't sure whether Daniel's information was reliable. However it turned out that there were indeed 1881 and 1882 editions published in Boston by Roberts Brothers.

As usual, Walter's Christmas present to Christopher was a book. This time it was Walter's latest publication - a further account of his travels on the *Blue Bird* for which he had been delighted to find an appropriate quotation from Oscar's *The Decay of Lying* which describes how "over our heads will float the Blue Bird singing of beautiful and impossible things". After he had read the account Christopher lent it to Alan (who was then living on Furzey Island in Poole Harbour) before writing to thank Walter for his gift: "Ever so many thanks for your delightful little brochure... A really interesting and fascinating little work in all ways. I know most of the places you visited". He was "particularly pleased to read your approbation of St Augustine's, Ramsgate, built by Peter Paul" as this had been built by "the father of a very dear young friend of mine, Welby Pugin, himself the fourth in direct descent of a family of architects." The friend he referred to was almost certainly the seventeen year old Augustus Herbert Welby who was one of the sons of the architect,

Edmund Peter Paul Pugin. Christopher might well have introduced Augustus to Alan at around this time and they would later run a school together.

CHAPTER TWELVE

REPLAYING OSCAR

"And the end thereof no man can foretell." - Christopher in a letter to Walter 26 December 1913

Even before Christmas 1913, events in Alfred Douglas' vendetta continued to unfold. Charley was due to be released from prison on Wednesday 10 December and shortly before this he wrote to his mother requesting, "Dear Mother, Please send me a clean shirt, a clean collar, and a pair of navy blue trousers."

Christopher was informed that Charley would be at the gates of Pentonville Prison at seven in the morning and he was there to meet him. He could see immediately that his friend had lost weight - a result both of the prison diet and of the manual labour he had been forced to undertake. Charley quickly revealed that he had been visited in prison by a clerk sent by Cecil Bruce Holt, the solicitor employed by Alfred, who had showed him a photograph of Robbie and tried to persuade him to admit that they had been lovers though Charley convinced Christopher that he had refused to do this because it was untrue. Disturbed by his story, Christopher asked him to accompany him to Ely Place in Holborn where they met Robbie's solicitor, George Lewis, who asked Charley to make a statement about exactly what had happened.

Charley spent his first evening of freedom with Christopher and they had dinner together at The Globe. Whilst they ate Christopher might well have urged Charley to leave London for a while, primarily to get him out of Alfred's way, although apparently he could not persuade him to go. Instead Charley slept that night in a local rented room in Marylebone Road, which Christopher could have found for him.

At this stage Christopher must have assumed that Charley could be trusted, and that the young man was as committed as he was to supporting Robbie's cause. But (not for the first time) Christopher overestimated another person's loyalty and in fact Charley was not being entirely straightforward in his dealings with Christopher. Two days later, on Friday 12 December, almost certainly without Christopher's knowledge, he made his way to Cecil Holt's office at 24 Upper George Street in Bryanston Square. Why did he decide to do this? His main motivation was likely to have been financial. He had only a few shillings left and he knew he had little chance of finding work. He might not have felt he owed much loyalty to Christopher - or to any wealthy friend of his - and he was certainly still resentful about his imprisonment.

At the solicitor's office he met Alfred Douglas for the first time. Alfred was quick to grasp the need to get Charley out of the reach of "Millard and my other friends" so he accompanied him by taxi to collect his small amount of luggage from Marylebone Road and when he found out the young man only had 4s 2d in his pockets, he gave him half a sovereign. He took him to Victoria Station where they left his luggage at the cloakroom and went to a restaurant for lunch and "2 large lager beers." Alfred then summoned Thomas Crosland who soon appeared at the restaurant and between them Thomas and Alfred drew up a statement in pencil in order to implicate Robbie. Alfred repeatedly told Charley that Robbie was a "dirty beast" and eventually the young man agreed to sign the statement, though he later claimed that he had never even met Robbie.

After lunch Alfred took Charley to Scotland Yard and left him there to make a statement telling him to "rub it in well about Ross" whilst he went off to arrange a room for him at the Wilton Hotel in Victoria. Then that evening, when Alfred and Thomas took Charley for dinner at the Grosvenor Restaurant, money was discussed for the first time. Charley was assured that Robbie would be willing to pay him a thousand pounds in order to avoid a court case and this must have provided a huge incentive for a destitute young man who probably felt he deserved the money. No doubt he assumed that the man he was accusing would never actually be prosecuted and that he could well afford to give Charley the kind of sum which would transform his life.

On Saturday all three men had lunch together again and Charley went twice more to Scotland Yard to continue his statement. In the evening he met Alfred at Victoria Station and they dined with a man called Mr Carew, who was a private detective, before at about 11.30 pm Charley returned to his hotel room in the Wilton Hotel leaving Alfred behind in the much grander surroundings of the Grosvenor Hotel. However Alfred did not entirely trust Charley and might well have sent the detective to keep an eye on the young man. About half an hour later he turned up in person at the Wilton Hotel claiming that he had seen Christopher and another man arriving. He insisted that Charley should pack up his things and leave immediately. They changed cabs three times as Alfred was convinced they were being followed, and finally ended up at Edwards' Hotel in Euston Square.

On Sunday Alfred, as a devout Catholic, attended a service at Westminster Cathedral taking Charley with him. The two men then lunched with Mr Carew at the Grosvenor Restaurant. "After lunch he [Alfred] took 3 tickets for us to go to Kensington to the Commissioners but I then refused to go." Perhaps Charley now felt things had gone too far. His refusal infuriated Alfred: "Lord Alfred Douglas said 'You are no good except to be f-d at' Carew said 'Hosy posy'. Lord A Douglas was in a frightful temper." Charley started to walk away but Mr Carew grabbed him and pulled him back.

The Grosvenor Restaurant

On Monday Charley was taken back to Cecil Holt's office where he was eventually convinced to visit the Commissioner of Oaths and to make an affidavit, although he later said he had told Alfred that what he had sworn was untrue. He then returned to Scotland Yard at about 3 pm. He didn't stay long though, because he was in a hurry to get to a suffragette meeting at Knightsbridge Hall which must have discussed the previous day's demonstration at Bow in the East End of London that had been broken up by mounted police. Charley had hoped to hear Emmeline Pankhurst speak, but she had been arrested at Victoria Station on Saturday (whilst Charley was dining at the Grosvenor) on her return from France. After the meeting ended Charley returned to Scotland Yard and went back once more on Wednesday to complete his statement.

Scotland Yard

Meanwhile Alfred's associate, Thomas Crosland, had not been idle. He had travelled up to Leicester where he tracked down Charley's mother, Elizabeth, to Countesthorpe. When he arrived at her home he did not immediately discuss matters with her, but asked if there was someone he could talk with man-to-man. He clearly felt that "he could not very well explain" the situation "to a woman." Elizabeth suggested they should go to see her son-in-law, Edward Flude, who lived close by, and when they arrived at his cottage Thomas explained that Charley "had been charged with loitering and speaking to gentlemen" and that Christopher and Robbie had been "doing" to him "the same way as he would to a girl." This was Thomas' attempt to explain that the two men had had sex with Charley, but it apparently confused both Elizabeth and Edward, who

130

concluded that he must have been dressed as a woman and wearing scent.

Thomas was keen to depict Charley as an innocent and exploited young man who had never consented to sex and told Elizabeth and Edward that Robbie and Christopher were together when they first met Charley at the corner of a street in London. They claimed acquaintance with him saying "Hullo young man, we've seen you before" before taking him out drinking. Eventually he passed out and could remember nothing about what had happened before he woke up at three in the morning. Christopher and Robbie had taken advantage of him and had sex with him whilst he was unconscious.

This story quickly convinced Charley's relatives that it was really Christopher and Robbie who should have been jailed, not Charley himself. They were further encouraged by Thomas' offer of money. He gave Elizabeth a pound note (which for her represented nearly three weeks earnings) and promised that Alfred would give her ten shillings a week to support Charley if he returned home to live with her. This was something that Thomas was keen to arrange, because he wanted him in Countesthorpe to keep him out of Christopher and Robbie's reach. He then made Elizabeth and Edward the same promise that he and Alfred had given to Charley - if an action was brought on Charley's behalf then Robbie, who was a very rich man, would have to pay him a thousand pounds for ruining him, and this money could set him up in business. Both Charley's mother and his brother-in-law were keen on pressing for compensation and it seems likely that they were more swayed by the thought of this money than by any abstract notion of obtaining justice. Gradually Edward's enthusiasm waned though, and he came to think that it was not really worth pursuing the matter. However Elizabeth seems to have been more malleable and Thomas and Alfred saw her as a useful ally in their campaign.

Back in London, two days after Charley had completed his statement, Alfred wrote to Scotland Yard for the second time urging the police to act on the information they had received. "The boy Garratt has made a statement on oath incriminating Christopher Millard & Robert Ross. What he alleges against the latter is not so serious as what he alleges against the former but it is quite sufficient to get him convicted if proved. As regards corroboration, in the case of Millard this already exists for Millard has admitted in the witness box that the boy has been in his flat

& has been publicly rebuked by a magistrate for his conduct. ... In the case of Ross the corroboration is that he is Millard's constant associate & employer & that like Millard he is well known to the police as an associate of sodomites." In his letter Alfred also drew police attention to another one of Christopher's friends, Frank Hughes claiming that he "frequents the streets & other places where stage people congregate." In fact the police might already have been aware of Frank because it was suggested that at least one police officer, Sergeant Stevens, knew him well by sight. Alfred claimed that Frank was Robbie's "particular friend", that Robbie "continually takes him out to dinner & has given him presents including silver dressing things", and that it was common knowledge that Robbie had "continually committed acts of immorality" with him. It could have been true that Robbie had a sexual relationship with Frank, but it seems more likely that Alfred was confusing Frank Hughes with Freddie Smith, who had indeed been Robbie's lover until very recently and was himself an amateur actor.

On Saturday 20 December Alfred informed Scotland Yard that Charley and his mother were now instituting civil proceedings and three days later Charley's mother duly issued a writ on her son's behalf charging Robbie with improper conduct and claiming damages for assault and for the "ruin of his character and prospects in life." A similar writ was issued against Christopher. Both documents had been prepared by Alfred and Thomas and sent to Elizabeth for her to endorse although it is unclear whether she really understood what she was signing.

By now Charley had been persuaded (or bribed) back to Countesthorpe and he spent the next seven weeks there whilst money was sent to his mother for his keep. He had virtually no money of his own and without this allowance (and probably some additional money from Thomas and Alfred) he had "nowhere to turn." However he was very unhappy at home in "this awful beastly place" and desperate to return to London. He rather forlornly hoped that he might get a position at the Selfridge's store in Oxford Street, which had opened with a flourish in March 1909. It is easy to see how the glamour of this shop must have captured Charley's imagination with its air of luxury and its enticing displays of merchandise. But this dream, though it was modest enough, was firmly out of reach for a young man with no references and a criminal record.

It is true that Charley was not completely isolated in Leicestershire and he did have some friends there. Most of these were women and although some might have been friends from school or family friends, others (perhaps including two older married women named Mrs Cox and Mrs Edith Warburton) could have been W.S.P.U. members whom he had got to know through his suffragette activities. Charley was friendly too with two women of his own age who both worked as glove hands. Beatrice Alice Lines was one of his neighbours at Peatling End, whilst Harriet Laura Gilliam lived a little further away in a house on the road that led into Leicester.

Charley probably passed Harriet's house quite frequently because he escaped from Countesthorpe to go into Leicester as much as he could. Here there was at least something resembling the excitement of London and there were restaurants and hotels as well as a cinema and a concert hall. Additionally there was the Palace Theatre, a grand building where if he could afford a ticket he would have been able to see many of the top music hall artistes perform. When this theatre had opened nearly thirteen years before, it had been the largest one outside London and it boasted not only a grand auditorium but also a winter garden with rockeries and fountains. Whilst in Leicester Charley might also have seen something of his friend, Frederick Kendrick, who was then living at 164 Fosse Road. He, too, had spent time in London where he had worked as a warehouseman for a draper, and he was probably a welcome reminder of life in the capital.

However it was not long before two more of Charley's London friends turned up in Leicester in person - Frank Hughes and Aylmer Clerk. It is possible that Frank was working briefly at the Palace Theatre, but it could also have been that the two men had travelled to Leicester specifically to see Charley and to urge him to return to the capital. Perhaps Christopher had asked them to go. He must quickly have learned first of Charley's disappearance and then of Alfred and Thomas' latest conspiracy and when he wrote to Walter on Boxing Day he therefore had serious news to impart. Alfred had "taken the most amazing step against R.R. and myself, of which I will tell you something when we meet. It seems almost incredible. And the end thereof no man can foretell". Christopher was now directly involved in the struggle between Oscar's two former lovers.

Alfred was soon trying to bribe a waiter to steal papers from Robbie's rooms whilst Thomas wrote to Robbie demanding his resignation as Oscar's literary executor and telling him to state publicly that he had been wrong to try to restore Oscar's reputation. However as far as Christopher

133

was concerned, 1914 actually began quietly enough. He went "to a Charles I tea-fight at Westminster" on 30 January which marked the date of the king's execution - evidence of his continued interest in the Jacobite cause – and he had a telephone installed at Molyneux House and began adding his telephone number, PADDINGTON 5743, to his stationery. He completed work on a volume of selected prose by Oscar for Methuen's shilling library, which Robbie had begun, but could not finish in time. (It was published on 19 March.) He did succumb to one of his colds and had to send for a doctor, but felt well enough to see Walter when he came up from Wimbledon to visit the British Museum and to go to a lecture.

At the start of February there was still "no particular news about the A.D. case" as far as Christopher knew. He was not yet aware that on 31 January the police had finally informed Alfred that they would not be taking any action against either Robbie or Christopher because there was no corroboration of Charley's statement and in any case the young man was "untruthful, of bad character, and not to be relied on." So on 4 February the writ against Christopher was dismissed as was that against Robbie a week later. Christopher must have been relieved when he eventually heard the news. But despite this setback Thomas and Alfred did not give up. Alfred decided that his best plan was to drive a wedge between Christopher and Robbie, who was his real target. Through a combination of threats and bribes he tried to persuade Christopher to turn against his friend and to join in the conspiracy. He thought that Christopher's need for money, added to his fear of being prosecuted himself, would combine to override his loyalty towards Robbie. But in this he badly misjudged him.

Alfred's first tactic was to ask the private detective, Mr Carew, to offer Christopher money if he agreed to steal some of Robbie's letters. Christopher indignantly refused and immediately told Robbie about the incident. But Alfred persevered. Next he arranged a meeting with Christopher at the Café Royal. This was familiar territory for both of them. Christopher and Robbie, like other gay men, often used it as a meeting place and Alfred had himself dined with Oscar there. But times had changed and now in the richly decorated room with its large gilt mirrors, Alfred repeatedly urged Christopher to betray Robbie, as they sat at one of the small oval tables provided for tête-à-têtes. Plaster female figures wearing garlands looked down on them. The table linen was crisp and white, and the cutlery and glasses gleamed as Alfred warned

Christopher that he would use Charley's statement to ensure that Robbie was arrested. He offered Christopher money if he would provide information against Robbie and tried to convince him that Robbie had treated him badly and did not deserve his loyalty. However, unknown to Alfred, the entire conversation was witnessed by a private enquiry agent employed by Robbie, who was sitting at a nearby table.

Three days later Alfred invited Christopher to his house at 26 Church Row in Hampstead. Christopher agreed to come, possibly either hoping that he could still dissuade Alfred from continuing with his scheme, or merely to find out what he had to say. Alfred repeated his offer of a bribe, as he did when the two men met for the third time at Paganini's restaurant. This time Alfred was accompanied by Mr Carew. Although Christopher remained resolute, by now Robbie had panicked. He regarded Christopher as a weak link, whose lack of discretion made Robbie himself vulnerable and he knew that one way or another Alfred was determined to exploit Christopher in his campaign against Robbie. So he decided (probably reluctantly) to distance himself from Christopher by ceasing to employ him as his secretary. Christopher accepted the decision and remained friendly with Robbie, but he had lost most of his income and he was understandably upset. He blamed Alfred and accused him of ruining him. He felt betrayed not only by a fellow Catholic but by a man who had once shared his sexual identity. Although his plea failed to move Alfred, he did acknowledge something of Christopher's feelings in his reply, which was a little more understanding than might have been expected. "God forbid I should judge other people. If it were merely a question of yielding to temptation, I should sympathise with you and your ex-employer Ross, but it is a question of deliberate propaganda in the exaltation of vice."

Meanwhile Thomas was still working on Charley and his mother. He travelled up to talk to them both and had a long chat with Charley as they walked together in Hickling Road. On Friday 6 February he travelled down with them on the train to London where they went first to Cecil Holt's office and then to Marylebone Police Court though by the time they arrived there the court was closed for the day. The private detective, Mr Carew, treated Charley and Elizabeth to an evening at a picture palace and then Charley spent the night at the detective's flat. When he tried to escape, he found that he had been locked into his room.

On the following day he was taken back to Cecil Holt's office where he was told they were going back to Marylebone Police Court. But he had had enough and he told the solicitor that he was having nothing more to do with the scheme. He must have been frightened by Alfred's threat to swear an affidavit against him, as well as against Robbie and Christopher, and he was probably worried about perjuring himself as he had already admitted to his mother that he didn't actually know Robbie. He could even have been feeling guilty about getting Christopher and his friends into trouble. As Charley protested, Cecil telephoned Alfred urging him to come round to talk to the young man. But Charley did not wait for Alfred's taxi to arrive. He ran down the stairs and out of the office and then jumped onto a bus down to Oxford Street. Although the detective, Mr Carew, pursued him for the rest of the day Charley refused to return to Bryanston Square.

Instead he left for Brighton where he stayed at the Royal Albion Hotel with a friend called R. Baker (who remains unidentified). His hotel bill was paid by a wealthy American gentleman named A. C. Flowers. Charley had met Mr Flowers in London (where he was staying at the Strand Palace Hotel) and he might well have been another one of his lovers. Charley sent a postcard from Brighton to someone in Leicester whom he addressed as "My dear F". This could either have been Frederick Kendrick or Frank Hughes, who also seems to have had some connection with Leicester. Charley was open enough with 'F' to give him details of the Brighton trip: "Staying here till Monday with R. B. Lovely time at a splendid hotel and everything else." He signed himself affectionately with one of the aliases he used for his political activities: "Yours always, Carl Garratt Tuke." He sent another postcard to his sister and a letter to his mother in which he asked her to pack up his clothes and told her that he was planning to head for Glasgow. But it seems unlikely that he made this journey and he could just have been trying to set a false trail to confuse Alfred because a few days later in fact he was back in London.

At 12.25 am on Saturday 14 February he was arrested again. He was charged with importuning in Piccadilly, and remanded in custody in Brixton Prison for a week. It is not clear how soon Christopher heard of Charley's latest arrest and when he was made aware of what had happened he must have felt ambivalent about it, because in some respects it undermined Alfred's campaign, which rested heavily on Charley's evidence. Charley must have realised this and, as he was no

136

longer certain that he could count on Christopher's support, he contacted Cecil Holt. Cecil's clerk, Gustavus Fairall, visited him and promised that Alfred would get him legal representation if he continued the proceedings against Christopher and Robbie, but it seems likely that this representation never materialised. After a week on remand Charley appeared at Marlborough Police Court on the following Saturday where he faced the same magistrate who had convicted him the previous year. This time he was sentenced to six months' hard labour and again sent to serve his sentence at Pentonville Prison.

Charley's experience was far from unique. It was part of a much wider pattern of attempts to control gay sexual activity in the early years of the twentieth century. The numbers of men arrested and convicted had gradually risen after 1890 and then increased significantly between 1910 and 1914. A clause against men soliciting had been included in the 1898 Vagrancy Law Amendment Act and action was increasingly being taken against men behaving in ways that were not explicitly sexual. The Marlborough Police Court Register shows that along with Charley seven other men were convicted for importuning in the West End during February 1914. Possibly Charley knew some of them, at least by sight. William Martin aged twenty one was arrested on Friday 6 February at 10 pm, John Godfrey aged twenty, was arrested at Piccadilly on Wednesday 11 February at 12.30 am and Frank Courtney, who was the same age, was arrested at Hyde Park on 10 February at 10.50 pm. John Eingland, also aged twenty, was arrested at Shaftesbury Avenue at 1.20 am on Thursday 12 February. An older married man, Cecil Cook, who worked as an outfitter was arrested at Piccadilly at 12.30 am on 17 February whilst George Albricht aged twenty five was arrested in the same location at 1.20 am on 23 February. Finally Albert Fletcher aged twenty two was arrested at 1.30 am on 27 February. All were sentenced to hard labour and both George and John Eingland (who were probably German) were subsequently deported.

Charley's conviction must have given Alfred and Thomas pause for thought, but they quickly concluded that it need not put an end to their plans. Thomas had already sent Robbie a letter in which he repeated his allegations and challenged Robbie to issue a writ for libel. And Alfred (or someone representing him) went to see Charley in Pentonville Prison and asked him to make another statement incriminating Robbie. Charley was reluctant to do this and at this stage (if not before) he did contact Christopher, who agreed to visit him and was told about Alfred's latest actions. Because of his own experiences of arrest and imprisonment Christopher was probably fairly sympathetic towards Charley, though he cannot have been comfortable with the way he switched sides to his own advantage and the fact that, despite this interview, he later signed another statement implicating Robbie.

It must have been an unedifying sight for Christopher and his friends to watch as Alfred exploited the homophobia that imbued contemporary society in order to try and bring about Robbie's downfall and displayed little concern for the other gay men who were caught up in his vitriolic campaign. No wonder George Ives, who had been a good friend of Oscar's and who knew Robbie well, scrawled "traitor" in his diary next to Alfred's name. However things were not going all Alfred's way because his father-in-law had decided to continue his own separate action for libel against him. In response Alfred fled to France and Thomas followed him there. With considerable satisfaction, Christopher acquired a copy of the green poster issued by *The Star* newspaper and stuck it up on the wall of his flat in Molyneaux House. It read:

"LORD
ALFRED
DOUGLAS
GONE"

Christopher was greatly relieved. "It seems almost incredible. I may not have shown it as much as R.R., but the strain has been pretty bad for the last six months since A.D. began including me in his campaign. There is a great deal more in his flight than appears on the surface. ... The Custance case was brought up again in order to give Douglas an opportunity of bolting on that charge and so saving his face to some extent ... The summons was served at 5 pm on Wednesday: at 7 he was at the Café Royal with his luggage: and at 9 he left.... Crosland himself is in hiding... I would gladly see the whole thing dropped now that the arch-conspirator has fled....I went to the Old Bailey and had the satisfaction of hearing the ushers calling through the corridors 'Alfred Bruce Douglas surrender!' The proceedings were quite brief and formal...It appears that his blackmailing has been much more subtle and successful than one had any idea of." Christopher went on to claim that "there has been no limit to his debauching of little girls." This was an interesting accusation as it served to associate heterosexual activity not with social approval but with unsavoury practices.

In prison Charley was having second thoughts about the statement he had made. He now claimed that Alfred had told him what to say and that it was Alfred who had concocted the story that Robbie had burnt "my lips with a cigarette when trying to kiss me" and Alfred who had suggested that Charley say he had met Robbie "at the Café Royal, at Millard's and at the bar in Shaftesbury Avenue." Christopher arranged for him to see Robbie's solicitor, George Lewis, again. Charley apparently "confessed on Saturday to Lewis that he had never met R. in his life; but to what extent his confession further implicates Douglas I have not yet heard. I fancy that D. realised a fortnight ago on Garratt's conviction that his game was pretty well up." At the same time Charley was protesting his own innocence, declaring that his convictions had been unjust and had been based merely on the evidence of police officers (which was indeed the case): "The officer said he followed me for an hour thro' various streets and that I was smiling at gentlemen all the time. That was not true."

Although Alfred had left the country, Robbie was still trying to decide how to respond to his and Thomas' campaign. Finally on 24 March after much deliberation Robbie resolved (very unwisely as it turned out) to file for criminal libel against Alfred and to issue writs against both Thomas and Alfred for conspiracy and perjury. He probably hoped neither would actually return to face the charges.

But Alfred had not given up. He continued "to pester from Paris!" and almost immediately sent Christopher a copy of *Letters to my father-in-law No 1* which contained "gross abuse of R.R. and myself!" This folded A4 pamphlet bore the date 20 March 1914 and a London address - 19 Royal Avenue, Sloane Square. It was addressed to Colonel Custance and included gratuitous insults about his "grocer ancestors." In particular it warned him that George Lewis was "using you as a catspaw" in the interests of Robbie "the notorious Sodomite" and Christopher, "Ross's 'private secretary'", who "has already been convicted and has served a term of imprisonment for indecently assaulting a boy." Alfred claimed that Colonel Custance's proceedings had effectively prevented Robbie and Christopher from having "been brought up to answer a disgusting charge." But "Sodom Ross" and "Gomorrah Millard" could not be protected for ever. Alfred referred to the sworn statements that had been made by Elizabeth Garratt "the mother of one of their young victims" and by Charley himself. These were held by Alfred's solicitor and Alfred intended to "take every measure" to bring Robbie and Christopher "to justice sooner or later."

Christopher had hoped to get away from London for Easter, but events rumbled on. On Easter Sunday Thomas dramatically returned to England and was arrested. Christopher now seemed resigned to the legal proceedings that would inevitably follow. "It is all very horrid but it had to come sooner or later. I hear that documents found on T.W.H.C. were most important."

The preliminary hearing on fourteen counts of conspiracy took place in front of the Magistrate Paul Taylor at Marylebone Police Court. It opened on 13 April but it dragged on until 2 June as both sides sought to untangle fact from fabrication. Ernest Wild presented Robbie's case that Thomas and Alfred had concocted a plot as part of a conspiracy to ruin Robbie's reputation and had tried to use Charley to achieve this. On Monday 27 April Christopher went to the court "but heard only the opening of [Ernest] Wild's speech, as Crosland asked that I should not be allowed to stay if I was to be called later. The best report seems to be in the *Daily Citizen*. ... Today the evidence & cross-examination of the mother took up all the afternoon. I do not expect to be called till next Monday. To-morrow they will try to finish the mother and go on with the rest of the family so that they may be sent back to Leicester." In fact Charley's mother was still in court on Wednesday.

"It is very sickening," wrote Christopher, "seeing my name dragged in after all these eight long years!" Robbie was "fairly well but of course nervous and jumpy." First Robbie appeared in the witness box and then Christopher was called. He gave an account of the events of the previous 17 September and of his subsequent dismissal from his post as Robbie's secretary. He described how he had written to Alfred to protest against his actions and he told of the meetings at which Alfred had urged him to help secure information against Robbie.

Marylebone Police Court

Thomas was called to give his evidence on 28 May, but Christopher did not attend to hear his defence. He was exhausted and he half-envied Walter his much less fraught life filled with "bottling and botany and *Blue Bird.*" To try to recover Christopher went to Ramsgate where he stayed with Vyvyan and Violet Holland for "a short change and rest." By now he had managed surreptitiously to get hold of an advance copy of Alfred's book *Oscar Wilde and Myself* (which had been co-authored by Thomas) and he might have taken this to Ramsgate with him, though it would not have made comfortable reading as it was a sustained attack on both Oscar and his work.

The Magistrate's hearing ended on 2 June with Thomas's cross-examination and he was committed for trial at the Central Criminal Court. Whilst Christopher waited for the hearing to begin he did hear at least one piece of good news when Alfred's solicitor, Cecil Holt, was arrested for embezzling money.

141

Despite the approaching trial, Christopher was still putting the finishing touches to his definitive bibliography of Oscar's works (*Bibliography of Oscar Wilde*). On 25 May he completed the preface in which he acknowledged Robbie's help with the book and continued, "Scarcely less gratitude is due to Mr Walter Ledger who, at one time, it was hoped would have collaborated in the work. Mr Ledger's collection of Wilde is almost without an omission and certainly unrivalled, and he has ungrudgingly shared the results of his own researches and lent his own volumes for inspection." After thanking his friend, Christopher expressed his gratitude to various people who had allowed him to reprint material. They included Thomas Bird Mosher "the producer of beautiful books in America," Charles Ricketts and Charles Shannon, the collector Richard Butler Glaenzer, the late Reverend Matthew Russell, a Jesuit priest who had edited *Irish Monthly*, and Christian Karl Bernhard, Baron of Tauchnitz, who had inherited his father's publishing business in Leipzig.

After many years of work, Christopher's bibliography finally appeared that July and went on sale at twenty five shillings. It was published by Thomas Werner Laurie and turned out to be a substantial volume of six hundred pages. Christopher had produced a thorough and painstaking account of Oscar's work. The physical appearance of every edition was carefully described in a way which conjured up visual images of treasured volumes, and there were facsimiles of title-pages and manuscripts as well as notes on textual variations. Christopher referred to reviews of Oscar's work and reproduced correspondence and advertisements. He even included details of parodies of pieces by Oscar and adaptations from Oscar's work such as the setting of parts of *The Happy Prince* and *The Selfish Giant* to music. There were numerous notes on a whole range of subjects, which bore witness to Christopher's wide-ranging research, including the fact that the description of the embroideries in the eleventh chapter of *Dorian Gray* came from a book titled *Embroidery and Lace* by Ernest Lefebure which Oscar had reviewed in 1888. Towards the end of the book there was a list of all the biographies and studies of Oscar to date.

Christopher was extremely proud of his bibliography: "It is my life's work and the only thing I am likely to be remembered by to my merit!" Robbie had agreed to produce the introduction and wrote that "I learned more about Wilde's writings than Wilde himself ever knew." The words of praise which followed seem somewhat backhanded, although

Christopher (who knew him so well) presumably appreciated the sense of humour: "To those versed in the science of bibliography, Mr Stuart Mason's labours require no praise or commendation from me. But I want to assure those such as myself, who are entirely ignorant of enthusiasm for fourteenth editions or of the aesthetic excitement over a misprint of twenty years ago, that there is an enormous amount of diverting reading under these heavy-looking headings and that Mr Stuart Mason's book is not nearly as dull as it looks."

When Charles Scott Moncrieff wrote about Christopher's book many years later, he was more straightforward and fulsome in his praise writing, "Shortly before the War he crowned the labours of ten years by publishing his Bibliography of Wilde, a book invaluable not only to students of that author in all countries, but to anyone in search of a model on which to frame a bibliography of any sort. Indeed it is the first good bibliography, and still the best, in our language."

However at the time of its publication the reviews of Christopher's book were rather mixed. *The Library Association Record* described it as "minutely detailed" but although the reviewer acknowledged that it was a "comprehensive" bibliography which had evidently involved "solid labour and thoroughness" it was an "outrageously ill-proportioned volume" which had "been spoiled by the most useless and uninteresting padding" and was much too long. It was also poorly organised, and lacked "a well-compiled index" whilst its cost put it "beyond the pockets of all but the few specialists." Nevertheless despite these criticisms, the reviewer thought that Christopher's book was "perhaps the greatest tribute that has been paid to the memory and to the genius of Oscar Wilde" and Christopher must have been delighted by this assessment. He must have been even more pleased with the review by Ernst Paulus Bendz (who lived in Gothenburg and who later corresponded with Christopher). This appeared in the January 1916 issue of the periodical *Englische Studien* and it described Christopher's book as a "stately volume" which exceeded "every similar attempt on behalf of any other Victorian writer." The work was the "outcome of ten years unflagging enthusiasm and patient investigation" and was full of interesting information which would appeal to a wide range of readers.

The book sold quite well, though several years later there were still a number of unbound copies held by Thomas Werner Laurie, who decided eventually to use them simply as packing paper. Christopher was understandably annoyed. "It is enough to choke off anybody doing bibliographical work, isn't it?" He thought that his book should have been produced as a limited edition of just five hundred copies. This would have sold out so it would have been just as profitable for the publisher and made each copy more desirable. But Christopher was disparaging of Thomas Werner Laurie who had "no soul above a 5s novel."

Whilst the publication of Christopher's book had been reasonably successful and had been followed by a plan to produce *An Oscar Wilde Dictionary* for George Routledge and Sons (though this probably never materialised) the court case at the Old Bailey had gone badly. It opened on 27 June with Frederick Edwin Smith leading the prosecution for Robbie. He was an eloquent and intelligent speaker. But the judge, Horace Avory, who had been a member of the prosecution team when Oscar had been tried, seemed prejudiced against both Robbie and his barrister from the start. As expected, Christopher was called as a witness and he was cross-examined by Cecil Hayes, who produced a copy of *Dorian Gray* and asked him whether it was a moral book. Christopher refused to be drawn and insisted he saw nothing immoral in it even when Justice Avory joined in with the line of questioning. Christopher would have been acutely aware of following in Oscar's footsteps as he spoke because Oscar had been asked to explain and justify the same book at the Old Bailey nearly twenty years before. No doubt Christopher saw his answers as a belated form of homage to his hero.

When it was his turn in the witness box, Thomas successfully presented himself as an upright citizen acting in the public interest in exposing vice. The closing speeches began on 6 July and as Justice Avory started summing up, he sealed the outcome of the case. His hostility towards Robbie's barrister was obvious as he told the jurors they were not there to admire either Frederick Edwin Smith's eminence or his eloquence. He went on to stress Robbie's association with Oscar and to suggest that Robbie could not then complain if others drew their own conclusions from such an association. He described Charley as a "debauched and degraded human being" and said it would be idle for the jury to "shut their eyes to what Millard was by his own admission." The jury took only half an hour to find Thomas Crosland not guilty.

Christopher was appalled. "The horror of the Old Bailey is still upon me and I am in a state of collapse and chaos. Avory did for Crosland what his own counsel was incompetent to do: namely he made a violent, bigoted and ignorant speech for the defence – it is a monstrous miscarriage of justice." Robbie, too, was devastated. He could not face London. He went to stay with his sister in her home in Pangbourne and he resigned his position as Assessor of Picture Valuation. Meanwhile Christopher faced an uncertain future and Alfred Douglas (who had been in constant communication with Thomas throughout) boasted that he would be back in the country within a week.

To celebrate Thomas' acquittal, Alfred published a poem in Boulogne entitled *The Rhyme of F double E*, which ridiculed both Charley and Christopher: "There's Charlie Garratt he's in jail/For offering himself for sale.... Then there's 'Chris' Millard, such a dear/ You <u>will</u> like him; he too, I fear/Has done a little bit of time/For what the silly law calls 'crime'." Alfred mocked Christopher's distress at the outcome of the trial which caused him to shed tears which "fell like rain" and crowed over the fact that the result was a blow for "The fairest Gitons of the town,/ With scented locks, fair, red or brown,/ Curled <u>a la Garratt</u> and rouged lips,/ And powdered cheeks and rolling hips,/ And sweet shrill voices…"

Behind the scenes the attempt to gather evidence against both Christopher and Robbie intensified. Police officers watched Christopher's flat and contacted the Leicestershire Constabulary to make enquiries about Charley. They began tracing Christopher and Charley's friends and on 25 July they interviewed Aylmer Clerk, who had enlisted and was with the 1ˢᵗ Herts Regiment Territorial Force camped at Ashridge Park in Hertfordshire. Aylmer denied any improper conduct by either himself or his friends and when the police declined to give him a copy of his statement, he refused to sign it. Scotland Yard decided, "It is perfectly clear what Clerk is from his associates" and his evidence was considered worthless by the lawyer they consulted for advice: "Having regard to the class of person he manifestly is, we should sweep his evidence aside."

The police attempted to track down Frank Hughes too. They knew his letters were forwarded by *The Stage* newspaper and they traced him first to Miss Grace Muriell's company and then to Mr T. Edward Ward's company, which was currently producing *The Slave Girl* at the Oldham Coliseum Theatre. However they eventually seem to have decided not to bother pursuing him. Nor did they interview Gerald Souter. However they did speak to Cecil Howard Turner, who had joined the 1ˢᵗ Life Guards and was based in the Hyde Park barracks, and they tried to trace Charles Leopold Boulenger too. On 12 August they went to his father's house in South Kensington. George Albert Boulenger was a renowned zoologist who worked at the museum nearby and he was willing enough to tell the police where Charles was living without knowing why they were trying to find his son. But the police seem to have abandoned their investigation without travelling to interview Charles Leopold. He was no longer in London because he had been appointed to a post at the University of Birmingham. (He later became Professor of Zoology at Bedford College in London and spent the rest of his life in a house in Nottingham Place, which he shared with another man, Frederick Thomas Riley.)

Although they did not interview Charles Leopold, on 22 July the police did talk to two of Christopher's neighbours in Molyneux House. Neither had anything to say against Christopher. Mrs Daisy Bacon was now living in flat two but she had previously lived in the flat next to Christopher's. She had seen him receive a few visitors, but never any young men "and everything was always very quiet." Mrs Margaret Josephine Stewart lived in flat eleven three floors above Christopher's. She was responsible for lighting the gas on the staircases and keeping the front clean as well as reporting any irregularities or complaints. She knew Christopher and occasionally took parcels in for him and cleaned his flat. She did not recognise Charley's photograph and had never seen any of Christopher's visitors. The police also contacted Christopher's landlords, Burgoyne and Osbourne, who rather resented being questioned. Mr Burgoyne senior said stoutly that Christopher was "a good tenant who paid his rent regularly" and was a "thorough gentleman." William Barber, who had been employed to clean Christopher's flat for well over a year, said that he went in every day except Sundays between about ten and one to tidy up and sometimes to wash up the breakfast things, whilst Christopher worked at his typewriter. William had never seen either Charley or Frank at Molyneux House and the only visitors he had seen were middle-aged men. He knew that Christopher occasionally went away from Saturday to Monday but he never knew where he went.

Scotland Yard's final attempt to obtain some independent evidence against Christopher involved a trip to Westcliff on 23 July. But here, too, the police were unsuccessful. When they interviewed Susan Elizabeth

Humer, the widow who had let the apartments to Frank and his friends at 7 Windsor Road, she could tell them nothing of any real interest.

CHAPTER THIRTEEN

WAR

"life pretty busy and death rather near" from Back in Billets by Charles Scott Moncrieff

Less than two weeks later, on 4 August, Great Britain declared war on Germany. (Coincidentally on the same day Alfred's *Oscar Wilde and Myself* was published in both London and New York.) Two days afterwards Christopher wrote to Walter, "I wonder where you are at this deathly time. I hope the war has not prevented you from cruising, though I should think it is a dangerous amusement. It really is too awful to contemplate the results of what is happening." He was soon admitting, "I am frightfully depressed about the war" but he hoped "if we can hold out long enough the Allies … ought to crush the vile monster."

He spent a weekend at Westgate, where Vyvyan and Violet Holland entertained him, but his planned river trip with Charles Scott Moncrieff, had to be abandoned: "My companion-to-be has been mobilised with his regiment." Back in 1908 Charles had joined the Officer Training Corps Artillery at Edinburgh and in 1913 he became a second lieutenant in The King's Own Scottish Borderers. So when war was declared he was immediately ordered to Dumfries to join his regiment and from there was sent to Portland in Dorset where he worked in the wireless telegraph station. Here a friend from London (presumably either Christopher or Robbie) sent him a copy of *The Times* with Thomas Hardy's verses in it (as well as *The Times Literary Supplement*) and Charles amused himself by reciting them. Soon Christopher came down to visit him, but quickly ran into trouble: "I was immediately suspected of spying out the land; at 11.30 pm I received in my bedroom at the inn a domiciliary visit from two inspectors of the Dorset Constabulary who demanded my credentials. I was able eventually to satisfy them that I was a comparatively harmless individual. However the next day I fled me to the mainland and retired on Dorchester, determined during war time to avoid coast towns and fortified places." Meanwhile Charles spent his twenty fifth birthday in Portland marching his men off to bathe, and on 7 October, accompanied by his stout cherrywood stick, he left on the *Thespis*, an old liner which took about thirty six hours to make the crossing to France.

The outbreak of war resulted in Alfred Douglas making the journey in the opposite direction. When he disembarked at Folkestone on 4 September he was arrested and taken to Brixton Prison. Christopher was disappointed that he had returned: "I would much prefer him to be in Boulogne, where at least there would be a chance of the Germans shooting him as an undesirable."

Alfred's return meant his trial for criminal libel would go ahead and Christopher was pessimistic about the outcome. "I believe he has made arrangements with the authorities and that the Recorder will merely have him bound over again at the Old Bailey on Tuesday morning; in which case he will be brought up at the Marylebone Police Court in the afternoon on the R.R. libel case, and I fear I shall have to give evidence again. I don't think there is much chance of his being convicted, much less sentenced. The aristocracy is popular just now after the Duke of Westminster's deed of bravery." Quite whether that deed had really taken place was a moot point and Christopher suggested there were those who were saying that the Duke was not even at the front and "the story was circulated to encourage the young idea to get shot." Here Christopher was giving an ironic twist to a well-known quote from the eighteenth century poet James Thomson which spoke of his delight at the opportunity "To teach the young idea how to shoot". Alfred duly appeared in court, first on the charge of having libelled his father-in-law. He apologised and agreed not to repeat the libels. He was now free to focus on his defence against the charges brought by Robbie.

In October, as he waited for the trial to begin, Christopher offered Walter some advice about using the telephone. Christopher had been quick to learn how to use the new technology, but Walter was much less confident. "As for the telephone: of course you are welcome to use mine, but you must be quick as I am giving it up on the 26th as I cannot afford another year's rental. It is no good using it, however, unless there is some one at the other end to speak to. I suggest that you begin by ringing me up from Wimbledon post office: it is quite simple. Speak in your natural voice and do not talk loudly. The greater the distance the more clearly one can be heard as a rule, as the lines are clearer."

If they did discuss the war during their telephone call, the news would not have been good. Christopher was despondent: "The war news is very disheartening. I cannot see the use of the papers pretending that the Germans are not sweeping all before them. I think Antwerp ought to have surrendered at once without waiting to be bombarded." But his friend, Charles, at the front might not have agreed with him, and similarly Walter thought that it was important to contribute to the war effort. He came up to London for drill and began working with the searchlights that tracked across the skies above the capital.

Christopher can only have heard from Charles sporadically once he was involved in the fighting though presumably they must have occasionally corresponded. Charles was certainly writing relentlessly jaunty letters to his parents stressing the fact that his men were cheery and recounting wounds and deaths with a matter-of-fact air. But already men he knew personally were dying and on Sunday 1 November he received his first wound when part of a shell hit him just above the right eyebrow. Nevertheless whilst Christopher back in England was despondent about the war, Charles still thought the hostilities might end quickly. In addition he had "a strong presentiment that I am going to come out of this war alright." Soon, though, he began to have nightmares and although he tried to console himself: "I'd rather spend a night under fire; there are so many places bullets can't reach, and if they do there's a comfortable hospital, and bed socks from the Queen Mother", he was beginning to feel that the war "may go on for ever at the present rate." He soothed himself by reading. He had *The Oxford Book of English Verse* with him and he "used to spend the dark hours trying to piece together Keats' *Nightingale*, there are some lines in the middle that I never can remember" John Keats' poem could have had a particular resonance for Charles with its desire for escape from a world in which "youth grows pale, and spectre-thin, and dies;/ Where but to think is to be full of sorrow."

Even as the war went on, the legal processes that had been set in motion by Robbie continued to play out in London. Alfred's new solicitors, Currer and Bell, suggested further names for the police to track down. One of these was William Beavis Adams who lived at 26 St Augustine's Villas, Archway Road in Highgate. He worked as an artist's model and had been sentenced for importuning on 17 May 1909. Another was

Adolph Birkenruth an artist described as "an alleged habitual sodomite living with his mother at 28 Kensington Square". Scotland Yard found no evidence of Adolph in their files but perhaps he was regarded with some suspicion because he was the son of German parents.

On Thursday 19 November Alfred appeared at the Old Bailey before Justice Coleridge in a case that was reported only briefly in the newspapers thanks to the imposition of the Defence of the Realm Act. He pleaded justification for the alleged libels and put together four main pieces of evidence that Robbie had had sexual relationships with other men. The first was an incident that was supposed to have taken place twenty years before. The second involved Charley. The third involved Freddie Smith, and the fourth was an allegation that in 1908 Robbie had seduced a young man called William Edwards. It was also suggested that Robbie had attended "a New Year's eve party in 1911 at which 20 or 30 men danced together."

Alfred's case was helped by the fact that Robbie did not make a very good impression on the jury, whilst Alfred was more successful in presenting himself as a reformed character. Defence witnesses offered evidence in support of Alfred's claims, whilst the prosecution witnesses were not particularly effective. Indeed when the author Herbert George Wells appeared, his own moral and literary reputation was called into question. Neither Freddie nor Christopher was called as a witness, but Christopher followed the proceedings closely and was well aware that Robbie was "not very hopeful of winning his case."

When it was time for Justice Coleridge to deliver his summing-up he made much of the fact that Robbie had never been critical of sex between men. The jury deliberated for some time, but failed to agree on a verdict. This meant a date had to be set for the trial to be resumed. But before the date scheduled (11 December) Robbie seems to have accepted that his position was hopeless, and he decided not to proceed further. So the case ended with a 'nolle prosequi' in which Robbie agreed to pay Alfred's costs and Alfred agreed not to attack Robbie further – though he soon reneged on this. Christopher met Walter just before Christmas to tell him about the "inner history" of the matter. He wished Walter "as happy a Christmas as is possible under all the depressing circumstances of the present time" but it was a fairly muted celebration, although at least Charles was home on sick leave and was able to spend Christmas in Scotland.

Christopher, still without proper employment, was out of pocket and uncertain about how he would be able to earn enough to support himself. He needed to "freshen up my minus balance at the bank" and "when I am hard upper than usual I always worry myself into a decline!" But at least he enjoyed spending the Christmas period with his books. "I am reading Samuel Butler's *The Way of all Flesh* – a most delightful book." It was a work that attacked Victorian hypocrisy and focused on the relationship between a son and a domineering father which could have resonated with Christopher. He also read George Gissing's *Private Papers of Henry Ryecroft*, which had been published in 1903 and which purported to be the papers of a deceased writer who never wrote his planned novel. He wondered if Walter knew both books and assured him, "I am sure you would like them."

He posted Walter a little booklet called *Christmas Hymn 1914* which he thought he would appreciate. It contained a satirical poem by John Collings Squire written in response to the Lambeth Guardians decision not to give the pauper children the egg they usually received for breakfast on Christmas morning in order to help the children to appreciate the national situation. However at the same time the Guardians funded increases in the salaries of the poor-law officers and enjoyed their own luxurious Christmas meal: "Eggs is eggs, and eggs is dear,/ They shall have no eggs this year!.../ But, my Guardians, why, I beg,/ Go no further than an egg?/ If you'd have them not ignore/All the full effects of war,/Sell their beds and let them freeze/ Like the Belgian refugees;/Go the whole instructive hog,/Shell the workhouse, burn and flog./...Thus when they .../Cease to treasure/A vain and empty life of pleasure,/Duly chastened they will sing:/'Glory to the new-born King!/I am sorry, Jesus dear,/ I don't deserve an egg this year."

Things remained difficult in the new year both at home and abroad. Despite the agreement made at the Old Bailey, Alfred continued to pursue Robbie, writing to the Prime Minister, Herbert Asquith, and to the Reform Club, although without effect. It seemed for a time that the Director of Public Prosecutions might take some action against Robbie when the papers from the trial were forwarded to him, but eventually he decided against it. In the meantime Robbie's friends rallied round him to draw up a testimonial in his support. This infuriated Alfred. "Did you see Douglas's letter in the *Globe* on Tuesday in reply to the testimonial?" Christopher wrote. "It had evidently been severely 'edited' and was rather pointless, but showed how green the affair must have made him."

There was no sign of improvement in the war situation when in January Charles wrote one of his early poems about the war, *The Willow-tree Bough*, using the voice of a woman speaking about the good-natured rifleman that she loves. He has gone off to war leaving her with nothing but his name carved "on the willow-tree bough." She is proud of him, yet anxious about whether he will return: "How can you wonder that I in my anxiousness/Weep with my eyes on the willow-tree bough?" In some ways Charles' poem seems to offer a conventional reassuring ending suggesting that her lover will indeed return and they will have children together who will stand "around like young shoots in a row." The couple will visit the willow-tree where one of their children will read out the carved inscription. But these are imagined children who lie in a possible future. There is no real certainty about the soldier's return and, significantly, in the final line the words on the bark are "Worm-eaten" which could be the rifleman's fate too. Edward Joseph Dent, who was hostile towards the war, was certainly taken enough with *The Willow Tree Bough* to set it to music.

Christopher, too, remained despondent. In November he had written despairingly, "Two of my best friends are at this moment in the trenches (unless already dead)." By February he found such despair was widespread, "The war seems to have a depressing effect on every one and lowers one['s] vitality." He was not particularly keen to get involved in war work telling Walter, "I admire your courage in going to camp. I lack the necessary nerve and pluck to offer my services for anything, knowing how incompetent I should be, but under any definite request or compulsion I would gladly do anything to help." He added one, rather patronising, provision that he "was not put to work with the Women's Emergency Corps who dress up in khaki." The W.S.P.U., largely abandoning its earlier campaigns in favour of a fervent patriotism, had been responsible for founding the Women's Emergency Corps and led partly by Eveline Haverfield and her lover, Vera Holme, it organised women as doctors, nurses and motorcycle messengers.

Fortunately Christopher was almost certainly unaware of the ongoing police interest in his activities as this would have increased his anxiety. In fact it was only now that Scotland Yard finally abandoned any plans to charge him for gross indecency with Charley. The leading lawyer Archibald Henry Bodkin had been twice consulted as to the chances of such a case succeeding. He had little sympathy for either lesbians or gay men and was particularly hostile towards literature he regarded as

153

obscene so as Director of Public Prosecutions, he later strongly opposed the publication of Radclyffe Hall's lesbian novel, *The Well of Loneliness*. However on 2 February he reluctantly had to admit that, despite the evidence the police had gathered since the previous July, the case against Christopher had not really been strengthened. The "respectable" witnesses had offered nothing that supported the allegation, and the other witnesses could not be relied upon. Charley was presumably unwilling to give evidence against Christopher and "It can hardly be supposed that this coterie of sodomites will be found to support the tale of one of the number against another member of the party." He continued, "To expose a nest of sodomites may from one point of view be desirable, but it is not the duty of the police, unless in the course of a serious prosecution deliberately undertaken and on satisfactory evidence of criminal conduct." If a group of gay men supported each other and were careful to keep their activities hidden from outsiders it was, in fact, difficult for the law to act.

In April 1915 Christopher returned to court to see Robbie face the charge of bringing a malicious prosecution against Thomas Crosland. This time, however, the judge, Justice Bray, was more even-handed. He accepted that Robbie had been goaded into taking action and he was duly found not guilty. Christopher was relieved. "I have just come back from the law courts where I have been for the last four days. You will see that Crosland has lost his case, which is virtually (though not legally) a reversal of the monstrously unjust verdict given before 'Justice' Avory in July. It was good to hear the whole story of the vile conspiracy exposed before a just judge, who made no bones about the fact that C. and D. were both trying to blackmail Robbie. He emphasised many of the points which Avory swept aside because they were in favour of R.R. I hope now that R.R. will be left in peace – at long length some sort of justice has been awarded to him."

Feeling free to leave London at last, Robbie spent most of the summer with his sister. And Christopher spent a weekend walking with a friend in the Chilterns. But there was bad news from the front during May. Oscar's elder son was dead. "You will be sorry to hear that Cyril Holland was killed in action in France on Sunday last [9 May]. The news reached London yesterday. He would have been 30 next month." Cyril left most of his money to his brother leading Christopher to comment drily that Vyvyan "will now be well off enough if he is not shot."

Christopher continued to correspond regularly with those like Vyvyan who remained at the front because one of the few ways in which he felt he could support those friends who had enlisted was by writing to them: "I have so many friends at the front clamouring for letters that it is difficult to find time for them all." Then when his friends came home on leave he was eager to meet up. He managed a river trip with one of them - George Elwick Jemmett, who had previously studied law in London: "I went up the river above Oxford for Whitsuntide (70 miles from Sat to Tuesday, there and back)."

Without regular work he was still struggling financially and in mid-June he wrote to Walter, "I am very hard up and would sell you <u>almost</u> anything." However at some stage Robbie did begin employing him again and seems to have paid him an allowance for several years. There was also more good news about Robbie's persecutors. "The latest news is that Douglas and Crosland have quarrelled. C. is suing D. for a share in the royalties of *OW and Myself* of which he claims (as I have always suspected) to have written a part! They are abusing one another now like cats & dogs. C. has abandoned his appeal against Bray's just judgement and 'having been deceived throughout by Douglas' is not going to have any more to do with him or his attacks on R.R. I suppose Douglas and the Q. family got tired of financing T.W.H.C."

Vyvyan Holland came for a few days leave, following his brother's death and Christopher spent time with him before he "returned to the front in rather depressed spirits." At their meeting Christopher offered Vyvyan a manuscript by his father which had been copied out by his mother, Constance, but Vyvyan's wife, Violet, dissuaded him from purchasing it. Christopher commented derisively, "I suppose she prefers that the money should be spent on hats etc!" However when Vyvyan expressed an interest in buying some of his father's books back from Walter, Christopher was actually reluctant to assist. "I persuaded him (and More Adey supported me) that it was much better for them to be preserved in your collection. If anything happened to poor V. the books might be scattered irretrievably."

Charles, like Vyvyan was back at the front in June where he wrote his poem *Domum*, which opens with a lyrical description of the doomed town of Ypres that is abruptly followed by a rousing three verses which urge the "Little sons of Wykeham" to fight the good fight. But doubt has not been fully suppressed: "What was it you fought for, whose profit that you

155

died?/Here is Ypres burning and twenty towns beside." At the heart of the poem lies the question Charles, and those like him, must have faced over and over again. "Where is the gain in all our pain when he we loved but now/Is lying still on Sixty Hill, a bullet through his brow?" An answer of sorts comes from the reassuring internal voice which claims that what mattered was that the dead soldier has died doing what was right. "'He died one thing regarding that is better worth/Than the golden cities of all the kings on earth./Were right and wrong to choose among, he had seen the right,/Had found the thing appointed and done it with his might.'" Was Charles fully convinced by the reassuring voice? Well the poem ends, as it began, in lyricism. It acknowledges the possibility of failure as Ypres burns: *"Thus I muse, regarding, with a pensive eye,/Towered Ypres blazing, beneath the night sky.../This way may lie failure"*. Nevertheless it ends with a patriotic flourish. *"but Towers there are that stand,/Hence, it may be, guarded, in our own green land."*

Another of Charles' poems, *The Field of Honour*, is his most outspoken about the harsh reality of war. At first it appears that the sonnet's title is ironic. The octet focuses on dead bodies and the rats that live on them: "His grave will soon be ready, where the grey rat knows/ There is fresh meat slain for her." But the sestet counters this with the claim that the dead "Died radiant." The scene shifts to a remembered England of Windsor and of Eton, described in a gentler rhythm: "as he sees/ For a moment, Windsor Castle towering on the crest/And Eton still enshrined among remembering trees." And this is worth dying for. Thus the title is apparently not ironic after all.

Christopher had no first-hand experience of life at the front and could hardly have imagined how dire conditions could be for his friends. It is difficult to know how much they revealed to him, though he would have shared their constant anxiety about the fate of those they cared about. But life in London went on. The summer was hot and close. Christopher re-arranged his books and got "in a frightful muddle in consequence." Walter was away. He had been employed by some wealthy people to look after their boat. "Your adventures on shipboard sound very exciting," Christopher commented. "But I hate 'monied' people and could not live with them even as a pantry boy". However he was pleased to learn that Walter was at least allowed "a holiday from your rich employers" and to amuse him he wrote him several humorous poems which he called *Legends for Ledger*. Although they are light-hearted they are full of death. One reads: "Eating more than he was able/Jack died at the breakfast table./'Mother dear' said little Meg,/'May I have his other egg?'" and another is "Roller skating little Willie/Lost his life in Piccadilly./Father said that for a treat/Jack might skate in Lombard Street."

Christopher was kept busy entertaining friends back from the front. He protested that he never seemed to have time to himself and that really he loved "being alone for hours at a time", but he clearly also enjoyed being the centre of a social circle, which included a number of other gay men. They in their turn were happy to have places to socialise which were free from the prejudice they generally encountered. Christopher's flat in Molyneux House became one of these safe havens. Homophobic prejudice remained rife and it frequently emerged when Oscar's name was mentioned. Christopher received a letter from an Alice Westlake, who had once written to Oscar thanking him for his contribution to a bazaar for the New Hospital for women in Euston Road. In her letter Alice was adamant: "I should very much dislike having my name printed in connection with that of Mr Oscar Wilde and therefore hope that you will not publish this postcard." Despite Christopher's hopes expressed in his *Three Times Tried*, "virtuous hatred" still condemned Oscar.

Nevertheless gay support networks still functioned and one of their beneficiaries seems to have been Christopher's former lover, the young 'invert' Charley Garratt. After leaving Pentonville Prison, Charley does not seem to have approached Christopher for further help. Instead he was taken on by the White Cross League a moral organisation which aimed to "rescue" boys left to their own devices in London and who, "prey to the worst kind of scoundrels", fell "into vicious practices." He ended up in their home at 9 Clapham Road, apparently declaring he had "turned over a new leaf." But he did not last long there. The White Cross League soon decided he was "irreclaimable" and he probably agreed with them. At this stage someone seems to have intervened with the suggestion that Charley should enrol in the Campden School of Arts and Crafts in Gloucestershire. This would remove him from London, but to congenial surroundings, and would give him an education and prospects. It seems possible that Christopher had something to do with this intervention as it must have come from someone with knowledge of the Arts and Crafts pioneer, Charles Ashbee. Perhaps it was arranged through Robbie's friend, George Ives. He certainly knew Charles Ashbee whose love of art and architecture had been developed at Cambridge. Like Christopher, Charles Ashbee had been influenced by Edward Carpenter's view of homosexuality as a progressive force and this formed part of his vision for the Guild of Handicrafts which he set up at Mile End in the east end of London to provide workshops for a variety of craftsmen. Although mainly attracted to men, Charles Ashbee married, and in 1901 he and his wife along with over a hundred workers from the Guild moved to the rural peace of the medieval wool town of Chipping Camden. Here they established offices, craft workshops, a library and museum, and later a bathing pool. In 1904 a School of Arts and Crafts was set up by Gloucestershire County Council mostly run by members of the Guild.

Once enrolled at the school, Charley Garratt could have attended practical craft classes in a variety of subjects including drawing, design, carving, carpentry and gardening. He would have had opportunities to listen to and to perform music. And he could have attended the regular lectures on subjects such as history, crafts and architecture. Perhaps he even heard Edward Carpenter give one of his lectures at the school.

And in Chipping Camden, he probably also felt safe from the war at least temporarily. However men (even older men like Christopher) were coming under increasing pressure to contribute to the war effort. The National Registration Act established a register of all civilians between 15 and 65 in order to help the military authorities choose who should be called up and who should be employed in the national interest. Christopher decided he was willing to do farm work but admitted, "I wasn't able to give much information on my Nat. Registration form I fear. I don't think amateurs would be much good to farmers for corn gathering: at least so I've been told in the country. I would gladly put in a week or two at it if I could get my board and lodging for it."

Despite the propaganda which encouraged men to play their part in the war, those men back from the front could be reluctant to return. "I have had a couple of friends over from the front the last week: neither wants to go back to France, but both hope to get into the Flying Corps and get out to the Dardanelles." Perhaps they thought that was a better option than the trenches. The war continued unrelenting. On 13 August a German torpedo sunk the *Royal Edward* carrying troops to the Dardanelles and about a thousand men were killed. Christopher was shocked by the news: "I am frightfully grieved over the transport being sunk: it's about the biggest blow we've had for a long time." And the war was coming to London itself with Zeppelin raids. On 13 September Christopher wrote, "I saw the Zeppelin on Wednesday night: it was really rather thrilling to see our anti-aircraft shells bursting all about it. I believe a good deal of damage was done at Liverpool Street station where the signalling control apparatus was wrecked which necessitated all trains being run into Fenchurch Street."

At the front Charles had converted to Catholicism and Christopher must have been pleased when he heard the news that his friend had "found sooner or later that I was a Roman Catholic. It wasn't anything to do with the sensuous appeal of music, flowers, lights, vestments etc … But … I felt quite sure that I was at home." He was given a conditional baptism and his confession was heard so he felt he had become "a proper Papist." His conversion made him feel "very contented."

As the second Christmas of the war drew nearer, Christopher was still short of money. His finances were not helped by the fact that he had lost the royalty payments from three of his books - the revised *Art and Morality* (published in September 1912), *The Oscar Wilde Calendar*, and *Three Times Tried* - because "Palmer, my publisher, has gone to smash, which mean, I suppose, no more royalties from him!" The "little half-yearly cheque was always very welcome when it did come." Nevertheless he sent a gift to Walter: "Here is a duplicate *Dorian Gray* which I think you lack. Please accept it for Christmas with all good bibliographical wishes."

CHAPTER FOURTEEN

ON THE RUN

"I, in my haven, see the hills around/ Still white with winter's snow." from To One Falce an unpublished poem by Christopher

A week or so before the Christmas holiday, two officers and three young men visited Christopher at his flat at yet another of the frequent social gatherings when "crowds of officers (including a General!) ... inundated my flat." Several gay friends seem to have regularly attended these events and no doubt there were often opportunities for sex. This occasion appears to have been no exception. But unknown to the guests Christopher's flat might still have been under police surveillance and possibly those seen leaving Molyneux House were followed or questioned. Certainly soon after this particular party, one of the young men who had attended gave a statement to the police alleging that men had had sex with each other at the flat. The police were quick to act on the information and on 18 December an indictment against Christopher was prepared, though apparently he was not made immediately aware of this.

Even in early January 1916 the storm had apparently not yet broken and Christopher's main concern was still the war. "I am fairly well except for general depression which will probably last until we are wrapped in the perils of a prolonged peace." He dined with Vyvyan's wife, Violet, and they discussed a drawing, which Christopher thought might depict Oscar. But by 21 January Christopher was already making plans to get away from London, because he knew what was coming. "I may be going away for some time – possibly on Red Cross work in France, possibly only to the far north of England to stay with a friend who runs a skunk farm! .... I want a thorough change." Within a couple of days he had moved all his possessions out of his flat and put them into storage. Some he sold, including his set of the Winchester College magazine, *The Spirit Lamp*, which he later regretted losing.

160

In the same month Alfred Douglas' poem *The Rossiad* appeared. It was intended to be a scurrilous attack, both on Robbie and on those (like Herbert Asquith) who had supported him and indeed it proved to be a nasty piece of work couched in patriotic terms. It contrives to be both homophobic and xenophobic and ends with the words, "Two filthy fogs blot out thy light: The German, and the Sodomite." (Two further editions followed later that year. A fourth, with a new introduction, appeared in December 1920, after Robbie's death, when Alfred was still angry with those who had "whitewashed" Robbie's reputation.)

By 31 March when *The Rossiad* was in general circulation a warrant was issued by the magistrate, Paul Taylor, which charged Christopher for the second time in his life with gross indecency. But he could not be located. In fact he had been far away in Northumberland for over two months by the time the police tried to arrest him and the authorities never managed to trace him there.

Christopher did not contact Walter until late May, and then he was not completely honest with him about the reason for his flight telling him, "It was all along of 2 officers who were to be court-martialled over an alleged incident with which I was connected." He thus did not reveal that he had himself been charged. He claimed that he still wasn't sure "such a desperate remedy was necessary" though really he must have believed it was the only way to avoid another spell in prison. He did acknowledge that life in London was becoming "too complicated" and he made it clear that he needed to be careful to cover his tracks. In Northumberland he was calling himself 'S Millar' and he was cautious about revealing his address even to Walter – "only two or three people are supposed to know it." One of the few was Robbie, who had sent his luggage on and who generously continued to pay him an allowance of sixty pounds a year. Christopher had virtually no other income.

Life in London had been expensive and at least Christopher was pleased that in Northumberland "for the first time in my life, since I came to years of indiscretion, I am living within the bounds of my very meagre income." Later he wrote, "It was, moreover, the only place where I have ever been able to save a little money (now, alas! all gone). We had the house, coal, lights all free: we could get butter from a farm at ½/- a lb; home-made jams at 1/- for 2 lb; country bacon ½/- a lb, and milk at 3/- a quart (or latterly, from our goats for the milking!)"

He had escaped to a northern winter that seemed to last until the end of May. But then came the "delights of spring" with the "primroses ... still in bloom and the may ... not yet fully out." And Christopher, unexpectedly, found this time one of considerable happiness. He was not alone in Northumberland. Instead he was sharing the four-roomed bungalow and its four acre plot with his friend Alan Alington. It was in an isolated spot about eight hundred feet up on the Cheviot Hills with the nearest train station (Kirk Newton) four miles away and the nearest town, Wooler, eight miles away. Even the closest shop was about six miles across the hills in the little village of Yetholm, where there was a welcoming public house too. Christopher later looked back fondly at another local hostelry as well - the "old fashioned commercial inn at Kilso ... with an aged German waiter who might have come straight from Tennyson's *Cock*". Alfred Tennyson's poem describes a plump head-waiter who brings perfect pints. Significantly he seems to come "like Ganymede,/ From some delightful valley" and no doubt Christopher had the reference to Ganymede in mind when he made the association. In Greek mythology Ganymede was the beautiful young man abducted by Zeus to serve as the cup-bearer to the gods and he had thus become a symbol for gay desire. Perhaps Christopher also liked the poem's suggestive title. He certainly appreciated the beer at Kilso: "such beer, altho' it <u>was</u> 6d a pint against the 5d or 4d of inferior beers!"

Alan and Christopher lived a self-sufficient life together. "We do everything for ourselves, needless to say, from lighting the stove in the morning to feeding the animals at night. Two goats supply us with a sufficiency of milk (and destroy all garden produce, if they get a chance): hens give us eggs, from which we have hatched two lots (5 out of 13 in March, and 9 out of 9 last week – but the six weeks of snow ... made it unfavourable!)" Alan was responsible for the skunks on the farm which were kept for their fur: "it is Alington's hobby to look after them". Christopher was less keen: "The skunks don't interest me much". The two men's provisions arrived "on a pack-saddle on the back of a cuddy (ie donkey) from the bottom of the hill where they are deposited by the grocer about once a fortnight."

Christopher seemed to enjoy "the lonely life" despite the poor weather. And he relished learning new domestic skills. "I have become quite an adept at cooking – 'What an art it is!' – and bake bread (generally quite successfully), make cakes and scones, and all the more ordinary dishes – we live chiefly on vegetable stews and seldom see any meat except

162

smoked pig's flesh." He and Alan were growing some of their own food and perhaps this was Christopher's first real chance to indulge an interest in horticulture. "There is a nice bit of garden which occupies us fully as, of course, it is all virgin soil. It is awkward being on a slope, and it is impossible to dig a foot in any direction without coming on a rock – hewn out of the mountain side in some prehistoric age – some of them so big that two crow-bars rather than faith are required to move them." The clocks had been adjusted (which Christopher found rather annoying) but they lived a life of early rising and a regular pattern. "We get up about 5 am (6 am), breakfast an hour later: lunch at 11 am (12 noon); tea at 3 pm (4 pm) and go to bed about 10 pm (9 pm) after a light supper of herbs."

There were things that he missed in Nothumberland though, including his books and his friends. "Mentally and morally it is stagnation. I have ceased almost all correspondence, cancelled all my book catalogues etc. and get no letters forwarded." However he still received his press cuttings (in monthly batches) and catalogues. Perhaps Robbie passed these on to him. He did manage to read three new books. Two of these were on Thomas Hardy - one by Harold Hannyngton Child which Christopher thought "fairly good" and the other "a clumsy compilation by one Duffin at 5/- (Longmans)." The third book was "an absurd *Romance* by John Gambril Nicholson (of the *Chameleon*) privately printed to give it a superfluity of naughtiness which it entirely lacks!" Its author was a teacher and a member of the Order of Chaeronea, the society of gay men organised by George Ives. He wrote poetry addressed to young men and his *Romance of a Choir Boy* is a chaste love story between a young curate and a country boy with a beautiful voice.

The events in London continued to play on Christopher's mind. "Indignation inspired me a few weeks ago to write a sonnet," he declared. The poem is certainly heartfelt and is addressed *To One Falce*. This was Cecil Roy Leon Falcy who had been present at the party in December. Christopher had regarded him as a friend and felt let down by him.

Cecil had been born in Ramsgate, the son of a Swiss man who ran a private school at his home, Cranmer House. By the age of seventeen he had left home and moved to London where he worked as a clerk and boarded in a large club in St Pancras at 34-38 Cartwright Gardens.

34-38 Cartwright Gardens

Moving to the capital must have given Cecil opportunities to explore his sexuality and to meet other gay men although it is not clear when he actually met Christopher himself. At the outbreak of war Cecil joined the Royal Berkshire Regiment and a few months later transferred to the Royal Flying Corps. On 6 March 1915 he married. His wedding at North Weald was conducted in military style and reported favourably in both the *Chelmsford Chronicle* and the *Essex Newsman*. Seven months later to the day he qualified as a pilot in Birmingham flying a Maurice Farman biplane. Although he had married, when he was on leave in London towards the end of the year he had sex with other men in a flat in Edgware Road, at a hotel in Marylebone, at another hotel in Oxford Street and at Christopher's flat in nearby Molyneux Street. The man he had sex with in the Oxford Street hotel was a young Russian waiter called Maurice (or Morris) Rothfarb (who was also known as J. M. Rothwell.) Maurice subsequently turned to blackmail and was remanded at Marlborough Police Court on Saturday 1 January 1916 for demanding money with menaces from Cecil. Presumably Cecil made a complaint against Maurice, but his own name appeared in the report in *The Times* on 3 January and the subsequent case brought his sexual activity to public attention. It is possible that it was Maurice who was also responsible for the allegations made about the party at Christopher's flat which Cecil had attended.

164

When the army became aware of Cecil's activities he was tried by a General Court Martial and on 14 March 1916 he was stripped of his officer status. Another officer was also cashiered – possibly a nineteen year old second lieutenant in the Middlesex Regiment named Saville St John Nutt. Both men seem to have tried to shift the blame for the events at Molyneux House onto Christopher who, yet again, felt he had been betrayed by people he had trusted: "I was so badly let down by my two friends."

He turned to poetry to express his feelings and in *To One False* he angrily rejects the accusation that "I 'was the centre of corruption': I/'Seduced the youthful soldier from his oath/'Of manly purity and made him loath/'To fight for King and country and to die.'" In the next four lines he accuses Cecil of lying to try to protect himself: "Such to his captors was the desperate lie/Told by the helpless prisoner in his cell –/Vainly, to salve himself from utter hell,/He stains his soul with foulest treachery." But in the sestet comes the realisation that Cecil, too, is suffering. Christopher at least is free: "I, in my haven, see the hills around/Still white with winter's snow." Meanwhile "The wretched friend,/That once was mine, stone walls a captive keep/In Pentonville or Wandsworth gaol fast bound,/Hungered, athirsty, outcast to the end:" The final line links the two men again in their unhappiness: "While I, an outcast too, but weep and weep." In twice using the word "outcast" in his poem Christopher deliberately evokes Oscar's *The Ballad of Reading Gaol* and the inscription chosen by Robbie for Oscar's tomb and draws on the association of the term with his fellow gay men who were excluded from society.

Cecil seems to have spent some time in prison and he was still in disgrace when his brother Humphrey died later that year in France. But he was subsequently called up again for military service and allowed to re-join the Royal Flying Corps as a sergeant at the beginning of January 1917. He was back at the front from May and a few months later was awarded a medal for Distinguished Conduct for his photographic reconnaissance of enemy kite balloons. During 1918 he flew bombers on night raids from Dunkirk and for this he was awarded the French Medaille Militaire. He returned to Ramsgate after the war and in 1925 he changed his name by deed poll from Falcy to Vallance. When he died leaving two young children and a second wife, he was buried under that name.

Having explored, and perhaps resolved, his feelings towards Cecil in his poem, Christopher does not seem to have ever referred to him again. He was content enough in the Cheviots, despite the disadvantages of life there, and seemed happy to stay and to hope that the difficulties in London would blow over in his absence. But the interlude was not to last. Alan was already restless. "I don't much think Alington will stay here through another winter, so I shall have to find another abode. I don't much want to be in London again this year, and possibly not before the end of the war: but nothing is certain in this life or the next." In June he wrote, "I fear I shall be leaving here next month as Alington is fed up with it. … I don't quite know what I shall do; but I have some hopes of getting a job on a farm near here. In any case I will keep you cognisant of my whereabouts if I move."

Within a matter of weeks Alan had gone. He spent the rest of the war in Mesopotamia (now Iraq) where Allied troops, mainly from India and Australia, were fighting troops from the Ottoman Empire. There he began working on an Indian hospital ship for the British Red Cross.

Alan's departure left Christopher adrift in Northumberland. He spent most of July working on a farm at Yetholm and then in early August moved to another farm in the next village, Morebattle. His lodgings at the inn were uncomfortable, but more difficult to deal with was "the fact that the workpeople seemed to resent my assistance: I think they thought me either a spy or an absentee. … At last I received a visit from the local constable who wanted to know who, when and why I was." Christopher was too anxious to remain in the area and the next day he fled to Edinburgh, a city he knew from his visits to Charles Scott Moncrieff.

He had been sad to leave the fur farm "where I found real peace, with, I admit, occasional moments of depression" and unhappy to leave the countryside for the city: "I am much happier in the country, or would be if only people would mind their own businesses and leave me alone." However at first things looked promising in Edinburgh and he anticipated settling there. He found lodgings with a Miss Combe at 36 Grindlay Street and had "great hopes of getting work at Grants' in Princes Street as soon as their present man is called up. They are booksellers (new) and want someone to look after their lending library: it may suit me till the war is over." And in Edinburgh he was able to catch up with literary news again: "I hear that … Douglas's new book (*The Wilde Myth*, I believe) is in the press!" The book had indeed been delivered to the publisher Martin Secker, but it never appeared in print. It was considered both libellous and repetitive and contained several diatribes against Robbie, and his supporters.

Unfortunately the post at Grants' failed to materialise and on 1 September, feeling that he was running out of options, Christopher attempted to enlist. (Because of his age – he was then forty four - he was exempt from conscription.) At first he was rejected as permanently unfit. Two weeks later he went down to York to try again. Here the Medical Board eventually passed him fit for general service but the army officials refused to enlist him on account of his age, although they offered to send him to an Officer Training Corps. He returned to Edinburgh and was finally allowed to enlist when he falsely gave his age as forty. Like many new recruits, he donned his army uniform to have his photograph taken. The resulting image shows someone much altered since his days at Oxford. He has lost weight and his face looks drawn. There are deeply marked lines around his mouth and his eyes no longer look out confidently but gaze warily at the photographer.

Photograph accompanying Christopher's letter to Walter 16 October 1916
Robert Ross Memorial Collection MS Ross 13/3

CHAPTER FIFTEEN

DULCE ET DECORUM HALO

"It was a pretty rough 3 months I can tell you" from Christopher's letter to Walter 5 April 1917

Christopher was assigned to E Company of the 29th Royal Fusiliers and he began military training at Gillespie Schools in Edinburgh. "It is a very rough life – but nothing seriously to hurt one. The training is pushed through very rapidly: so if I keep fit I may be out somewhere in the spring!" However he did not always find the training easy. "Some things are rather trying: for instance we go for an hour's route march from 9 till 10 am, if fine, and get pleasantly warm; and then stand for two hours in the wet grass of the meadows doing our musketry." But he persisted. "I passed the first test – 'triangle of error' - without difficulty; but it doesn't necessarily follow that I shall become a good shot, I fear." And apparently he appreciated "the discipline and regularity of life", which was similar to that which he had enjoyed on the farm, and which he thought "very good for one of my temperament."

In Edinburgh he occasionally attended mass at John Gray's church – St Peter's in Falcon Avenue. John had been one of Oscar's lovers and he was now living with his wealthy male partner, Andre Raffalovitch. He looked "the picture of sacerdotalism" wrote Christopher, and Andre had built him "a charming little church." But Christopher was not keen to meet the two men. Robbie disliked them both and Christopher blamed John for having "'chucked' Oscar about 1893". More comforting was the club run for the battalion "by the good ladies of an episcopal church hard by. I don't know how I should endure without it." He wrote more than once of the women's generosity. "People are so kind – for example the worthy ladies who devote their evenings to our service in the Church Club – that it almost makes me weep with gratitude that I cannot express." He also appreciated the "tin of excellent cigarettes" which Walter posted to him.

In December he had a few days leave. He went back to London for the first time since his flight and stayed with his brother at a house in Paddington, 77 Westbourne Terrace. Paul Elwin seems always to have been the sibling who was closest to Christopher. He was generally tolerant of his wayward older brother and although he doubtless often disapproved of his actions, he never abandoned him, and always felt a responsibility for his welfare. Christopher trusted him to carry out his wishes and at this time wrote him a memorandum stating that if he died at the front Paul Elwin was to give Walter first refusal of any of his remaining Wildean items.

In 1912 Christopher's brother had joined a Christian community known as The Community of the Resurrection and he remained a member for the rest of his life. This community had been founded in 1882 emerging out of the Oxford Movement. Sixteen years later it took over a large house in Mirfield, Yorkshire and began using the adjacent quarry for sermons, bible classes, plays and political meetings. Subsequently a college was established and a church constructed. In 1914 the community had set up a London mission and Paul Elwin became one of the first residents at its initial base in 8 Grenville Place in South Kensington moving to 77 Westbourne Terrace when the community was given the lease of this grand stuccoed villa. He spent many years there and from time to time Christopher joined him.

The Community of the Resurrection attached considerable importance to ritual and to the liturgy, which Christopher might have found congenial, but whether he participated in any of the community's activities is uncertain. Many members, including Paul Elwin himself, were Christian socialists. A Christian socialist movement had begun in Europe during the middle of the nineteenth century and its followers tried to apply Christian principles to contemporary industrial society and to question the ethics of capitalism. There was a significant revival of the movement in England towards the end of the nineteenth century when a number of Christian socialist organisations were formed. With their commitment to the ideals of cooperation and social justice, these had a considerable influence on the Independent Labour Party when it was set up in 1893. Inevitably Christopher would have been exposed to Christian socialist ideas and it seems highly likely that this conception of socialism influenced his own political and religious views.

77 Westbourne Terrace

During his time at Westbourne Terrace, Christopher made arrangements to meet up with some of his friends including Walter and they had tea together, but "not at one of Lyons's places, please." However it was not long before it was time for him to take the train back to Edinburgh. He knew he would then be sent to France and must have wondered whether he would ever see London again.

On the day after Boxing Day he began a thirty six hour journey. He was "wet through" when he arrived on 29 December at 4 am in Etaples - an army base camp for those on the way to the front which was already notorious for its harsh conditions. A few months later things would be bad enough to provoke a mutiny. On New Year's Eve Christopher started the programme of intensive training in gas warfare, bayonet drill and marching across the dunes. He soon found life at Etaples a struggle: "It was a pretty rough 3 months I can tell you, to say nothing of the semi-starvation. My clothes were never once dry from the night we arrived".

He was hoping for a commission as an officer and on 10 January 1917 he was interviewed by the general in preparation for this. But six days later he came down with influenza. He spent nearly two weeks in the hospital, where apparently conditions were not much better than in the rest of the camp, before being moved to the convalescent camp and it was mid-

February before he was well enough to resume light duties at the base. The general planned to interview him again at the end of the month, but before that meeting could take place Christopher came into contact with a case of measles and was moved to a segregation camp. On March 12 he succumbed again to influenza. This time the attack was severe: "The second attack was much worse, of course, and caused considerable internal pain for some ten days or so." His heart was permanently affected and he would never fully recover. Ten days later, without ever having fought in the trenches, he left for England on a stretcher and he was sent to the Voluntary Aid Detachment Military Hospital at Eastbourne.

He was not unhappy about the situation: "I'm not sorry for most reasons to be getting out of the army, though it was rather sickening just missing that commission the <u>second</u> time – if it hadn't been for the quarantine I probably shouldn't have got influenza again as I should have been at the Training School within a week or so, with 10 days' leave at home into the bargain." However although he had not enjoyed army life he did admit that it was "pleasant enough to swank about London in a well-cut tunic when on furlough." Perhaps he had enjoyed the attention he had received on his visit during the previous December.

In Eastbourne he slowly began to recover and soon, as long as it wasn't snowing, he was able go out for a while each day. People came to visit him, including his friend 'R' of whom we will hear more later. Even though he was uncertain about what the future held, Christopher looked forward to the spring, which was so late that year that he hoped that he could still "catch it in my adventurous arms!" He had no immediate plans to return to London and for a while he anticipated borrowing a cottage near Dorking, but this seems not to have materialised. Instead he spent most of May and June in the barracks at Newhaven waiting for his discharge. He had a few days leave and went first to London – where he had a look at some letters at the sale-room of Hodgson & Co. in Chancery Lane - and then to Hampshire to see his mother and sisters. Back in Newhaven he was very bored: "I do absolutely nothing all day beyond answering to a roll call at 6.30, 8.30 & 1.30 – at 4 pm (Sats & Sunday from noon) I retire to a room which I have taken in the town & can rest or read or write or refresh myself there till 9 pm, which is a great relief after the discomforts of the camp. I suppose the authorities think I'm ornamental if not useful – that's the only imaginable reason why they keep me. The hot weather seems to affect my heart a good deal - the last

172

two or three nights I have carried my straw bedding outside the hut and slept under the searchlighted heavens."

With little else to occupy him in Newhaven, Christopher resumed his reading of works about Oscar including a section of the recent book by Coulson Kernahan, *In Good Company*. "I thought Kernahan's chapter on OW very poor and wrote to point out various anomalies and misstatements, for which he wrote very gratefully." He had already read Frank Harris' first version of *The Life and Confessions of Oscar Wilde* which had been written in about 1910 and privately published in New York in 1916. Frank had sent him a copy to thank him for his loan of some photographs and the book turned out to be a readable and reasonably fair account. After he read it Christopher lent the book first to Osbert Burdett and then to Walter. However Walter was still keen to acquire his own copy and Christopher advised him to order one through "Hatchards, who would run the risk of F.H. himself and submarines!" (The book was reissued in 1918 by the New York publisher and bookseller, Brentano's, and in the same year Frank issued a second version in two volumes with further contributions by Robbie and an appendix by George Bernard Shaw.) Because the book firmly blamed Alfred Douglas for Oscar's disgrace, it had to be published in America, as Alfred was poised to take legal action if it appeared in Britain.

Originally Christopher had not intended to return to London for some time, but at the end of June when he was finally discharged as "unfit for further service" and his "dulce et decorum halo" was exchanged for a state pension, he did go back to the capital to stay with his brother at 77 Westbourne Terrace. He undoubtedly thought that by going into the army he had "drawn the teeth of the enemy" and felt safe to pick up the threads of his old life. He began visiting his favourite auction houses and bookshops including the foreign language bookshop at 78 Charing Cross Road run by a German man called Richard Jaschke: "I went to see Jaschke in the Charing Cross Rd yesterday and found he had collected a bundle of transactions for me."

On 4 July he was interviewed for a position at the War Office as a civilian decipherer of telegrams and he began working "every day from 4 pm to midnight (with one day off in seven)" which meant he found himself unable to organise the afternoon tea parties he enjoyed. But nevertheless now he was in London he might have seen something of Charles who had been severely wounded on 23 April at Manchy-le-Preux during the

173

Battle of Arras when a shell exploded nearby. With a badly damaged leg and suffering from shell shock, he was sent back to England arriving in London on 9 June to recuperate at Lady Ridley's Hospital in Carlton House Terrace. Robbie came to see him bringing a novel and promising him more books, and probably Christopher visited too. By August Charles was able to move himself about in his wheeled chair and by October he was walking with a splint. Later he convalesced (as Christopher had done) in Eastbourne. He walked painfully with a limp for the rest of his life.

CHAPTER SIXTEEN

PRISON RHYMES WITH SORROW

"And that each day is like a year, a year whose days are long" from The Ballad of Reading Gaol by Oscar Wilde

During October 1917 Christopher began making a new life for himself in London by taking rooms at 4 Melcombe Place "almost adjoining the Great Central Hotel and opposite Marylebone Station."

Melcombe Place

The rent was high. He was paying about £55 a year for the rooms and he then began renting the attic above to stop anyone else occupying it and disturbing him. That cost him another 10s 6d every week. He was pleased with the location, which was only a short distance away from his old flat in Molyneux House, but actually he had made a major error of judgement and would have done better if he had avoided the area entirely.

For now things seemed settled enough. Christopher combined his deciphering work with further visits to auctions. During the autumn he bid for some books of newspaper cuttings and bought copies of *Irish Monthly* to resell. He managed to acquire some more of Oscar's letters. "I only wish I could have got them in time for my Bibliography. I knew they existed but old Fr Russell said he couldn't find them at the time." However they were only temporarily in his possession: "I can't afford, of course, to keep these letters." He hoped to get thirty pounds for them and offered them first to an antiquarian booksellers at 11 Grafton Street: "If Quaritch won't give me that I shall put them in Sotheby's and let the vultures fight for them." This price put them beyond Walter's means: "I imagine that even you are not rich enough to buy them!"

As the winter drew on in London, Christopher was fairly contentedly browsing in the bookshops: "In Farringdon Street to-day I picked up a very nice clean copy of *In a Good Cause* for three pence!" This was an 1885 collection of stories, poems and illustrations compiled by Margaret Tyssen-Amhurst and published in aid of a children's hospital in Hackney. It includes Oscar's poem *Le Jardin des Tuileries*. But then probably just before Christmas, he received the sad news that his friend, George Jemmett was dead. He had been fatally wounded at the battle of Cambrai and died at the age of thirty seven on 17 December becoming yet another of the long list of war casualties.

Both the police and the court authorities might well have hoped that Christopher, too, would never return from France and certainly seem to have assumed he was still at the front. Meanwhile he, in his turn, supposed that he had escaped their clutches: "I had been going quite freely about London for 6 months & more after leaving the army." But his luck was about to run out. He must surely have realised that moving back to the Molyneux Street area was something of a gamble, though he seems to have underestimated the risk he was running. On 9 January 1918 by "mere chance" he was recognised by a detective and arrested. He was charged with gross indecency and taken first to the police station in

Kentish Town and on to Brixton Prison where he was held on remand (as both Charley and Alfred had been).

A few days later he appeared at Marylebone Police Court. At some stage Charles had been informed of the proceedings and on 23 January he attended in order to speak on Christopher's behalf. Charles had not fully recovered from his experiences at the front but when he stood up in the court room he was still an impressive and attractive man with his strong jaw, heavy eyebrows and dark moustache. However his efforts were largely in vain and whilst Christopher found himself committed for trial at the Old Bailey, Charles left the court in a rather sombre mood and went on to attend the wedding of the writer, Robert Graves. He was uncomfortable in the crowded church of St James in Piccadilly but then at the reception in 11 Apple Tree Yard in St James' Square he encountered the poet, Wilfred Owen. Wilfred had come back from France in mid-1917 both physically and mentally fragile. He was gradually recovering "though his dreams were still nightmares, and his thick hair was shot with white" and he "returned with fresh enthusiasm to the reading and writing of poetry." He had already become friendly with Robbie, who invited him to dinner at the Reform Club and introduced him to members of his circle. Charles fell in love with him almost at first sight: "I was too sore at first, in mind and body, to regard very closely the quiet little person who stood beside me in a room from which I longed only to escape. But that evening I met him again after dinner, and found that we had already become, in some way, intimate friends." He began writing a series of sonnets addressed to 'Mr W. O.' and there were soon rumours that the two men were having an affair. But Charles' feelings were largely unrequited, primarily because Wilfred was already in love with Siegfried Sassoon.

Whilst Charles pursued Wilfred, Christopher had his own difficulties to face. He was particularly unfortunate that the prosecutor he faced at the Old Bailey was Archibald Bodkin. Sir Archibald (as he now was) must have viewed Christopher's presence there with considerable personal satisfaction. Three years before, he had been forced to accept that there was insufficient evidence for the police to take Christopher to court. Now he was confident of a conviction.

Central Criminal Court (Old Bailey)

Christopher's barrister, Richard David Muir, did his best to defend his client and argued strongly that he had rehabilitated himself after his previous conviction. However that conviction certainly counted against him and it was probably no great surprise to anyone that Christopher was found guilty on Saturday 2 March. The Recorder Sir Forrest Fulton duly professed himself horrified that in 1915 "such conduct was rife in London" and that "the condition of things at that time was truly appalling". He regarded it as particularly shocking that "in many cases the persons involved were educated men" who presumably should have known better. Nevertheless he acknowledged the fact that Christopher had undertaken military service – service which was made to sound more impressive than it actually was - and although he sent him to prison for twelve months he did not sentence him to hard labour, both because of his poor health and because he would have lost his army pension of 13 shillings and 9 pence a week.

Christopher's trial was reported in *The Times* of Monday 4 March in an article which again connected him with Robbie and naturally Alfred Douglas was quick to exploit this latest development. Robbie wrote to Walter asking whether he had seen the latest attack which Alfred had "sent ... around very freely" and acknowledging that "Of course the disaster to Millard was for him a very good opportunity." Meanwhile in Wormwood Scrubs, Christopher, for his part, seethed against the injustices he felt he had faced. "The only witness of importance against me – i.e. the one who perjures himself most heavily – was available only as he happened to be arrested as an absentee! I found it useless to try and put up any defence: bail was practically prohibitive: my solicitor foolish & incompetent: my counsel nearly as bad: the prosecution bitter and unfair: while the Recorder, deaf & in his dotage, was quite incapable of administering justice 'indifferently' or in any other way: I had to correct his unjust remarks more than once!" Over the following weeks Christopher continued to criticise the "unprincipled powers such as unjust judges, venal magistrates, bald-headed K.C's, prowling police, dissolute detectives, incompetent solicitors."

At the same time outside the prison walls, a new attack on those who breached society's conservative moral code was unfolding and yet again Alfred Douglas was heavily involved. On 26 January, within a matter of weeks of Christopher's arrest, an article by Noel Pemberton Billing appeared in a magazine called the *Imperialist*, which Noel himself owned. It was a scathing criticism of the Government's handling of the war but more significantly it included the claim that part of the German military strategy was the compilation of a *Black Book* of 47,000 prominent English men and women who were engaging in lesbian and gay sexual activity. Lesbians and gay men were thus making England vulnerable to the enemy.

Noel Billing's piece was followed by another article, this time by Captain Harold Sherwood Spencer - a "dangerous man" in Christopher's eyes. It was headlined *The Cult of the Clitoris* and published on 16 February in the same magazine now re-named *Vigilante*. It not only criticised the Asquith government and its German-Jewish friends, but explicitly linked government corruption with gay sexuality and particularly with Oscar Wilde and his followers. The article focused on the private performances of Oscar's *Salome* (to which Robbie had agreed) that were currently taking place at the Independent Theatre which were produced by John Thomas Grein with the dancer Maud Allan appearing as Salome. The government ignored the accusations, but John Grein and Maud Allan decided to take action against Noel Billing for libel.

Almost certainly Christopher initially knew nothing of this. Soon after his conviction he was moved to the prison hospital where, after several

179

weeks, his health began to improve. "Fortunately I now am sleeping better at nights. For several weeks I had brandy every 4 hours night and day." He always dreamt "of course that I am free (reason presumably why sleep has been called 'the prisoner's release')". However his heart was still very weak and he had to spend most of the time resting: "I shall never be fit for much again, I fear, unless God will create a new <u>heart</u> within me."

He continued to resent the loss of his freedom. When he began learning Richard Lovelace's *To Althea, from Prison* he complained, "Lovelace lies when he says 'stone walls do not a prison make' – I doubt if he wrote from experience – ... the <u>truth</u> is with the poet [Oscar] who said 'Every[sic] day is like a year, a year whose days are long'" in *The Ballad of Reading Gaol*. But conditions in prison were not too bad. Christopher's cell was not uncomfortable and his life was "much as if I were 'interned' – monotonous to a degree but not unendurable and probably not much worse than being a prisoner of war in Germany." He had "a sufficiency to eat" though he missed the food in France "where bully beef was thrown away as not worth eating" and good French bread was plentiful. Nevertheless "no man could possibly complain of the diet provided in a prison hospital: the dinner especially must be much better than many of the men are accustomed to outside – meat (or as today, a good piece of boiled fish with parsley sauce) and 2 vegs with bread, and a really excellent rice pudding – which could not be obtained at present prices outside, even at a modest eating house where you see 'Good Pull Up for Carmen,' for less than 1/- or 1/6 I am sure." And, very importantly, he had enough to read. "I try by reading a great deal not to let my thoughts dwell on my awful disaster: All I look forward to is Library day, so to me 'Wednesday is the sweetest of the week.'" He was allowed three or four books every week. Without them he felt he would have gone mad.

His voracious reading included Lord Frederick Sleigh Roberts' *Forty-one Years in India*, Charles William Chadwick Oman's *A History of Greece*, and a travel book - Paul Wainemann's *A Summer Tour in Finland* which was published in 1908 and had "delightful Japanesey colour plates." He read books on history - Edward Gibbon's book on Roman history, John Lothrop Motley's three-volume *Dutch Republic*, which was "much better reading than most novels and easier than Gibbon," and John Malcolm Ludlow's *American War of Independence*. He even had access to books on the current war - *Antwerp to Gallipoli* by a pro-German American correspondent, Arthur Ruhl, John Buchan's *A History of the Great War* (published in 1915) and the popular novel by Herbert George Wells, *Mr Britling Sees It Through*, which he though "poor stuff tho' much more true to the war than Buchan's." John Buchan's book indeed gave a completely false impression of the progress of the war on the Western Front claiming that in 1915 the Germans were on the brink of defeat and that British losses were minimal.

Christopher's reading continued with essays by Jean-Jacques Rousseau, Charles Lamb, James Henry Leigh Hunt and Thomas Babington Macaulay and the letters of the diplomat Robert Bulwer-Lytton. There was Charles Darwin's *Origin of Species*, poems by Alfred, Lord Tennyson and Sir Walter Scott, and numerous nineteenth century novels including some by Thomas Hardy and Mary Crawford, George Eliot's *Mill on the Floss*, Jane Austen's *Emma* and Anthony Trollope's *Last Chronicles of Barset*. He particularly enjoyed James Boswell's *Life of Samuel Johnson*, Charlotte Bronte's *Villette* and "a jolly yarn" by Frank Thomas Bullen, who wrote stirring sea stories. He liked the 1901 book, *The House with the Green Shutters*, by George Douglas Brown as well because it contained "really admirable character studies of the natives of a small Scots town." Perhaps it reminded him of Charles. He gave Lord John Russell Morley's *The Life of Richard Cobden* "a +" and read Voltaire's biography of Charles XII of Sweden too. He found the book on the English novel by Charles' old tutor at Edinburgh, George Saintsbury, as well as Andrew Lang's *History of English Literature*, but only gave the latter "d-". Joseph Henry Shorthouse's *Life & Letters* had been edited by the author's wife "so there is too much of 'my beloved husband' all through, but Christopher enjoyed the unedited pieces. He also read the *Short History of the English People* by his father's old pupil and adversary, John Richard Green.

As he read, he resolved to write an article for the *Clarion*. "Certainly prison libraries must be very much improved since 1895-7 when Wilde complained so bitterly of them," he thought. In Oscar's time they had consisted mainly of mediocre theological books selected by the prison chaplain. But now "There are more books here that I want to read than I can get through in my time." And he received at least one new book from outside when his friend R. sent him a copy of Herbert Asquith's *Lecture: Some Aspects of the Victorian Age*. Christopher was keen to look at this: "It will interest me to see if his literary style is up to his political." This short book contained the lecture Herbert Asquith had given on 8 June at the Sheldonian on some of the developments in ideas and literature of the Victorian period - particularly the social criticism of

Matthew Arnold and John Ruskin and the scientific breakthrough made by Charles Darwin.

Christopher's brother occasionally visited him in prison and kept Walter informed about how he was faring. One of these visits took place on 10 June and two days later Paul Elwin met Walter in Bolton Street (close to the hospital in Charles Street where he was chaplain) in order to give him the latest news. Christopher was allowed to send and receive a limited number of letters as well as having visits: "I am allowed one letter every 28 days, and a 2nd in lieu of a visitor once a month, if I prefer it – which means writing and receiving a letter at fortnightly intervals, which isn't bad." Christopher asked his friend R. for a letter on large paper - "sermon paper or foolscap, please" – which meant a longer letter - and he wanted him to send the letter on to Paul Elwin so that he could add a postscript.

His main correspondents during his time in Wormwood Scrubs seem to have been Charles and the friend whom he addressed as "My dear R" and warned to write legibly as otherwise the censor might suspect he had "something to conceal!" However he was keen to stay in touch with Osbert Burdett too, particularly because "He & his wife were most kind & hospitable to me last year & were never unduly shocked at my 'crime.'" With R. Christopher wanted to discuss political matters and was eager to find out what was going on in the world beyond the prison walls. "What do you think of the prospect of enforcing conscription in Ireland? of the Sinn Fein position? of Lady Randolph Churchill's marriage? of Lloyd George's prospects?" His questions continued: "Has there been any contested by-election since March? or any notable deaths? … or any books published of special interest apart from this silly war".

R wrote back about his visits to Oxford, which led Christopher to reminisce about his old university town. "Oxford was, no doubt, lovely as ever in spite of its being June – filled with 'strange enchantments from the past' and 'memories of the friends of old.'"

View of Oxford across Port Meadow

He remembered "visiting you at Abingdon in '94 or '95 & have been there many times since – those excellent inns the Lion and the Queen used to vie with each other as to which could supply the better 2/6 lunch ad lib." By October he was writing that "Oxford ought to be glorious this weather" and quoting again from Andrew Lang's poem *Almae Matres* "autumn with its crimson pall/About the towers of Magdalen rolled,' though he acknowledged that "Summertown by the Chervil, where you are, must be less rural than it was when we first knew it a ¼ of a century ago!"

His mind was filled with poetry because he was spending much of his time learning poems by heart. "It passes the time, soothes the mind, helps me to fall asleep at night; and at exercise, when I repeat it to myself, prevents my thoughts from dwelling on my fate." He learned pieces by Sir Walter Scott and William Wordsworth as well as Thomas Gray's *Elegy Written in a Country Churchyard*, but avoided poems by Robert Burns, which he described as "scarcely lyrical or English!" From another poetry collection in the prison library which was "absurdly called *Bridges to Kipling*" he learned pieces by Andrew Lang and Robert Bridges' *Eton Jubilee Ode* which was intended as an inspiring piece both for schooldays and for life: "O ye, 'neath breezy skies of June,/ By silver Thames's lulling tune,/ In shade of willow or oak, who try/ The golden gates of poesy;/ ... Or whether with naked bodies flashing/ Ye plunge in the

183

lashing weir; or dashing/ The oars of cedar skiffs, ye strain/ Round the rushes and home again". He also liked *Silver Thames*, which offers a picture of the river flowing past meadows with dreaming anglers and ancient labourers, and considered it "both delightfully dignified and scholarlike." He learned William Watson's 1903 "prophetic warning to England's to restrain her conquering feet" entitled *Rome and Another* whose second verse read "Imperial power, that hungerest for the globe,/ Restrain thy conquering feet,/ Lest the same Fates that spun thy purple robe/ Should weave thy winding sheet". When he felt despondent about the war writing, "I know the Germans are near Paris which is bombarded by a gun 70 miles off! … my own opinion has always been that we shall never beat the Germans in the field or on sea or by blockade," this poem came to mind: "England has for centuries delighted in little wars of oppression or annexation & she will now find that the Fates which hitherto have weaved her imperial robe will spin her winding sheet! I dare say we shall be none the worse off!" Another piece he could recite was Oscar's *Ave Imperatrix* "which, now that we have again suffered from 'the treacherous Russian' might once more become popular in quires & places where they sing." He went on to tackle Matthew Arnold's *The Scholar Gypsy*, which recounts the story of an Oxford scholar who went off to join the gypsies, Percy Shelley's *Ode to a Skylark*, John Keats' *Ode to a Nightingale* (which Charles had learned during his time in France) and a shorter piece, William Blake's *Tyger, tyger*.

After his hours spent reading, Christopher switched to making "on a wooden frame woollen scarves for wounded soldiers: the work is very restful for the mind and the eyes after much reading; and my eyes, alas! are not as good as they used to be." Whilst he made scarves he could either "meditate on my sins" or, presumably more enjoyably, "recite to myself poetry that I've been learning by heart."

As he learned poetry and made scarves, his friend, Robbie, was again becoming enmeshed in legal matters. Robbie, who was probably regarded at the time with considerable suspicion because he continued his friendships with several conscientious objectors and went to see German prisoners-of-war, was visited by detectives from Scotland Yard. Then on 29 May the trial of Noel Billing for criminal libel against Maud Allan opened at the Old Bailey. The defence was determined to fuel anti-German and anti-gay sentiment and used the alleged existence of the *Black Book* at every opportunity to whip up public hysteria.

Whilst Noel Billing argued forcefully that fighting the sexual immorality of Oscar and his followers was a patriotic duty, when Alfred appeared as a defence witness he accused Oscar of being "the agent of the devil" and named both Christopher and Robbie as part of his cult. Although Judge Darling's summing-up was actually in Maud Allan's favour, the jury returned a verdict of not guilty and the spectators in the packed court were jubilant. Both Alfred and Noel Billing were greeted with rapturous applause. Robbie sadly observed the pleasure the English seemed to take in "kicking the corpse of Wilde" and found that there were those who thought Robbie himself was an appropriate substitute. Lord Beaverbrook, for example, tried to have him removed from the British War Memorials Committee. For his part, when he heard about the outcome of the trial Christopher wrote drily of the role Alfred had played in the proceedings: "The prosecution might have put in his eulogy of *Salome* to be found in Vol. IV, No. 1 of *The Spirit Lamp* dated May 1893!"

Christopher's own future was still uncertain: "'Think what ills the scholar's life assail – Toil, envy, want, the garret & the gaol!'" he quoted from Samuel Johnson's 1749 poem *The Vanity of Human Wishes*. But he anticipated that when as in William Watson's poem, *Autumn*, the summer was over: "June's 'virgin rapture' stilled and 'August's panting heart of time cold'" he might "begin to hope" again. And by early October he was indeed starting to look forward to his release. "My time is up in less than 3 months now – 12 weeks tomorrow, to be exact – so it is possible almost to count the days tho' the most consoling way is to reckon backwards & note that it is 268 days since my arrest, 216 since my conviction and "only" 85 to my release!." But he still chafed against his imprisonment "Yet would I gladly change it all for a crust of bread and that noble thing called Liberty or Freedom! I would say that 'prison rhymes with sorrow', only I believe a tramp once said it of a workhouse."

From time to time he seems to have decided to move abroad once he was free. "I think to retire to Holland in peace; tho' the doctor here advises Algiers or some sunny island in the South Seas." But really he never seriously intended leaving London. Shortly before his release his brother wrote to Walter, "I am afraid it is quite evident that he intends to live on in London, & I do not think that any one's advice will alter his purpose." However life in London would never be the same because he would no longer have Robbie's support and friendship to rely upon. On 5 October his friend died of heart failure in his rooms in Half Moon Street. He was only forty nine.

It was Paul Elwin who broke the news in a letter to Christopher which caused him considerable distress. He had lost Robbie's "devoted friendship and help of every kind" and grieved that "I can never again expect to have such a dear good counsellor and friend: he seems to have [been] universally lamented by all good men." Not only that, he had lost Robbie's regular financial support and Robbie had left only an unsigned draft of his latest will. It might have been that Robbie's brother, Alec, carried out Robbie's plan to set up a trust fund to support Christopher (amongst others) - which would have meant that he eventually received an annual annuity of £50 which he badly needed. However comments made by Christopher do not entirely support this and he only acknowledged that Alec helped him out with an allowance of £10 towards his rent. Still at least that was better than nothing.

Robbie's death hit Christopher particularly hard because he felt guilty about it: "I feel too in some ways responsible for his death: for it appears that he had decided to go to Melbourne some weeks ago in order to be away from London on my return to it, fearing that those blackguards Billing & Douglas & Co would renew their attacks. ... According to the evidence at the inquest, it was on account of his asking for a passport to Australia that he had to be medically examined, and he worried himself so much about the doctors' bad report on his health that it seems to have hastened his end."

Unlike Robbie, Christopher was reasonably fit. "My general health is really very good." In a way prison life had been good for him with the "long rest and regular hours" and no smoking or drinking helping his recovery. And there had been no sex either. Prison had meant "More than 9 months' entire 'abstinence' (unbridled chastity, as it might be said)". His wry comment suggested that abstinence had not generally been a feature of his life!

But his heart remained weak. "My heart unfortunately still thumps and throbs as loudly as the beating of the wings of the angel of death which John Bright <u>almost</u> heard, tho' it does not cause as much actual inconvenience." John Bright had been a politician whose most memorable speech had been in opposition to the Crimean War when he had warned, "The angel of death has been abroad throughout the land. You may almost hear the beating of his wings." Christopher seemed resigned to the idea of dying: "I suppose I shall drop down dead of a sudden one of these days."

In fact death seemed omnipresent. Whilst Christopher continued to mourn Robbie, his friend, Charles, heard the news that three of the men he had loved had died in quick succession. Philip Bainbridge was killed in September, Ian McKenzie died a few weeks later and on 4 November Wilfred Owen was killed just a week before the Armistice.

Christopher was still in Wormwood Scrubs when the war ended and spent Christmas Day there too. His mood was no doubt lifted both by a Christmas box sent anonymously by Walter and by the fact that he was soon to be freed. Three days later he was met outside the prison by his brother who took him back to Westbourne Terrace and on the following day Christopher relished being able to scrawl a brief letter to his friend R. "It is a treat to be able to write to you freely – yet this will be but a scrappy letter on a still scrappier bit of paper."

Christopher's prison letters to R. were published in facsimile as *Five letters and A Catalogue* and in his introduction Timothy d'Arch Smith suggests their recipient was a man called Roderick Sinclair Meiklejohn. Christopher certainly knew Roderick, who was tall, thin and rather striking in his appearance. Although he was shy, he was a kind man and he enjoyed food and wine as well as playing bridge. He loved books and his reading ranged from the classics to risqué poetry. He was just a few years younger than Christopher and was the eldest son of a Scottish naval doctor. He was educated first at St Paul's School in London and then at the age of eighteen he won a scholarship to Hertford College, Oxford. It seems feasible that it was whilst he was at Oxford that he first met Christopher - which would explain a reference in the letters to the men meeting in Abingdon a few miles south. After university he joined the War Office as a clerk and then moved to the Treasury before being appointed private secretary to Herbert Asquith. He became part of Robbie's circle and their mutual friends included Reggie Turner and the writer, Edmund Gosse.

When Christopher wrote to R. on 1 January 1919 he said, "I am sorry to hear of your mother's death." But perhaps this was a slip of the pen because it was Roderick's *father* who had died on 31 October 1918 after a long illness. (His mother had died several years earlier.) After his father's death, Roderick moved into the rooms in Half Moon Street which Robbie had occupied and here he organised Monday evening gatherings and, as Robbie had done, gave opportunities for his contemporaries to mix with young artists and writers, including Siegfried Sassoon, who shared his poetry with Roderick and also confessed his sexual attraction towards other men.

So was it definitely Roderick to whom Christopher wrote in 1918? It is certainly a reasonable suggestion but it is difficult to confirm. Christopher recalled visiting his correspondent at Abingdon in 1894 or 1895, which would have been the time that Roderick was at Oxford. The letters further reveal that in the summer of 1918 R. was hoping to let Little Munstead, a Lutyens house in Godalming in Surrey. Back in 1905 Christopher had stayed with someone at a country house in Surrey, and in 1921 he visited an "old friend" who lived near Godalming. But there is no evidence linking these locations with Roderick. Then Christopher generally addressed his friends by their surnames, which suggests 'R' might be the first letter of a surname rather than a first name.

Whoever R. was, Christopher was willing to flirt with him: "I was most delighted to get your letter – all too short – of June 24th – my dear person – and have pored over it ever since like any lovesick maiden with her first billet doux." He was open with R. about his sexuality and asked him if had seen the article in *The Winning Post* of 16 November 1918 which consisted of "a violent attack on Ross in which I'm sorry to say I figure largely? Obviously inspired, if not written, by Douglas." It contained "two pages of filthy abuse of him and me and Freddy Smith." The main targets of this newspaper attack on "unnatural" and "German" vices" were Robbie and his lover Freddie, but the first person to be named in the article was Christopher whose sentence for "unnatural offences" was described as unduly lenient. The writer commented sarcastically, "It is true that Christopher Millard had the advantage of being a 'gentleman of superior education,' a graduate of Oxford, the nephew of a bishop, and the private secretary of the late Mr Robert Ross, who described him as the greatest living authority on the works of Oscar Wilde. One or more of these circumstances may have had a mitigating effect on the mind of the Recorder."

Whilst 1918 had certainly been a hard year for Christopher, it had been a worse one for his former lover, Charley Garratt – though Christopher probably knew nothing of this. Before the war Charley seems to have been a confident young man, not easily cowed by the authorities. This was evident from his behaviour in court when a judge reprimanded him for his rudeness and threatened him with another spell in prison. Charley replied coolly, "I shall not go to prison for telling the truth, I think." His self-assurance irritated the judge who snapped back, "But you may go to prison for behaving insolently in this court." Sadly this youthful self-confidence was not to last.

Charley probably spent about a year at the school in Chipping Campden before briefly re-joining his mother, Elizabeth, near Rugby where she was living with her eldest son who worked as a lock keeper on the canal. By the spring of 1916 Charley was back in London and it was there that on 11 April he enlisted using his middle name, Nehemiah Garratt. He had little choice in the matter. Until the end of 1915 the British government had relied on voluntary enlistment. But the Military Service Act of January 1916 had introduced conscription and as a young man of twenty Charley would have been automatically called up for military service. When he was examined by the army doctor he was classified only as Class II Field Service and was assigned to duties "at Home" so he must have had some significant health problems which prevented him from being sent to the front. He spent the next seven months with the Fifteenth Middlesex Regiment, but by 6 November he was unable to stand garrison life any longer so he absented himself and was subsequently declared a deserter. He remained on the run for four months before being apprehended in Northampton on 16 March 1917 (a few days after Christopher had succumbed to influenza in France). He was found to be suffering from neurasthenia and depression, which had been aggravated by the hardships of military life, though the army doctors did not consider that the conditions he had experienced (which involved no actual fighting) would "have caused a breakdown in a normal man."

Charley's mental health did not improve. He had spells in several hospitals and in November 1917 spent nine days in the Military Hospital at Clipstone Camp in Nottinghamshire suffering from "delusional insanity. He "imagines he has done something very wrong & that if he does anything out of the ordinary sentries will stick him with bayonets" and he was "unable to concentrate his attention on anything". Significantly the hospital doctor noted in addition that he "Admits to being a Sexual Pervert". From Clipstone Camp he was moved to Wharncliffe War Hospital in Sheffield where he remained until 28 December. His medical records stated that he was suffering from "moral imbecility" and was "a moral defective" though he showed no "signs of intellectual deficiency". He was transferred to the Fourth Northamptonshire Regiment and posted on 12 January 1918, but on 21

March he again absented himself. He was apprehended for a second time on 13 April and subsequently returned to his unit to await trial for desertion. Four days later he was transferred to the psychiatric section of the Second Eastern General Hospital in Brighton suffering from "hysteria" and he remained there until 10 June. Because of his previous brushes with the law he was regarded as "a deliberate criminal" and although it was admitted that he "does actually suffer from hysteria & neurasthenia depression at times" the doctor at Brighton rather unsympathetically considered that he "makes the most of it." More ominously he thought he "would be better in an asylum for life."

Again Charley was briefly returned to his unit, but tried to kill himself in the guard room by swallowing buttons so he was sent back to Brighton suffering from "Mental instability" with his moods swinging between "depression with definite suicidal tendencies" and "temporary periods of cheerfulness". When he was at his worst he repeatedly declared "that his one idea is to die; that when he sees medicine bottles[?], nails, or any means of suicide an impulse to commit suicide comes over him. He also states that he has written letters to friends asking for poison, and that if he were discharged from hospital he thinks he could not face life & so would kill himself." He "threatened to smash a window and eat the glass" and seemed "hopeless in his outlook on life." There were times when "he brightens up for a while" but these alternated with periods when he lay on his bed crying and with times when he was "restless & excited saying that he must die." Usually he was "inert, silent & sullen."

He was discharged from the army on 23 November 1918 shortly after the armistice, but he was not free to resume civilian life. Instead he was confined in the Warwickshire County Lunatic Asylum at Hatton (just north of Warwick). Considerable emphasis was placed on Charley's homosexuality during the assessment of his mental state and this must have played a part in the decision to send him to the asylum. He was variously described as of a "bad" character, "degenerate" and "morally defective" and it was recorded with disapproval that "He appears to have lived as an invert for many years; this he admits, but that such misconduct has not occurred in the army."

Consequently Charley found himself confined in the large gothic Victorian asylum, which formed almost a self-contained community with farms, sports pitches and a chapel. (Its buildings are now part of a housing estate.) It is true that he could have found himself in a worse place. Hatton was a reasonably progressive institution where the patients were allowed some freedom and were able to watch and act in plays and to take part in social activities. But once a person was sent to an asylum it could be difficult for them ever to be released. There are many examples of people who should never have been confined, but who spent the rest of their lives in such institutions. Charley might have been one of them.

CHAPTER SEVENTEEN

THE BUNGALOW

"a very quaint and cosy little abode" from Christopher's letter to Walter 2 January 1919

On 2 January 1919 Christopher wrote to Walter for the first time since his arrest, though their friendship had clearly survived this latest crisis: "It must be more than a year since I wrote to you. Very many thanks for your letter of Decr 27th and also for kind messages that reached me from time to time. You have indeed been loyal to me in spite of everything." He knew Walter shared his sadness about Robbie's death which "has robbed me of my chief interest in life: apart from the loss of his ever devoted friendship and help of every kind, it affects my financial position considerably as he gave me (this in confidence) £50 a year for many years past as 'salary' for my assistance whenever he wanted anything done. Apart from that actual sum he was constantly giving me books: and various things which he discarded were readily saleable."

In the world beyond the prison walls Christopher found that "Food is more plentiful than I expected – but the price of everything is appalling. Until I can get my goods unwarehoused all my 'capital' is locked up: which is awkward." Nevertheless he was already making plans. Until 8 January he stayed at Sutherland House, "a sort of 'hotel for gentlemen'" in London Street very close to Paddington station. He then moved "to a small bedsitting room" at 23 Beaumont St near Baker St and quickly began meeting up with friends. On the afternoon of 13 January he met Walter at the Central Hall and he met a friend visiting from Oxford that same week.

He was soon looking for somewhere more permanent to live. "Within a few weeks from now I hope to be settled down again in a hole of my own. I found a few days ago and have now taken in St John's Wood – 3 mins from Maida Vale <u>tube</u> – a tiny <u>bungalow</u> which is situated in the back garden of some flats – a very quaint and cosy little abode. It is so small that I shall have to get rid of a great many books & my big shelves: but I had already decided that it would be necessary to sell the best part of my books partly to pay for the cost of moving from Melcombe Place, warehousing and settling into a new home, and partly to make a nucleus wherewith to begin life again. … My pension for 1918, my allowance from home, were both stopped, though now being renewed, whereas if they had been allowed to accumulate there would have been something to look forward to and some consolation for what I have endured during the past year."

Organising the move cost money and, as ever, he was hard up. "At present all my things are stored and I have had to buy all sorts of socks, collars, a[?] thick scarf, and many other odds & ends that I could not get from the warehouse." He could not afford to reclaim them from Druce (who was charging 25 shillings a month to store them). However he was far from destitute. His mother was still giving him a monthly allowance of £8 and his army pension was about £30 a year. R. helped him out with £5 and he was able to raise enough money for the move to St John's Wood.

Christopher spent the rest of his life in this little wooden bungalow which belonged to Mrs Joseph Lupton (the mother of an actress called Marie Studholme) who initially charged him a rent of £40 a year. The bungalow no longer exists but it was located behind the stuccoed house at 8 Abercorn Place (known as Abercorn House) and accessed by crossing the front garden, going down some steps and then along an alley. It provided just enough space for his business and for entertaining his friends. Anthony Powell, who later visited several times, described how Christopher "lived his life in one of the minute rooms; in the other he slept. There was an exiguous kitchen-bathroom. The whole place must have been dreadfully cold in winter. Books were everywhere: on shelves; on tables; stacked on the floor; stored away in boxes; all neatly arranged, because Millard was intensely methodical."

193

8 Abercorn Place

Christopher liked the location: "It is sufficiently near for me to get into London when I want to, and, what is of greater importance, remote enough to choke off casuals and undesirables visiting me." He repeatedly stressed his desire for a more peaceful life. "By living quietly, I suppose I shall be able to get along: the blessing is that a solitary life does not bore me ... I never want to return to my former mode of living; the "West-End" life had long ceased to amuse me." Whether this was genuinely what he believed or just a way of making the best of things is difficult to tell. However he was not really isolated in Abercorn Place. He was very close to Lord's Cricket Ground and friends on the way to see a match would look in on him. West End life was only a short journey away as Christopher was close both to the tube at Maida Vale and to the underground at Marlborough Road whilst buses regularly ran down towards Oxford Street. He had a telephone (Maida Vale, later Hampstead, 3559) installed so he could easily be contacted, and in fact he travelled to the bookshops and the other attractions of central London on most days.

But he did enjoy being self-sufficient and having his own little garden for the first time in London. He told Walter, "When you come to my bungalow I will give you a spade or a trowel and you must show me how to dig up my little garden – it is only a few inches but big enough to plant some nasturtiums or some quickly growing creepers." In mid-April he wrote, "My flower border is panting for plants and ferns!" and by the end of the month, "My garden grows apace in spite of the cold weather." There was indeed something rural about this wooden home and it might have reminded Christopher both of his childhood and of the time he had spent in the Cheviot Hills. Michael Davidson thought the bungalow resembled a "country cottage in the middle of London" whilst Charles Scott Moncrieff described how in his garden Christopher "speedily gathered a volunteer following of squirrels, birds, and other humble admirers, who would come to his call and with whom he delighted in sharing the more edible fruits of his labours."

By late spring he was happily settled and he wrote to Walter. "I don't know if you have a Sunday post in your district but in any case I hope this won't be too late to wish you very many happy returns of the day". He enclosed a penny Omar as a birthday present. This was a volume of translations by Edward Fitzgerald of poems by the Persian eleventh-century poet Omar Khayyam. Edward's translations had become highly influential but there was an added significance to Christopher's gift. Edward had almost certainly been gay and he had had close emotional relationships with other men once admitting, "My friendships are more like loves I think."

Christopher had begun his bookselling business in earnest and Walter was one of his regular customers. In January Christopher drew his friend's attention to an 1893 specimen copy of *Lady Windermere's Fan* which Robbie had seen shortly before he died. It cost £4 10s and was "far beyond" Christopher's own means, but he earned a commission on the sale. His first major venture was to sell his collection of editions of *Dorian Gray*. He could not afford to be sentimental about these, nor about the manuscripts and a book of cuttings, which Robbie had given him and which he had not wanted "to part with while he lived."

It was also at this time that he started sending political notes to New York at Frank Harris' request. These were intended for *Pearson's* magazine, which Frank was now editing, and in return Frank sent him some copies of his book on Oscar to re-sell privately. Initially Christopher was not keen on the assignment. Frank had annoyed him by losing some photographs he had lent him and failing to pay him for some proof reading. In any case: "I'm not really sufficiently interested in politics to write about them; and if I wrote about them as I feel, I should probably be arrested under the Defence of the Realm Act... I am not a journalist ... and can never write anything unless I'm frightfully keen on the subject. I would much rather write on literature than on politics." However he did eventually send several batches of notes and some duly appeared in the June issue.

One evening that April Christopher dined amidst the lush greenery of Princes' restaurant in Piccadilly with Tancred Borenius and his wife Anne-Marie. Tancred, who was Finnish, worked both as a diplomat and as an art historian and might well have met Christopher at the *Burlington*. Tancred had known Robbie well. Through Roger Fry he became involved with London's art circles and with the Bloomsbury group and from 1914 he lectured at University College London. Christopher liked Tancred and Anne-Marie and subsequently invited them for tea at the bungalow.

Another encounter at the end of the month was much less welcome. Christopher found himself in the crowded coffee room of a hotel in Lewes when he caught sight of Alfred, who was continuing to publish derogatory pamphlets about both Christopher and Robbie which he generally put on sale at the kiosk in the Café Royal. Determined to give him something of his own medicine Christopher stood up and shouted out, "My God, it's that bugger Alfred Douglas!" and there was something of a public slanging match. Afterwards he told the hotel proprietress that Alfred was a "notorious blackmailer" and she agreed to bar him. Christopher recounted the incident to Frank Harris and promised that if Frank ever wrote his book about Alfred Douglas he would offer him his own dossier. He was disappointed not to have a copy of Alfred's notorious letter, which described his sexual activity with an Arab youth in Biskra, but he was reassured to know that the original was safely held by George Lewis (who had been Robbie's solicitor).

Robbie must have been much in Christopher's thoughts at this time because 25 May 1919 would have been Robbie's fiftieth birthday and Christopher was always very good at remembering the birthdays and anniversaries of his friends. Osbert Burdett described his endearing habit of marking such occasions by giving "little presents to the tiniest of which he would give his cachet by adding to the thing some personal touch" so for Walter on one occasion he picked out "four very elementary penny books on *Plant Life*" which he hoped "may amuse you". This thoughtfulness was part of the charm which helped him make and keep friends. No doubt he saw the *In Memoriam* notice in *The Times* inserted to mark Robbie's birthday which described him as "Of ev'ry friendless name the friend". It must have forcibly reminded Christopher (who had certainly at times been one of those 'friendless names') of his loss.

That summer saw the national celebrations marking the end of the war, which Christopher viewed with considerable cynicism. "You will be lucky to escape the so-called 'Peace' celebrations," he wrote to Walter. "There are 23 wars going on and yet they say Peace, peace when there is no peace." Still when he was taken to *A Temporary Gentleman* by Henry Francis Maltby, which dealt with the war and which had opened at the Oxford Theatre in Oxford Street on 9 June, he did find it "quite an amusing play". It was certainly a hit amongst returning soldiers and its author claimed that it was the "first war play that attempted to tell the truth." Its 'hero' was a middle-class junior clerk whose army career gave him ideas above his station.

As well as a fortnight's holiday with his brother in Devon, Christopher spent some further weeks away from his bungalow during the summer when he stayed at a bookshop at 24 Museum Street (later renumbered as number 30), whilst the owners were on holiday. The shop was run by a Cambridge graduate, (Joseph) Irving Davis, and an Italian, Guiseppe (Pino) Orioli who both shared a love of books as well as a willingness to trade in controversial material, which was evident when Pino later organised the publication of *Lady Chatterley's Lover* and distributed copies through the Museum Street shop.

Pino had returned to Italy after the war (where he later met up with Charles Scott Moncrieff) and had left Irving to run the Museum Street shop. Irving, who was a shy man and often short of money, became a well-known figure in the bookselling world and specialised in early scientific literature. He might have suggested that Christopher go into partnership with him as Christopher was certainly considering such an arrangement at this time though it is unclear whether this was the shop in question and perhaps he merely helped Irving out from time to time. In any case he must have found Irving a congenial companion, who shared his interests in both literature and food.

30 Museum Street (formerly the premises of Davis and Orioli)

Christopher was also still involved with Robbie's affairs. He sent Walter "a little memento of R.R. for you (from the executors)" and he read Edmund Gosse's article on Robbie in the *Sunday Times* of 3 August with interest. At the same time he was annoyed by the plans to print a new edition of Alfred Douglas' *Oscar Wilde and Myself* with its chapter in which Alfred denied any gay sexual activity: "A.D. may be a 'Catholic' and 'pious' but he is still an unmitigated liar."

Another book which must have attracted his attention towards the end of the year was Charles Scott Moncrieff's translation of *The Song of Roland*. Charles had dedicated "my part in a book of which their friendship quickened the beginning their example has justified the continuing" to men he had loved – Philip, Ian and Wilfred - "three men, scholars, poets, soldiers, who came to their rencesvals in September, October, and November nineteen hundred and eighteen." In his preface he included a poem to each man. That to Philip addresses him directly and declares their intimacy. "Friend – nay, friend were a name too common, rather/Mind of my intimate mind, I may claim thee lover". Although the poetic forms and the conventional religious sentiments apparently made the expression of his feelings acceptable they are in fact quite strongly worded. Furthermore the poem dedicated to Ian refers back to his friend's own poem on desire and repeatedly likens him to fire evoking his physical and intellectual energy and also suggesting physical attraction with the first three lines reading: "Like fire I saw thee/Smiling, running, leaping, glancing and consuming;/Like fire thine ardent body moving."

Charles seemed to believe that his translation of this story of chivalry and death at the eighth-century Battle of Roncesvalles provided a suitable memorial to his friends but the story is not an unproblematic account of valour. The Frankish warrior hero, Roland, dies through treachery and it might be his arrogance which prevents him from summoning help in time. There is no evidence of Christopher's response to Charles' book, but as he was generally rather cynical about tales of valour and patriotism he was probably alive to the ambiguities of *The Song of Roland*.

CHAPTER EIGHTEEN

BOOKSELLING

"I am much too fond of books to be a successful dealer in them; but needs must." from Christopher's letter to Walter 13 December 1921

At around the same times as Charles' *The Song of Roland* appeared, Christopher's first catalogue was ready for distribution. "My Catalogue No. 1 has actually gone to the printers... I am quite broke over it but hope to recover by the time it is circulated!" It was the first in a series of catalogues, issued in small quantities and at infrequent intervals, for which Christopher re-used the design originally made by Charles Ricketts for the third edition of Oscar's *The Ballad of Reading Gaol.* This depicted a rose growing from a pierced heart which for Christopher was presumably both a Jacobite and a gay symbol. These catalogues were detailed and informative on the works of authors he admired, but equally Christopher was not afraid to express disapproval of books he disliked. Charles Scott Moncrieff appreciated the pages "teeming with his own witty comments on the nature and quality of his wares" which "were treasured by all who were so fortunate as to receive them. One memorable feature was the concluding half-page of 'unsolicited testimonials' from correspondents in all parts of the world from Eton to the Antipodes." Mostly these were positive but Christopher displayed his sense of humour by including those that were negative or double-edged such as "Prices more reasonable than usual" from a Wimbledon correspondent, presumably Walter.

To build up his stock Christopher regularly visited bookshops and auction sales. His circuit included Simpkin, Marshall, Hamilton Kent & Co's shop in Ludgate Hill. In 1913 they had published Haldane Macfall's *The Splendid Wayfaring* to which a young artist, Claud Lovat Fraser, had contributed illustrations and his name was soon to become a familiar one to Christopher. In addition Christopher attended Puttick and Simpson's auctions at 47 Leicester Square and made time for "book talk" with friends such as Walter. These conversations were important to him and he was annoyed when they were interrupted, apologising to Walter, "I'm sorry that silly girl turn'd up on Wednesday as we did not nearly finish our book talk. I was going to show you Stuart-Young's books," and warning him to come early the following week because people were coming and they would again "interrupt our book business."

Walter remained fascinated by Oscar's work, but had recently found another heroic figure to admire - Horatio Nelson. He began collecting memorabilia associated with the sailor and followed up his new interest by researching the history of the hatchments in his local church in Merton. One of these depicted the arms of Horatio Nelson who had regularly attended services there. Walter wrote an article about them for his parish magazine and sent Christopher a bound copy. When Christopher wrote to thank Walter, he began with an apology: "I am really rather ashamed of myself for not writing before now to thank you for the copy of the Merton Hatchments: there seems no end to the subjects on which you are an expert! And the delightful green buckram binding is yours also, presumably." He enclosed just a small Christmas gift for Walter - "a little Riccardi book of Carols but, as it is nicely printed you will appreciate it." Christopher had had enough of the "'festive' season" but he hoped his friend would "have a happy time" with his family and early in the following year as he worked on his second catalogue - "mostly rubbish, I'm sorry to say" – he did derive some satisfaction from the report of the fourth bankruptcy of Alfred's brother Percy. "They are a pretty crew!" he commented drily.

Christopher spent Easter 1920 alone in his bungalow commiserating with Walter over his problems with his landlord – "what brutes they are!" On the afternoon of Wednesday 31 March he headed for Sotheby's and as he passed through Oxford Street he "recklessly went into the shop called BUSZARDS and ordered some cold pie and coffee." He was shocked to discover that "After wondering what the pie could be made of I found that the pastry and the mixture were green with mildew! The 'A.B.C.' people own Buszards now but still keep the old name to deceive the unwary!" Indignantly Christopher decided to write "mildly to the directors."

Walter visited the bungalow a couple of weeks later and "didn't have to rush away as early as usual" which pleased Christopher, who was interested to learn that Walter was making a transcript of the details of *De*

Profundis material from the catalogue of the New York auction of the private library of John B. Stetson, Jr. The sale included numerous works by Oscar many of which were purchased at the auction on 23 April by the wealthy American collector William Andrews Clark, Jr. He was soon to become one of Christopher's regular customers. In his turn Christopher possibly shared some of the discussion about books contained in his correspondence with (Charles) Vincent (Emerson) Starrett, an American writer who lived in Chicago.

Naturally Christopher was still working on Wildean material and his new book, *Oscar Wilde and the Aesthetic Movement*, soon appeared in a limited edition of 100 copies published by Townley Searle in Dublin. It was a short volume (illustrated with images from Christopher's own collection) that dealt with the caricatures of Oscar in the music of the 1880s such as the song *The Flippity Flop Young Man*. The book provided another sympathetic account of Oscar and depicted him as a resilient figure: "Few young men have been more savagely criticised and satirised, more ruthlessly burlesqued and caricatured.... Wilde took it all in good part and lived on. He joined in the laughter against himself."

In August Christopher had "quite a nice holiday in different parts of the country" including "a very jolly time near the Thames" at Long Wittenham (a few miles south of Abingdon, which he had visited many years before with R.). But he was back at his bungalow for September where he began work on his third catalogue which was intended "to tide me over the coming winter." A few weeks later his friend Alan Alington arrived back in London apparently for the first time in four years because he had stayed on to work for the Indian Civil Service after the end of the war. He travelled back from Bombay in a second class cabin on the *Karmala* which docked on 8 November.

Within a fortnight of Alan's return, Christopher's eighty-five year old mother died at Wintney House and he wrote tersely to Walter. "Sorry to put you off but I am obliged to go down to Hampshire on Wednesday for a funeral." His visit appears to have been a brief one – he always found it particularly difficult to deal with his relatives en masse - and he does not seem to have been particularly distressed by his mother's death. Robbie's had certainly hit him much harder and it was probably at least partly as a memorial to his friend that in November he wrote an anonymous preface for an edition of Oscar's 1897 letters to Robbie which was to be published the following year (by Cyril William

Beaumont) as *After Reading*. He signed some copies of a longer version produced by Paul Reynolds in New York and was pleased when Max Meyerfield produced a German translation of the work. Oscar's son Vyvyan had insisted that the letters were edited to remove any homosexual references and when Christopher tried to replace the deleted sections, Vyvyan warned him that he would not allow the "Uranian passages" to be included, though he patronisingly forgave Christopher for trying "knowing how earnest you are in your devotion to the subject."

As 1920 gave way to 1921 Christopher's energies were mainly absorbed in acquiring new items that interested him. These included a copy of "A.D.'s *Perkin Warbeck* (privately printed), 1897(!)" Alfred had written this poem between 1893 and 1894 and it deals with a fifteenth century pretender to the English throne who is "Fore-doomed to splendour and sorrow." Christopher was delighted to find that this copy had "a presentation inscription from his mother in it!"

However all Christopher's activities were brought abruptly to a halt at the end of April when he had a severe heart attack. He lay unconscious alone at his home for several hours until he was discovered and taken to Charing Cross Hospital. The next day he was moved to the more congenial Hospital of St John and St Elizabeth's in Grove End Road run by the Sisters of Mercy, where he must have been happier both to be near his bungalow and to be in a Catholic institution. Christopher was kept in this hospital for a week and once he was well enough to leave he went to stay with some (unidentified) friends who lived nearby though he spent his days at the bungalow continuing to work. He was still far from fully fit though and his doctor soon informed him that he needed to spend some time at St Andrew's Hospital in Dollis Hill Lane "for 'a long rest and careful nursing'". This hospital, too, was run by the Sisters of Mercy and was in a peaceful location in "an extraordinary spot for so near London – the cuckoo sings all day. Luckily as only 6 beds out of 20 are occupied, I am able to have my bed at the far end where I can have all the windows open without the other patients complaining of too much fresh air." He had few visitors in this isolated spot and warned Walter, "The place is quite inaccessible except by Rollys [sic] Royce, so please don't attempt to find your way here."

His stay in hospital was not entirely tranquil though, because whilst he was there he appears to have been annoyed by "an appalling poem." It had been published by Blackwell and, according to Christopher, its author was sufficiently well-regarded to have his poems included in Arthur Quiller-Couch's influential *The Oxford Book of Victorian Verse*. Christopher told Walter that the offending poet was "a parson in the New Forest" and he might have been Canon Hardwicke Drummond Rawnsley, who had died recently and who had been in favour of the censorship of literature and art, speaking out forcefully against the depiction of sex and violence. Christopher might well have found his work annoying.

After a fortnight Christopher was allowed to leave St Andrew's and immediately spent "the week-end in the country near Godalming where an old friend of mine lives." Although he felt better when he got home, he was frequently exhausted. "My chief complaint now is indolence: I seem to lack energy even to get on with my next catalogue and prefer to spend most of the day lying on a sofa in my garden (or yard). However it may pass off with cooler weather. I have a great deal of work on hand and don't seem to do it."

Just a couple of weeks after his return, Christopher received the news that on 9 July his eldest sister, Magdalen, had died. Following their mother's death, she had set up home in a house called Up Green in the village of Eversley, a few miles north of the home she had shared with her mother, whilst her sister, Philippa, had moved to a house called Inglewood in Bembridge on the Isle of Wight. There is no evidence about the kind of relationship Christopher had with his eldest sister and they cannot have seen much of each other as he rarely visited Hampshire, but she did resemble him in a number of ways. In particular she, too, was devoted to her favourite causes. She was passionate about women's education and especially keen to help women gain access to training in horticulture and agriculture. She was an enthusiastic gardener herself and although it seems unlikely that Christopher ever introduced her to his friend, Walter, both gained similar pleasures from growing plants. Her interest led her to join the Women's Farm and Garden Association which ran training courses as well as an employment service before launching the Women's Land Corps at the start of the First World War – a scheme which was subsequently adopted by the Government. She also became a great supporter of Studley College in Warwickshire which was the first horticultural and agricultural college for women in Britain providing up to a hundred places. The training, taken up mainly by middle-class women, was intended to provide a route into employment and to give such women a measure of independence. The college had been founded in 1898 by Daisy Greville, Countess of Warwickshire, who was interested not only in women's rights but in socialist politics, which might also have influenced Magdalen too. Certainly the college was close to her heart and at her death she left a bequest (later incorporated into the Studley College Trust) to fund exhibitions or scholarships to enable clergymen's daughters like herself to study there. She also donated her books on horticulture to the college; like Christopher she was a great book collector.

Whilst Christopher had created a close-knit male social network, first in Oxford and then in London, his sister had established her own circle of local, primarily female friends. At her death she left small presents to many of them in a gesture that is reminiscent of Christopher's habit of giving little gifts to his friends. Magdalen's keepsakes included a number of pieces of jewellery – a pearl serpent brooch, a diamond brooch, a lapis lazuli chain, a turquoise locket (that had been her mother's), a pearl studded chain, a pearl brooch, and a curb chain bangle. Their recipients included the cleric Gilbert Stapleton (and his wife and daughters) whom she had known for twenty years, as well as a number of both single and married middle-class women such as her god-daughter Dora Christabel Finlinson, the daughter of a shipping agent (whom Magdalen knew from Basingstoke) and the Australian-born, Anne Grant Tindal, a neighbour of Magdalen's who lived with her elderly father in Eversley. Through her cousins, the daughters of Baron Basing, Magdalen had got to know young Diana Dashwood and she seems to have been supportive not only of her but of several other young women whom she encouraged with their education. One of these was Margaret Dorothea Sellon, the stepdaughter of Henry John Hardy, an assistant master at Winchester, and another was Sylvia Noel Stilwell, the niece of Magdalen's friend, Anne Tindal. Sylvia seems to have used the legacy she received from Magdalen to take a trip to Australia accompanied by another one of relatives, Beatrice Ellen Stilwell, who worked as a professional gardener.

Magdalen left most of her other possessions to her sister Philippa, but bequeathed her silver and plate to her sister Dorothy, and left keepsakes to Christopher and her other brothers. In addition she left firm instructions about what was to happen to her body after her death. She was to be cremated and her ashes scattered to ensure that her relatives would not be burdened with looking after her grave. When Christopher came to write his own will, his instructions for his burial indicate that he shared many of his sister's sentiments on this matter.

Following a prolonged convalescence Christopher finally felt well enough by the autumn to be able to go sailing again and he spent several enjoyable weekends with Alan, either at Burnham on Crouch or Fambridge, before it got too cold. Back in London he resumed his research on Wildean matters and met up with a Miss Farran, who had typed up Oscar's expanded version of *Mr W. H.* in 1894. He also continued buying and selling material. Sales from his fifth catalogue went well, but it took a long time to get payments from some of his customers – particularly those in America. The catalogue included the oil portrait of Oscar by Harper Pennington, which was bought for the substantial sum of £200 by William Andrews Clark, Jr. Oscar had given this painting to Robbie who had passed it to Christopher. When it was offered to the National Portrait Gallery they refused it, leading Christopher to comment sarcastically that they might have found space for it in the lavatory.

In November Christopher offered a book by Andre Raffalovich to one of his American customers for £5 but still felt defensive about such sales: "I fear you think I am a bit grasping now that I have 'commenced bookselling'" he wrote to Walter, "but it is my sole source of income (with the exception of my insignificant army pension)." His finances had recently worsened because he was no longer receiving the allowance which his mother had paid him: "Though my mother died just on a year ago, her will has not yet been proved owing to some ambiguous clause which has to be decided by Chancery, so I have been entirely without the allowance from her that I had been accustomed to." When the legal issues were finally resolved it emerged that Dora had left four of her children outright legacies. She bequeathed £4000 to both her unmarried daughters, Magdalen (though she died before receiving this) and Philippa, as well as all they needed to furnish a small house each. She left £2000 to Paul Elwin and £1500 to Baldwin (who had already received £1000 of this on his marriage). Trusts were established for the benefit of Dora's other three children. One trust of £2000 was set up for George Michael (and his wife and children) because he lived abroad. The same amount was invested for Dorothy to provide her with an income. This would have been done to safeguard her legacy because she was a married woman.

Unlike his other unmarried siblings, Christopher did not receive his legacy outright. Instead a trust of £1500 was established for him, which left him dependent on the annual income the executors paid him. Furthermore in July 1918, whilst he was in prison, his mother added a codicil to her will. "I desire that the money that I leave to my son Christopher Sclater should be placed in the charge of his brother Paul Elwin or any other person he or my executors may select." The income was to be paid to him "quarterly or monthly as may seem desirable." This must have felt humiliating. Having 'misbehaved' himself again (as his mother had seen it) Christopher was not to be trusted with even the moderate lump sum yielded by the trust each year. Instead his brother was to parcel it out in small amounts. No doubt Paul Elwin dutifully did so, but it placed Christopher in a permanently dependent position. Perhaps he resented this (which would have been understandable) or perhaps he merely accepted it as a continuation of the kind of arrangement he had had whilst his mother was alive.

Besides worries over money there remained the on-going annoyance of Alfred Douglas, who was back in court again. This time he was suing the *Evening News* for libel after it had published false reports of his death and allegedly defamatory remarks in an obituary. The newspaper employed George Lewis (who had been Robbie's solicitor) to represent them. He tried hard to argue the case for justification and produced incriminating letters from Alfred to Oscar. But when Christopher attended the court to hear his old adversary he thought things were going Alfred's way: "I heard Douglas in the witness-box the other day: his lies and perjuries were made to some effect this time. I think Lewis mismanaged the case – badly." The outcome was indeed in Alfred's favour and he was awarded £1000 damages.

Around the end of the year Christopher was pleased to be the temporary custodian of two paintings which had once been in Oscar's home. These were "the two pictures described in lot 123 of the Tite St sale catalogue … as '2 crayon full length figures, framed'". Christopher speculated, "One may be by Albert Moore (or even Rossetti possibly) and one by Simeon Solomon; but I have not had a chance of identifying them yet." Albert Moore's painting was no doubt one of his typical depictions of languorous women in a classical setting whilst the gay painter, Simeon Solomon, produced works on both literary and Jewish subjects.

These paintings soon moved on but in December Christopher also acquired an original Max Beerbohm cartoon of Oscar and his brother Willie to join his collection of images of Oscar which he had been compiling for more than a dozen years. (He added "a rather interesting miscellaneous collection of OW cartoons" later in 1922.) His collection has largely provided the material from which the popular iconography of Oscar Wilde has been composed and eventually it comprised 181 items (which in April 1927 were sold to William Andrews Clark for fifty pounds). The image of Oscar which Christopher constructed through his acquisitions was not of a tragic figure but rather of a man who was both a gay icon and a successful and powerful author who left an important literary legacy. Christopher assembled his material into a sequence that celebrated Oscar's life rather than dwelling on his trial or his suffering. He deliberately excluded any image that included Alfred who, in Christopher's eyes, had betrayed Oscar and many of the pictures depict a young, defiant and attractive man - as in the one Christopher chose as the frontispiece to his *Art and Morality*. The final image, showing Oscar in Dieppe, affectionately likened him to Queen Victoria and Christopher must have appreciated the way the association between these two well-known figures played on the meaning of the word 'queen', which already had gay connotations by the 1920s.

As well as purchasing images for this collection, Christopher was trying to acquire more books for resale. Hence Oscar's friend Ada Leverson arranged to visit him at the bungalow bringing some books with her that she thought he might buy. Christopher was sceptical about whether she would actually appear - "She is such an irresponsible person that she will very likely not turn up" - although he was interested in what she had to offer. Nevertheless he continued to have reservations about the whole business of selling books: "I am much too fond of books to be a successful dealer in them; but needs must; and I have kept myself entirely (since my mother's death more than a year ago) and very largely for three years' past from my earnings."

There continued to be a regular stream of visitors to his home including Elizabeth Gwendolen Otter, who subsequently invited Christopher to lunch in Chelsea. She was fascinated by spiritual matters and wrote a number of books about the notion that the world could be influenced by contact with heavenly forces. Vyvyan Holland was another visitor. Before setting off to spend two months in Spain, he came "to fill in the date" of the books by Oscar which had been published in America by Paul

Reynolds. Other friendships were sustained through correspondence. Christopher "wrote to a friend in Paris last week" (who might have worked at the branch of Brentano's there at 37 Avenue de l'Opera) and asked him "to call at Masson's to see if he could get the Raffalovich books" whilst other friends kept him up-to-date about the whereabouts of those associated with Oscar: "I hear that Sherard is taking his whiskies and waters at Alassio" - a popular resort on the British Italian Riviera.

Although Christopher liked living in his bungalow, at the beginning of 1922 he was contemplating moving out probably because he was having trouble with his landlady. He got as far as viewing a house nearby but found that "the expense of making it habitable" would be too much. So he was still in Abercorn Place when he wrote to Walter: "The date 22.2.22 on your letter looks too too utterly absurd! I suppose such a combination can occur only twice in a century – Nov. 11,'11 and Feb 22, '22, so <u>we</u> shan't see it again."

Not long afterwards and presumably as a result of his illness the previous year, he was summoned to a Medical Board at Chelsea for an assessment of his health and a consideration of the renewal of his pension. Walter was also unwell and Christopher wrote, "I am sorry you caught cold last week," before gently scolding him, "I warned you that you ought not to venture forth without your cloak!" More seriously Charles Scott Moncrieff's health, which had never really recovered after the war, had further deteriorated and he decided to move permanently to Italy both for its more favourable climate and because of its more sympathetic attitude towards gay sexuality. At first he settled in Florence where he became part of an expatriate literary community which included Robbie's old friend, Reggie Turner, as well as the lesbian writer, Radclyffe Hall.

When Christopher himself left London on 6 March, his destination was far less exotic. He spent the day in Welwyn Garden City "with a man who wanted to see if it was possible to live there." Christopher was not impressed with the new town: "The houses are nice enough but absurdly expensive and all crowded together as thick as thieves in Vallombrosa, and the surroundings are horrible. The method seems to have been either to cut down a tree if it was in the way or build as far from a tree as possible, with the consequence that there is not enough shade in the place to shelter a rabbit. Further it all reeks of *Daily Mail* advertisement."

CHAPTER NINETEEN

NEW INTERESTS

"really rather a temptation" - Christopher quoted by Anthony Powell in Infants of the Spring

But Christopher did not spend long considering the failings of Welwyn Garden City because he had a much more compelling new interest. He had recently met a young man, the future author Anthony Powell, whose family lived nearby and whose father collected books. Anthony, then at Eton, became a regular visitor at the bungalow during the holidays and greatly appreciated the way that Christopher addressed him "in conversation on absolutely equal terms." In his turn Christopher found the young man rather attractive and one day, whilst they were having tea, he voiced this: "You're really rather a temptation you know." He must have hoped for a response that would indicate that Anthony might be interested in taking things further. But although the young man was not particularly shocked, he laughed the comment off. His visits came rather abruptly to an end, however, when his father warned him against Christopher.

The visits ceased, but they left a rather unexpected legacy. Anthony was a keen admirer of the work of the artist, Claud Lovat Fraser, and although Christopher initially knew little about him, he was inspired to find out more and soon began making his own collection. He acknowledged his debt to Anthony by calling him as "the 'onlie begetter' of the collection which I am making" – a description which deliberately associated Anthony with the 'Mr W. H.' who had supposedly inspired Shakespeare's sonnets and who had been identified by Oscar as an attractive young Elizabethan actor, Willie Hughes. Christopher's new interest was further fuelled by a visit to the Leicester Galleries show and he wrote to tell Walter, "I am collecting everything by Lovat Fraser now and have about 80 items out of a possible or probable 800. It is a mad idea; but it seems to show that my mania for collecting OW was not due entirely to his

210

vices!" Drawing on his experience of collecting Wildean material, Christopher was aware of the importance of buying the smaller and more ephemeral items by the artist which would eventually become very rare. In April he wrote to thank Anthony for finding the print designs for MacFisheries Ltd, and to explain that he was concentrating on trying to track down the artist's Eno's Fruit Salt advertisements as well as the issues of two magazines – *Pan* and *Hearth and Home* – which included his work.

Claud Lovat Fraser had been an innovative and talented designer and illustrator. He began his artistic career at the age of twenty one and was taught by Walter Sickert. He produced the illustrations for Haldane MacFall's essay on art, *The Splendid Wayfaring*, and then in 1913 along with Holbrook Jackson and the poet Ralph Hodgson he established a small publishing firm to create illustrated poetry works. His other work included fabric designs for Liberty's, book illustrations, advertisements and theatre designs - most famously for *The Beggar's Opera*. He enlisted at the start of the war and in early 1916 was invalided home suffering both from the effects of gas (from which he never fully recovered) and shell shock. He subsequently worked for some months at the War Office on visual propaganda and during this time married an American-born actress, Grace Inez Crawford but he died suddenly in June 1921 at the age of thirty one.

As well as searching for items related to Claud Lovat Fraser, Christopher continued selling. Some items he sold on commission for people such as Cyril William Beaumont, who had a bookshop as well as a publishing business in Charing Cross Road. Other material he acquired for resale including "some rather interesting letters of Shaw, Barrie, Kipling and Max Beerbohm: the last-named I have promised not to catalogue, but the others should help to liven up my next list." The Max Beerbohm letters contained sensitive material which suggested he had had an affair with a married woman and Christopher was evidently uncomfortable about revealing this. It was a step too far even for someone who engaged in what he frequently described as "a sordid business as one is apt to value a book for its £-s-d-ness and not for itself; but it is amusing: and for me necessary in my present state of ill-health and impecuniosity."

That spring another talented young man, a fellow pupil of Anthony's at Eton, also found his way to the bungalow. This was Brian Christian de Claiborne Howard, a Jewish-American who had recently founded the

Eton Society of Arts and who strongly reminded Christopher of his former lover, Charles Scott Moncrieff. He was tall, dark and handsome, sensitive and witty, and a rebellious dandy. Like Christopher he enjoyed evading rules and along with his great friend and artistic rival, Harold Mitchell Acton, he seems to have modelled himself on Oscar and his fellow aesthetes so he and Harold appeared at the Alhambra in Leicester Square wearing full evening dress with long white gloves, canes and top hats. His school society published a single issue of a magazine *The Eton Candle* that March, to which both he and Harold contributed poems. It sold out on the day it was published and although it was a school magazine it was widely reviewed. Christopher later listed it in one of his catalogues and he seems to have taken to Brian (although Brian himself rather archly described Christopher as *"very* sinister") and wanted to find out from Anthony how he had "discovered" him after finding the "'aesthetic' part of the young man was more obvious at a first glance than the 'poseur' part." He admitted, "I hadn't the cheek to ask him to lunch – after confessing myself a bookseller." However Brian was already collecting books and pictures (as well as records which ranged from Wagner to jazz) and when he told Christopher that he was interested in collecting material about John Gray, Christopher was keen to send him his latest catalogue: "not that I in the least want him to buy anything. People never do buy John Gray and I catalogue his things only to annoy him and the Jew Raffalovich who lives with him!" Like Anthony, Brian was interested in the work of Claud Lovat Fraser and Christopher shared his duplicate material with both of them.

Another new acquaintance was Raymond Duff Lawford. Christopher met him at a Sunday supper which was apparently a convivial occasion at which plenty of champagne, white port and kummel liqueur was consumed. Raymond claimed to be an old Etonian but Christopher was suspicious and thought he didn't seem "quite the right thing" so he asked Anthony to look Raymond up in the Eton Roll to see whether his hunch was correct. In fact Christopher was wrong. Raymond had indeed been at Eton from 1909 to 1914. (He had moved on to Balliol before joining the Grenadier Guards.)

Despite his growing interested in Claud Lovat Fraser, Christopher had not abandoned his Wildean research and in early April he wrote to *Notes and Queries* (still under his Stuart Mason pseudonym) in an attempt to trace the publication details of a fragment of a manuscript by Oscar which refers to the success of a catalogue. In the same month he acquired some copies of the December 1921 issue of the New York magazine, *Century*. It contained a play titled *For Love of the King* which had also appeared in *Hutchinson's Magazine*, a London periodical. It was a work that was destined to involve Christopher in yet more controversy.

The spring weather came late that year and there was no real warmth or sunshine until early May when its arrival raised Christopher's spirits. He continued to write on bibliographical matters and to visit booksellers and by the middle of June he had acquired some manuscripts thinking they were genuinely by Oscar. But they turned out to be forgeries by "a man calling himself Sebastian or Dorian Hope" – Oscar's nephew by marriage, Fabian Lloyd (otherwise known as Arthur Craven). Christopher did not find much other material of interest that year and he had little money to spend. What money he did have, he mostly used to buy items for his Claud Lovat Fraser collection. However as the weather improved he enjoyed spending some time away from London sailing with Alan. He regularly took the train from Liverpool Street to Fambridge station and then walked the short distance down to the little village by the river Crouch with its inn and yacht club. This was an isolated area of stark beauty that even today seems a long way from London. It was a land of winding creeks and saltmarsh, of wide views across flat grazing fields, of big skies and dramatic sunsets, and of the calls of wading birds across the mud flats. As Christopher sailed along the Crouch he must have felt exhilarated by the sense of freedom and space. He had a ready sympathy with the natural world and no doubt would have enjoyed the sight of feeding lapwings and redshanks and the flocks of Brent geese that arrived with the autumn. As night fell the darkness here, unlike in London, would have been almost complete. Lamps and firelight would have shone out from isolated farmhouses and from the public house where Christopher might have led the other drinkers in carousing). But it would have been possible to find complete darkness only a short distance from inhabited buildings.

River Crouch at Fambridge

In October a parcel arrived from America which contained three copies of the first volume of the catalogue of William Andrews Clark's growing collection. *Wilde and Wildeana* included material that he had acquired from Christopher. In return Christopher sent him the copy of his own 1908 bibliography of Oscar's poetry which had belonged to Robbie. He then passed one copy of William's volume on to Walter and the second to Vyvyan.

In the same month *For Love of the King*, which Christopher had already seen in magazine form, was published in a book by Methuen, who had previously published Oscar's collected works. It was advertised as a newly discovered work by Oscar Wilde and issued in an edition of a thousand copies. Walter bought one for 8s 6d and was annoyed to find it advertised elsewhere at 15s. But Christopher quickly recognised a more serious fraud was being perpetrated. A woman called Mabel Wodehouse Pearse (also known as Mrs Chan Toon) owned the typescript of this play - along with a letter which she said was from Oscar. She claimed that she had been brought up with Oscar and his brother Willie in Ireland (although actually she was too young) and that Oscar had written the play for her. However Robbie had never mentioned *For Love of the* King and in fact it was not by Oscar. Christopher's robust exposure of the fact was eventually to lead him into further difficulties with the law.

But that lay in the future and for now Christopher spent Christmas (presumably with Alan) in Fambridge at The Ferry Boat Inn. This old timber framed pub with weather boards and handmade clay tiles was located just by the river Crouch (at the point where there was a ferry). It was just a few minutes' walk from the yacht club. He enjoyed himself there but was glad to get back to London where he wrote to Walter to remind him that it was "18 years ago almost to the day since I first called on you at Wimbledon!"

The Ferry Boat Inn, Fambridge

Perhaps it was during this Christmas break that he made the decision to sell the rest of his Wildean material: "I shall never do any more OW bibliographical work: life is too short." Early in 1923 he compiled his latest catalogue – his eighth – though in fact this mainly dealt with a selection of material on James Joyce. He was also hard at work on another project with quite a tight deadline. This was a bibliography of the printed works by Claud Lovat Fraser based on the material Christopher had collected and it was intended to accompany a biography jointly written by John Drinkwater and the artist Albert Daniel Rothenstein (or Rutherston), who was "staggered" by the amount of material Christopher had located. Christopher did not expect to make any money from this commission but enjoyed compiling the book.

He worked on it throughout the summer although he did spend 18 July in court as an observer. The *Morning Post* had published a letter which claimed that Alfred Douglas was making insulting and untrue allegations about Lord Kitchener's death. Never averse to litigation, Alfred sued for libel. Christopher "heard Douglas cross-examined : of course he got my name out but as far as I can see only the *Morning Post* has reported it, and that not in an offensive manner. Spencer was not called as you will have seen by to-day's papers." The jury decided that Alfred had acted in good faith and both sides paid their own costs. However Alfred, who was obsessed with Jewish conspiracies, continued to write a series of anti-semitic articles for *Plain English* claiming that Winston Churchill was guilty of war profiteering and that he had conspired with high-profile Jews to murder Lord Kitchener. On 3 August Alfred gave a public speech about high level corruption saying that the leading Jewish figure, Sir Ernest Cassell, had given Winston Churchill money to publish a report which falsely blamed the Germans for blowing up Lord Kitchener's ship. Alfred's speech was subsequently published in pamphlet form and sold in large numbers. People were keen to tell Christopher about it but he found it difficult to locate a copy. "I have searched the Strand and the purlieus of Villiers Street in vain." He finally tracked it down in the Strand but found it "very silly and uninteresting."

On 16 October Christopher's second substantial bibliography, *The Printed Work of Claud Lovat Fraser*, with five illustrations and describing over seven hundred items, was published by Henry Danielson. Christopher was clearly proud of it: "It is over-subscribed and a wonderful book for 15s – people say it looks like a two guinea book!" There were just 275 numbered and signed copies. Walter was keen to buy one even though it had almost nothing to do with Oscar, but Christopher had none to spare and suggested trying Hatchards bookshop for one. He had managed to reserve just five copies for himself and had given four of those away including one to Claud's parents, one to his widow, and one to Haldane MacFall whose *The Book of Lovat Fraser* was published in the same year. (Haldane wrote a number of other art historical books, including a study of the art of Aubrey Beardsley.)

No doubt Walter eventually managed to acquire a copy of his friend's book. He was continuing to add Wildean material to his library too and was currently searching for a copy of *Mr W. H.* which had been published by Duckworth. Christopher had sold his to William Andrews Clark for £20, but he negotiated with Vyvyan who proved willing to sell Walter his last copy (which had been meant for Dublin University). As well as tracking down Wildean material, Christopher remained on the look-out for opportunities to defend Oscar so that autumn he wrote to *The Sunday Express* to protest against the repetition of the false statement that Oscar danced over his wife's coffin. The letter was not printed, but at least the editor acknowledged it.

He sold two issues of *The Spirit Lamp* to Walter during October and continued to sell other items to William Andrews Clark. However there were few other buyers for Wildean material. Fortunately the wealthy William was a generous and rather gullible customer, if a slow payer. "His secretary called here a few weeks ago and bought three items for £40 — not yet paid for, alas! Indeed the higher the price that I asked, the better pleased she seemed to think Wm A. C. Junr would be." From Los Angeles William continued to issue regular catalogues of his mounting collection. Eventually Christopher became fed up with receiving them almost certainly because he resented the wealth William could lavish on his material. But the American collector was still his best client and that December Christopher offered him an 1894 edition of *Salome* for 15 guineas after William had unsuccessfully tried to buy a copy from Davis and Orioli.

London was foggy at the end of the year and Christopher enjoyed the sight of the fog overwhelming not only London, but the Tory party. The Prime Minister Stanley Baldwin had called an election in which the Labour Party won fifty more seats and with Liberal support, formed a minority government led by Ramsay MacDonald. Christopher must have been delighted to see his party in power for the first time. He was happy, too, about the outcome of the latest court case in which Alfred Douglas was involved. Although Christopher had dismissed Alfred's pamphlet as mere silliness it had led to his arrest on 6 November for criminal libel. Christopher visited the Old Bailey to see the start of the trial before Justice Avory at which Alfred was again represented by Cecil Hayes. "I hope Douglas will get 12 months at least," Christopher wrote. "All Hayes's muck throwing at Churchill is quite irrelevant and 1000 miles removed from the actual libel. I wonder that Avory lets him go on."

Harold Spencer, who had been central to the Billing case, appeared as a defence witness but was shown to be a liar and found to be suffering from mental illness. Eventually Alfred was sentenced to six months in prison. He served his sentence in Wormwood Scrubs and Christopher must have derived considerable satisfaction from seeing his enemy incarcerated in the same prison where he had himself spent time five years before.

Christopher's eleventh catalogue came out in December and included a collection of cuttings of Oscar's pieces that had been published in various periodicals. As usual he sent a copy of his catalogue to Walter and continued to encourage his friend's research into literary matters by offering helpful advice. He suggested that Francis Edwin Murray of Park View House in Ramsgate might be able to give Walter information about the Thomas Hutchinson books which he had published, but warned that Gordon Craig, then living in Florence, would be less forthcoming: "You will find it difficult to get a letter out of him, I fancy." Like Walter, Christopher was particularly interested at this time in the work of the Dutch Jewish writer Jacob Israel de Haan. (He was shortly to be assassinated in Jerusalem both for his anti-Zionist stance and because of his gay sexual activities.) Christopher sent Walter a letter (presumably written by Jacob) to insert in his copy of the author's *Pathologieen* - a gay novel which had been published in 1908. At the same time he shared the news that he had acquired a copy of the April 1912 issue of the Dutch magazine, *De Gids*, which had a poem by Jacob dedicated to Oscar in commemoration of his imprisonment in Reading.

As usual, Walter and Christopher exchanged Christmas presents that year. Walter gave Christopher a book by the poet Robert Laurence Binyon (who had known Robbie and had introduced him to Arthur Ransome). In return when Christopher sent Walter the two books by Thomas Hutchinson which he had ordered – *Ballads and Other Rhymes of a Country Bookworm* of 1888 and *Jolts & Jingles* of 1889 – he enclosed a manuscript poem as a gift. He then celebrated Boxing Day by dining with friends at the Café Royal. The "special 10/6 dinner (without wine) – my hosts not being content with the ordinary 7/6 dinner (without wine) – included mussells [sic] and bottled mushrooms and preserved French beans and imported turkey." Although after selling an expensive item from his catalogue Christopher always celebrated with food and drink, something in this particular meal did not agree with him. He was ill for several days "with a sort of ptomaine poisoning" and then succumbed to influenza. He was ill on and off during much of that winter and Walter came to visit him at the bungalow bringing him a volume of early poetry by Robert Sherard titled *Whispers*.

Christopher probably also saw something of Charles Scott Moncrieff when he spent time in England during the following year. By now Charles had found his metier as a translator and had published two further translations. The first was his version of the Anglo-Saxon poem, *Beowulf* which was followed by the first volume of his translation of Marcel Proust's massive work, *A la recherché du temps perdu*. He was currently working on further volumes and might well have been particularly attracted to this work because it features a gay man, Baron de Charlus, and openly considers homosexuality particularly in the fourth volume, *Sodom et Gomorrhe*. The translation was much admired and it made Charles famous.

Oscar's son, Vyvyan, was also trying his hand at literary translation and one of his early efforts was a translation of Paul Morand's witty 1922 French novel *Ouvert la Nuit*. Christopher read this and then passed it on to Walter. The narrator describes his encounters with women across Europe which end with a Baltic night spent with Aino, who calls him a "cosmopolitan swine" as he recalls lovers in Hyde Park (amongst other places) "swathed to their shoulders in mist, heedless of the clamourings of the Salvation Army".

CHAPTER TWENTY

POLITICS

"Why should they be grateful for the crumbs that fall from the rich man's table." from The Soul of Man under Socialism by Oscar Wilde

It was around this time that Christopher first met the twenty-six year old Michael Davidson, who moved to London during 1924 to work for a literary agency and a weekly paper. Michael had been comfortable with his homosexuality from an early age and had already fallen in love with the poet Wystan Hugh Auden. He and Christopher soon became friends and quickly established that each was (in the term of the time) 'so'. Not long after settling in London, Michael sold a story to *The Sketch* about a ship watchman in the London Docks, who fantasised that he was a seafaring hero. Christopher read it with pleasure and wrote, "Please allow me to congratulate you on your very remarkable short story... I would compare you to Joseph Conrad, only I could never stomach that much over-rated writer's halting sentences and slipshod English."

Christopher recovered only slowly from his influenza and it was not until mid-May that he felt better. He was then well enough to travel with Alan to Brightlingsea on the river Colne to look at a boat - the *Margery Daw* – which Alan decided to buy. Christopher was soon invited to sail it with him, although in early June Christopher was too busy in London to join Alan as he was arranging a display of Claud Lovat Fraser material drawn mainly from his own collection. This exhibition was held at 6 Little Russell Street, the premises of the First Edition Club, which not only published limited editions but arranged exhibitions of rare books and manuscripts. It had been established by yet another of Christopher's friends, Alphonse James Albert Symons, and Christopher regularly attended its events. His own exhibition ran throughout June and comprised seven hundred items. Many of these were from Christopher's collection whilst others were owned by the artist's father or by his widow. The exhibition featured in an article in *The Spectator* of 7 June and was reviewed by *The Times* on 12 June which thought "One of the most noteworthy features" of the exhibition was the set of sixty five designs for *The Shropshire Lad* which Alfred Edward Housman had "rejected as unsuitable." Christopher was "horrified" to learn that Walter did not know these poems and resolved to send him a copy for his next Christmas present. He was gratified by the interest in the exhibition and was pleased that the publicity helped him to sell a number of pieces to the museum at South Kensington. (He advertised further pieces for sale in a catalogue he produced during the following year.)

At home he was having his bedroom whitewashed and distempered. Whilst he lived and slept outside under his 'shed' his unsold books were piled high in his living room and he was giving them a dusting. However one book he did not need to store was a copy of a miscellaneous collection about Oscar - Martin Birnbaum's *Fragments and Memories* – which had originally been presented to Robbie. Christopher sold to Walter for two guineas.

Meanwhile Christopher remained a prominent and active member of the Marylebone branch of the Labour Party, which now had over two hundred members. Even from prison he had been aware of his party's campaign for a minimum wage of £5 a week and afterwards must have followed with interest as the party developed its new constitution and manifesto, *Labour and the New Social Order* - which advocated the nationalisation of industry and the redistribution of wealth – as well as the policy, *London Fit for Heroes*, which addressed issues such as housing and public services. His favoured newspaper was now *The Daily Herald*, which shared his political views and he tried (possibly unsuccessfully) to persuade Walter to read it too. The paper had been founded in 1912 to express the views of both strikers and suffragettes and during the war it opposed military action and backed conscientious objectors. Now it was the official organ of the Trades Union Congress and strongly supported the Labour Party in the 1924 general election campaign.

Unfortunately depite Christopher's efforts, and those of his fellow activists, the local Labour candidate was heavily defeated by Sir Douglas Hogg. Christopher must have been even more disappointed that nationally the Labour Party also did badly and the Conservatives were able to regain power. They had been considerably aided by a smear campaign which had followed the previous election and involved forged documents, published by the *Daily Mail*, which claimed links between the Labour Party and Russian Communists.

Even though his political activities kept him busy, Christopher did manage to make several visits over the course of the year to another friend and fellow bookseller, (Reginald) Norman Colbeck, who was then in his early twenties and living at Vernon Road in Bushey (near Watford in Hertfordshire).

Norman had been born in Islington, the son of a pharmacist, and had largely educated himself using the resources of the British Museum. He became a fount of knowledge about nineteenth century and Edwardian poetry and essays and in 1923 was hired to manage the Rare Book Room at Foyles in Charing Cross Road where he stayed for the next four years before launching his own bookshop at 24 Great Titchfield Street. Christopher's visits to see him sometimes had to be cancelled at short notice though, as there was much industrial unrest on the railways that year and a number of unofficial strikes were called. As might have been expected, Christopher staunchly supported the strikers: "To-morrow I shall go to Bushey for the day – if the Railway Managers allow me. No blackleg conveyances for me!"

As Christopher's health had worsened, he had become very anxious about contagion from germs. He hated closed windows and generally he preferred to sleep outside. So he was annoyed with himself when on one of these visits to Norman he "stupidly slept in doors and woke up with a streaming cold". As soon as he returned home he "managed to cure it during the week by my open-air treatment, still sleeping under my shelter where germs do not congregate."

At the end of the year William Andrews Clark sent Christopher three copies of his privately printed volume containing twenty five letters from Oscar to Alfred that William had purchased in 1920. Christopher wrote back, "The sumptuous way in which the book is produced is beyond all praise." Despite his resentment of William's wealth, he genuinely admired the book and relished the "beautifully made facsimiles." He sold one of the books to Vyvyan and a second one to Walter, who, when he heard how desperate his friend was for money, posted some to him. Although he was probably grateful, Christopher seems to have been embarrassed: "I hope you will soon put me out of your debt by purchases. It is only because people will not pay me what they owe me I'm hard up." He had

222

hoped to keep the third copy of Oscar's letters for himself, but his friend Alphonse Symons telephoned and reminded Christopher that he had promised him one. When Alphonse offered £7 10s for it, Christopher reluctantly decided to part with his last remaining copy. "One gets hardened to these things when once one begins to part with treasured books," he assured Walter. Really he never stopped feeling bitter about having to do so.

Originally he had planned to spend Christmas 1924 at Rochester with Alan, but he had no money, so instead he went to Norman's for two days and "had a very jolly walk in the country on the Friday which was a lovely day with bright sunshine." He was also rather gratified to read of the death of Thomas Crosland on Christmas Eve. By now Thomas and Alfred were themselves long estranged and Alfred did not attend his former ally's funeral.

Back at the bungalow one of the first visitors in the new year was Christopher's sister, Dorothy, who travelled up from Banstead in Surrey. No doubt he generally tried to keep her away from his friends and he certainly warned Walter: "I have my married sister coming up for tea to-morrow so I hope you won't turn up!" Dorothy mostly occupied herself in assisting her husband, Arthur, in his parish work. They had been settled in Banstead for several years and Arthur had set up a local horticultural society there, whilst Dorothy devoted time and energy to various Christian organisations including the Society for the Propagation of the Gospel and the Church of England Children's Society.

Although Dorothy's visit meant Walter had to be put off for the day, presumably the two friends soon arranged another meeting for the literary conversation they both enjoyed. In April they shared their thoughts about the reviews of a new play, *Oscar Wilde: His Drama*. Although the *Daily Mail* was critical of the work (which was by the German Expressionist playwright, Carl Sternheim) Christopher dismissed that paper as "notoriously inaccurate and anti – OW." He was much better pleased with the review in *The Observer* which found nothing offensive in the play, praised the character of Oscar, and thought that Robbie was depicted as "a figure of real charm, cultured and lovable." Christopher was delighted that his friend was so sympathetically shown and told Walter he was sure that from beyond the grave "Robbie does not object."

Even after Christopher's Claud Lovat Fraser exhibition was over, he remained one of the prime movers of the First Edition Club and he was keen to visit the displays prepared during 1925 for the centenary of the death of Lord Byron, the flamboyant and notorious Romantic poet who had had love affairs with both men and women. Christopher was photographed closely examining the exhibits and obviously found them fascinating.

His ongoing work with the First Edition Club kept him in close contact with its founder Alphonse Symons, who liked and admired him even though Christopher himself was rather dismissive of Alphonse's work and in particular his attitude towards the writing of bibliographical works, which seemed much less thorough than his own. Alphonse's first bibliography (which he published through the First Edition Club in 1924) was an account of the first editions of the work of William Butler Yeats and he was now planning a bibliography of the writers of the 1890s. Christopher realised that this would be a huge undertaking and although he acknowledged that it "should be an interesting volume if he can make it really accurate and complete" he was not convinced that Alphonse would achieve this because he "proposes to do in a few months, work that takes others as many years." In fact Alphonse never completed the project.

As usual Christopher continued to correspond with other literary figures. These included George Charles Williamson, the art historian and biographer, who wrote articles for the *Encyclopaedia Britannica* and made numerous contributions to the *Catholic Encyclopaedia* of 1913. Another of Christopher's regular correspondents was Max Meyerfield, who was then engaged in translating further works by Oscar (including *The Duchess of Padua*) into German. Max was as devoted to Oscar's memory as Christopher and they had a chance to meet up that year when Max paid a visit to London.

Although Christopher remained busy and active, he was increasingly anxious about his health and resolved to make his will. He particularly wanted both to set out the arrangements for his funeral and to ensure that the Labour Party would be his main beneficiary. So on 11 June his brief will was drawn up and witnessed by two men, one a labourer, F. W. Montagu, and the other a postman, John Joseph Dunn, who might well have been fellow members of his Labour Party branch.

With his will completed, Christopher could turn his mind to other matters. The next challenge was not long in coming.

CHAPTER TWENTY ONE

DEFENDING OSCAR

"my almost impromptu epigrams" from Christopher's letter to Walter 15 November 1926

Things began to develop further in the *For Love of the King* matter when on 26 June Mabel Wodehouse Pearse wrote to Christopher from The Garden Hotel in Craven Street, Charing Cross to tell him she had "six very interesting Oscar Wilde letters which for an immediate deal you can have a bargain." By now Christopher was so familiar with Oscar's work and with his manuscripts, he could readily judge whether or not new material was authentic and he quickly realised that the letters were not in Oscar's handwriting. They might still have been copies of genuine letters of course, but when Christopher probed further, it was evident that Mabel Wodehouse Pearse was unable to produce any originals. It soon emerged that she had no original manuscript of *For Love of the King* either. All she possessed was a typescript with handwritten corrections which she claimed had been made by Oscar. It was fast becoming obvious that the work was not by Oscar at all.

"A WOMAN BLUFFS TWO CONTINENTS. GREAT LITERARY FORGERY. EXPERTS AND FAMOUS CRITICS TAKEN IN. SENSATIONAL DISCOVERY. That is the sort of heading one ought to see in the papers soon if newspapers ever take any interest in literature – and if it wasn't that I dislike seeing my name in print," Christopher declared. "There are many points in the six letters which prove them to be fakes and obviously the whole thing was a colossal fraud, but it is not easy to produce proofs to satisfy a law court."

Nevertheless Christopher was determined to expose the fraud. He contacted Methuen which had published the work, and then on 8 July he drafted a letter to *The Times* in which he publicly questioned the authenticity of *For Love of the King*. He wrote to *The Times Literary*

Supplement about the matter as well (and also contacted the *Daily Graphic* about a purported Wildean poem.) He followed this up with a one penny pamphlet in which he reprinted all his correspondence and which he called *Who Wrote 'For Love of the King'?*. He sent a copy to Walter.

When he received a response from Methuen he found it unconvincing, although he was given permission to see the typescript. He arranged to view it with a handwriting expert and after careful examination they both agreed that the corrections had been written not by Oscar, but by Mabel Wodehouse Pearse herself. On 17 August, armed with this evidence, Christopher produced a circular letter for the bookselling trade in which he claimed that Methuen had "succeeded in foisting [the book] on an unsuspecting public." He was determined to defend Oscar's literary reputation and to ensure that his hero was not associated with this inferior work. But in his desire to expose the forgery he made a statement that clearly suggested that not only Mabel Wodehouse Pearse, but also the publisher, had been dishonest. However because the statement was made in a business context, Methuen at first took no action.

Not long afterwards an injunction was taken out to stop Mabel Wodehouse Pearse publishing any further material if she claimed it was by Oscar. Christopher hoped she would respond to his allegations of forgery by suing him for libel so he could expose both the manuscripts and the letters as fakes. But, knowing she could not prove that they were genuine, she did not.

When he was not occupied that summer with *For Love of the King*, Christopher frequently went out drinking in The Plough Tavern at the corner of Museum Street and Little Russell Street just a few doors away from Davis and Orioli's bookshop. Here he socialised with a number of broad-minded Bohemians including the composer Constant Lambert and the artist Nina Hamnett who had known Robbie and who had once acted out *Salome* with him - she had played the title role and Robbie had been Herod. At the centre of the group were Boris and Phyllis de Chroustchoff. Boris was a Russian intellectual, who worked as an antiquarian bookseller, whilst Phyllis was an artist, who made silver jewellery and enamelware.

The Plough Tavern

However Christopher did not spend all his time in London. Although he enjoyed his literary activities in the capital, he still relished his time away from the city and the freedom of being afloat so that September he readily joined Alan to go sailing in Hampshire.

He was pleased to see yet another step in Oscar's rehabilitation when it was decided to place a commemorative tablet on the façade of the hotel at 13 Rue des Beaux Arts where Oscar had died twenty five years before. In October Christopher offered William Andrews Clark almost all of the Wildean material which he still possessed. His main concern now was that it should be preserved even if that meant he could no longer keep it himself. At least he knew that it would be safe in the American's collection. The items he parted with included a rather personal article - Oscar's monogrammed wallet lined with crimson silk, which Robbie had given to Christopher. Another break with the past was the death of Harold Mellor whom Christopher had met frequently during his brief exile in France. Oscar had stayed with Harold in Switzerland for a time and originally wrote to Robbie that he thought him "a charming fellow, very cultivated, though he finds that Literature is an inadequate expression of Life." However within a few weeks they fell out and Oscar began complaining bitterly about Harold's meanness, which he ascribed to the "insanity in his family." When Christopher read of Harold's suicide at Cannes in the newspapers he was not much surprised by it. "I used to see a great deal of him in Dieppe in 1907 and later in London. He was always very nervy and eccentric, and I do not think that his marriage was a success."

Alfred Douglas, however, was still very much alive and at the end of December Christopher received his *New Preface to The Life and Confessions of Oscar Wilde* on loan from Alphonse Symons, who had been given it by the author. Christopher sold the book to Max Meyerfield assuming he could easily get a replacement to return to Alphonse. But it turned out that this particular book was one of only 250 copies which contained various misprints and Christopher had to frantically track down another one. When he sent a copy of the book to Walter he wrote consolingly, "It is awful rot, of course, and is not likely to have any influence." Certainly it was only scantily reviewed. The book came about after Frank Harris contacted Alfred and blamed Robbie for the attack in *The Life and Confessions of Oscar Wilde*. He then explained that he wanted to produce a new edition. Alfred was initially keen to cooperate and sent Frank a letter describing his relationship with Oscar. But Frank and Alfred soon quarrelled and Alfred decided to bring out his own book. Essentially his *New Preface* consisted of Frank's original preface along with a piece of his own. Frank responded by reprinting his original book with two additions – George Bernard Shaw's memories of Oscar and, much more controversially, the letter which Alfred had given him.

Christopher's next visit to a court room had nothing to do with Alfred though. Instead he was at Bow Street on 13 January 1926 in order to observe the trial of Mabel Wodehouse Pearse not for fraud, but for theft from her fellow lodger, Mrs Wood. Mabel, who was accompanied in the court by her green parrot, Coco, was found guilty although her conviction simply "made a heroine of her". An additional annoyance was that the newspaper reports of the case were full of errors: "It is quite useless writing to correct these things," Christopher complained. However he could not let "The worst article on Mrs Chan Toon" pass unchallenged. This had appeared in the *People on Sunday* with the headline WILDE'S SWEETHEART JAILED. Christopher wrote to the editor who merely thanked him and kept the letter "for future reference."

Not long afterwards, William Andrews Clark arrived in England. Christopher hoped to sell him "a few out-of-the-way things" but William returned to Los Angeles without visiting him. Although over the years Christopher had sold him many items related to Oscar, he still resented the fact that so much Wildean material had finished up on the other side of the Atlantic. He wrote to Walter, "It is sad, I admit, about the power of American dollars, but, after all, where should we have been if America hadn't provided us in the war with shells to blow our enemies to pieces? And where should I have been since 1919 but for American dollars? Also, you must remember that the competition of American dollars has increased the value of your own collection a hundred-fold, though as you don't intend to sell it, that doesn't help you much, I fear."

He also had some bad news to share with Walter about one of their old friends. William More Adey had been suffering from poor health for years and in 1925 he had seriously damaged one of his eyes in an accident. Now his condition worsened further. "You need not spread this," Christopher confided, "but you must not expect to see More Adey again, nor can you communicate with him. He is quite irresponsible and for many months past has been in a private 'home' near Bristol under constant observation and control. Further, I am told that he is suffering from advanced kidney trouble and may not live long. His last letter to me was quite unintelligible." It was probably at this time that William's kneehole writing table and his small mahogany bookcase with a glass door were passed to Christopher for safe-keeping.

Christopher issued his fourteenth catalogue that February. It included books from the library of the publisher John Lane (of Bodley Head) as well as eighteen unpublished letters and five postcards written by Frederick William Rolfe (known as Baron Corvo) which Christopher had acquired two years previously. Frederick Rolfe had been gay and a Catholic convert whose most famous novel was *Hadrian the Seventh*. Christopher had introduced his work to Alphonse Symons, who subsequently purchased the letters and they inspired him to write his own book, *The Quest for Corvo*. One of the books from John Lane's library had gay associations too. This was a copy of Gleeson White's 1890 anthology *Garde Joyeuse* which Christopher discovered was "inscribed EDWARD SHELLEY FROM JOHN LANE!!!!" The gift offered some evidence of a relationship between John Lane and Edward Shelley, who had been one of Oscar's lovers. John had chosen a book to give to Edward whose title referred to the castle given by King Arthur to Lancelot. It contains a collection of light, witty poems many of which deal with flirtation and the brevity of love. Sophie St G. Lawrence's *Last July*, for example, moves from "She really is a charming girl,/ And I adored her last July." to "I find the girl an awful bore - / So long it is since last July." Then *An*

Autograph mocks a lover who ardently gazes at a woman's signature explaining, "This is no scented billet doux, /... Her autograph is here inscribed/ To recommend a bar of soap."

On Friday 26 March, despite the cold weather, Christopher left London to spend Easter with Alan on his boat. Alan had already left Fareham (which Christopher liked) and had made his way to Woolston at Southampton. He was hoping they could sail round to Poole but in the end they spent the week by the Hamble enjoying the weather - which turned out to be lovely - before Christopher returned to London where he continued to encourage Walter with his research. He was interested to know whether the publisher Arthur Lee Humphreys, then based in Reading, could give Walter any information about the book *Confessions of a Book-Lover* written by the American writer Maurice Francis Egan. Arthur had published Robbie's *Masques and Phases* as well as Oscar's *Sebastian Melmoth* and Christopher had last seen him "at the John Lane memorial service when he nodded very affably."

Although Arthur Humphreys seemed friendly enough, other acquaintances could be malicious. At this time Christopher made a visit to the publishers, Elkin Mathews, at 4a Cork Street and as soon as he left a homophobic remark was made about him. No doubt Christopher knew such comments were often made behind his back, if not to his face. On this occasion it was apparently Alfred Edward Newton, the American author, publisher and book collector, who warned his friend not to encourage Christopher: "Don't you know that he's been in prison for a most disgusting offence?" Alfred Newton had written a book on Oscar's work which had been published in 1912 but although he had praised Oscar's literary achievements and spoken with approval of Robbie's kindness, he was clearly uncomfortable with those aspects of Oscar's life which he considered "not good" and "not pure." This had led him to declare that *Dorian Gray* was full of "general nastiness" and to ascribe Oscar's downfall to a "disease." On this occasion, though, his remark did not go unchallenged. The cashier at Elkin Mathews, Miss Rintoul, though apparently a strait-laced woman, boldly spoke up for Christopher: "Whatever Mr Millard has done, and I don't know what it may have been, if he's been to prison he's expiated his offence, and, personally, I find him a very nice gentleman."

Doubtless Christopher was unaware of this exchange and in any case he would have been too busy to take much notice of it. There were now other important matters which demanded most of his attention. Although he still made sure that he remembered Walter's birthday he was much occupied with the fact that Methuen had decided to go to court over the statements he had made about the publisher's involvement with *For Love of the King* and he was now carefully examining "Methuen's statement of claim" and drawing up a defence. The solicitors for Oscar's son, Vyvyan, were involved as well and they were "pressing" the publisher "for information as to the latter's rights in *For Love of the King*. However Methuen was "disinclined to reply satisfactorily."

At first Christopher thought that the impending court case would hinge on his ability to prove that the play was a fake – which he thought he could do. But gradually it emerged that the focus would not be on the play's authenticity, but on Christopher's use of the word 'foist.' It seems likely that it was the author Henry Watson Fowler who bluntly told Christopher that he had been ill-advised to use the same words to describe both Mabel Wodehouse Pearse (who had undoubtedly intended to deceive) and Methuen (who almost certainly had not).

The court case did not absorb all of Christopher's time and energy. He was also heavily involved in political activity as a result of the General Strike, which had been triggered by the struggle between the mine owners and the miners who were backed by the Trades Union Congress. He spent his evenings, red flag in hand, combining drinking with politics. Along with Michael Davidson and the young activist David Amyas Ross (then in his mid-twenties) he set out with piles of the *British Worker* which they attempted to sell in the bars, clubs and restaurants around Soho and Piccadilly Circus once the three of them had "drunk enough beer to drown the insults and rebuffs" which they "got in such strongholds of law and order." At times they faced not only insults but physical violence. On one occasion at the Hambone Club in Ham Yard "at the top of a steep and winding stone stairway" they were attacked by a group of volunteer strike-breakers and three of them tried "to crack Amyas's leg across a chair."

Christopher's fellow activist, David Amyas Ross, had been born in Somerset and, like Christopher, he was the son of a cleric. At Repton School he was particularly influenced by one of his teachers, Victor Gollancz, and at the age of eighteen he made his way to London and to the Labour Research Department, where he announced that he wanted to spread the Russian Revolution. Although he went on to study at New

College, Oxford, he remained committed to left wing politics becoming a tutor for the Workers' Educational Association and helping to found the Soho Gallery. His short book *100 Years of Working Class Progress* was published by the BBC in 1927 and in the following year he stood as the Labour candidate in the Marylebone by-election.

As the court case drew closer, it seems that there was some kind of disagreement between Christopher and Alan Alington though its cause is unclear. On 30 August Christopher told Walter that he "was hoping to have joined Alington by now, but the man with him (whom I dislike) is staying on, so the arrangements had to be cancelled. There is no other holiday that I care for except roughing it on sea or river, so I shall stay quietly on here where I am quite happy and fairly busy and enjoying the open air life (such as it is) and the nice weather.... Alington is up the Hamble somewhere and is going to lay up at Bursledon towards the end of September." Alan had returned to Woodford Wells to run a boys' preparatory school called Montclair in collaboration with two other men. One was an old friend of Christopher's, Augustus Herbert Welby Pugin, and the other was a young man in his late twenties, Henry Francis Joseph Wall. It might have been Henry who triggered the marked deterioration in Christopher and Alan's friendship. Perhaps Christopher was jealous of the fact that Alan was spending an increasing amount of time sailing with someone else. Or perhaps Christopher was simply less reliant on Alan now that he had met Michael who shared his political outlook and many of his interests and who clearly enjoyed his company. They went walking together that summer and it was around this time that Christopher gave the young man a pair of Robbie's pyjamas - an intimate and erotic gift. They were almost certainly one of the last few items which he owned that provided a tangible link to Robbie, because that summer (presumably to raise money for the approaching court case) he offered all his remaining Wildean manuscripts to William Andrews Clark, who promptly purchased them.

The Methuen case finally reached court in November and it turned not on whether the play was a forgery, but on whether Methuen had published it believing it to be genuine. The case was heard in front of Justice McCardie and a special jury, with E. F. Lever and Lionel Jellinek defending Christopher.

Ernest Webster, a managing director from Methuen, claimed he thought the work was genuine, as did the chairman Edward Verrall Lucas, who had written the introduction to the published book. The latter said he was very familiar with Oscar's work and although Edward thought the play was an inferior one – and indeed had described it as "awful tosh" – he still thought it was by Oscar. However Lionel Jellinek pointed out that Edward had apparently made no effort to investigate Mabel Wodehouse Pearse's (untrue) story that she had grown up with Oscar and had merely reproduced it in his introduction. He also demonstrated how Mabel Wodehouse Pearse had clearly mimicked phrases from Oscar's work in *For Love of the King* and suggested Edward should have realised this.

When it was his turn in the witness box, Christopher appeared confident and dignified, dressed in a blue shirt, grey flannel trousers and wearing his patched green jacket. He stressed his expertise in Wildean matters and said that he thought the publishers had been careless in not insisting on seeing the letter from Oscar that allegedly had accompanied the play. Nevertheless he did not believe Methuen were dishonest and accepted they had acted in good faith. However he felt it was his duty as Oscar's bibliographer to expose the forgery.

He was pleased with his appearance: "I had a great time on Wednesday: I was in the witness-box for three hours and floored [Boyd] Merriman, K.C., [who appeared for Methuen along with St John Micklethwait] on every point. Unfortunately the papers omit to report what the Judge called 'my almost impromptu epigrams!'" Naturally Christopher might well have felt more assured in court this time because it was not his sexuality, but his expertise, which was on trial.

He was followed into the witness box by Charles Evans a director of Heinemann's who had had his own doubts about the play when it had been offered to his firm and who had advised Heinemann's not to publish it. Christopher's friend, Alphonse Symons, also spoke on Christopher's behalf to say that he thought it was obvious that the play was spurious. It was poorly written with grammatical errors and even the stage directions were unlike those in genuine plays by Oscar.

However the judge ruled that Christopher had not confined himself to arguing that the play was inauthentic, but in addition had alleged that Methuen had been negligent and careless. And the jury subsequently decided that in using the word 'foist' he had accused the publishers of dishonesty. Christopher thus lost the case. He was asked to pay £100 damages to Methuen and to meet all the costs involved. He seemed resigned to the outcome: "I am quite satisfied with the result of the case, for at no time did I seriously anticipate winning." And he still thought his actions had been justified. "Until I used, what McCardie called, 'pretty strong language,'" the publisher had ignored him. "To my mind it is of much greater importance to have exposed Mrs Chan Toon throughout the length and breadth of the land – and abroad too, probably, than to prove that she wrote the masque." He still could not believe how gullible the publishers had been: "It is amazing that Methuen gave that woman £50 on her bare word and did not even get a typescript till six months later." He was disparaging about the firm: "Muller (the secretary) is stone deaf and Edward Verrall Lucas (the chairman) … is practically dumb and obviously sodden with drink; so my Counsel said it is not surprising that mistakes occur in that firm!"

However the financial implications of losing the case worried him and he admitted that if the publisher pressed for "damages and costs, I suppose they'll have to make me bankrupt." But his friends, led by Vyvyan, supported him by raising a public subscription. Walter gave £5 and other contributors included Reggie Turner, Osbert Burdett, Tancred Borenius, Boris de Chroustchoff, Holbrook Jackson, Robbie's brother, Alec, and Coleridge Kennard (a friend of both Robbie and Vyvyan, whose mother had paid for Oscar's monument). Enough money was raised to cover both the damages and the agreed sum for costs and thus the matter was resolved. Another friend, Henry Durand Davray, reported the case sympathetically for the *Mercure de France*. Henry had translated works by both Oscar and Frank Harris into French and although he was "nearly stone deaf and always pretends he can't talk English!" Christopher appreciated his loyalty and knew he could be trusted. He told Walter, "I cannot think of anything that it would be indiscreet for you to tell Davray: he always seems to me to be both safe and sound."

Walter commiserated with his friend over the outcome of the trial and was disappointed that it had not even established that the play was a forgery. However he thought that it should have been left to Vyvyan (as Oscar's literary executor) to take any necessary action over *For Love of the King*. But Christopher did not regret his decision to put himself at the centre of the controversy and had apparently relished the chance to defend his hero and to demonstrate his own Wildean wit into the bargain.

He sent a copy of his *Who Wrote 'For Love of the King'?* pamphlet to Michael, who was spending the winter in the Mediterranean, and inside he penned a hopeful message which quoted the *Song of Solomon*: "Shall look out for you on the feast of purification of our Blessed Lady" [the 2 February] "by which time 'flowers ought to appear in the earth and the voice of the turtle to be heard in our land.'"

CHAPTER TWENTY TWO

A LAST GOLDEN INTERLUDE

"None but wild flowers and evergreens" from Christopher's will proved on 20 December 1927 in the Principal Probate Registry

As soon as the weather permitted in the spring of 1927, Christopher moved his bed outside and began sleeping in the open air once more. His bungalow remained full of books and in March he offered Walter a copy of *Art and Letters* of April 1888 which was "the only copy I have ever seen except the bound volume in the BM. I must have advertised for it dozens of times... This copy that I have is practically as fresh as the day it was issued... to find a copy in mint state is a miracle. You can have it at the original published price of 25s to save it from going to the library of Wm Andrews Clark, Jr." However, despite its apparent rarity, Walter already had the issue and in due course the copy Christopher had tracked down found its way to Los Angeles. Walter did purchase John Moray Stuart-Young's *An Urning's Love*, but Christopher had little else of value to sell: "It is getting more and more difficult to find scarce things." And even when he did sell an item, it was not always easy to collect the money he was owed. He had had to pay a New York attorney $5 to collect an unpaid debt which only amounted to $1.67.

However he was excited to see Sotheby's latest catalogue, because it included two unpublished sonnets by Oscar. These might well have been sent to the sale by another friend of Walter's, the author and collector Geoffrey Dudley Hobson, who lived in Chelsea Park Gardens. Christopher also carefully scrutinised the catalogue of the sale (in New York) of John Quinn's entire collection of art and manuscripts before lending it to Rainforth Armitage Walker, who was collecting works by Aubrey Beardsley including his drawings for *Salome*. Christopher, always interested in new Wildean material but keenly aware of the possibility of forgery, was not convinced that all the items for sale were genuine. One he thought "suspicious, from internal evidence. The last sentence about Magdalen looks like blackmail!"

As he contemplated this latest evidence of fraud, it came to his attention that his bête noire, Mabel Wodehouse Pearse, was in London again and she apparently had not been put off by her experiences with *For Love of the King*. Indeed that turned out to have been just the latest in a series of elaborate hoaxes which included an episode in which she had posed as a widowed Russian princess whose husband had been killed by the Bolsheviks. Now she was trying to sell an interview which she claimed to have had with George Bernard Shaw. Christopher fervently hoped she would "get her fingers burned again."

He continued to sell a trickle of items himself. In May Walter purchased a copy of the 1920 edition of Oscar's *Sphinx*, illustrated by the artist known as Alastair. His drawings, which Robbie had much admired, were heavily influenced by Aubrey Beardsley. They were expressive and sophisticated, rich with pattern and decorative detail, and included erotic images of both men and women. Walter was familiar with Alastair's work as his own bibliography had been included in the 1922 edition of *Salome* illustrated by the artist, though Christopher admitted, "I really know nothing else about the book and Robbie would never reveal who Alastair was!" In fact he was a German whose real name was Baron Hans Henning Voigt and he was an attractive, flamboyant poet and artist. His illustrations inspired by Oscar's poems were amongst his best.

Christopher also found a manuscript of *The Harlot's House* on sale with a suggested date of April 1882. But he was sure it must have been written considerably later. Tongue-in-cheek he referred to the "letter quoted by Mason on page 55 of his frequently inaccurate and much over-rated bibliography shows that OW didn't offer it to the *Dramatic Review* till April (or March) 1885." In fact, of course, he trusted his own research much more than that of the manuscript's owner.

With few sales during the first half of the year, he was interested when he was approached with a proposal for a new project. There was a "scheme afoot for me to help a young woman to start a bookshop, but I don't know if anything will come of it." He was actually quite keen on the idea. "I have a great deal of rubbish that it might help me to get rid of!" Shortly afterwards the rich art collector Michel Salaman did indeed establish (Dorothy) Varda in the 'varda bookshop' at 189 High Holborn.

Varda was a great beauty – tall, elegant and well-dressed – and she had been working part-time as an actress. She was a lively and witty woman with a waspish sense of humour and although she often clashed with Christopher, they got on reasonably well together. He was soon spending much of his time in Holborn, where Varda would later keep her neighbours awake until the early hours with her renditions of the risqué song, *The Hole in the Elephant's Bottom*.

Christopher remained close to Michael during the course of 1927 and in June he took a break from London to spend a week with him on the river above Oxford. It would prove to be a last "golden interlude." The weather was lovely as the two men leisurely retraced a route which Christopher had last taken with Charles Scott Moncrieff, and along which he knew "every lock, reach and tavern." They arranged for their boat to be towed up from Oxford to Cricklade and they then slowly made their way downstream camping at night first at the market town of Lechlade, where Percy Bysshe Shelley had composed a poem in the churchyard, and then at Kelmscot, where William Morris had lived. They rowed under Radcot Bridge to spend the next night at Cumnor before reaching the sixteenth century inn, *Old Rose Revived*, which lay tucked behind weeping willows at Newbridge.

But whilst Christopher's relationship with Michael deepened, his friendship with Alan seemed to be over. Alan was also afloat that summer spending most of the school holidays on his boat sailing up and down the Hamble past Botley, Bursledon and Swanwick to Southampton Water but he had not contacted Christopher since Christmas and it seems that things remained tense between them. He probably never saw Christopher again. (He eventually retired from teaching in the mid-1930s and moved to the Isle of Wight where he lived out the rest of his long life.)

Back in London Christopher resumed his regular occupations as the summer gave way to autumn. Monday 7 November marked his fifty-fifth birthday. In the post he received a letter from Walter and wrote his reply the same day. Walter kept this letter (as he had all the others Christopher had written to him) and was soon to pencil a note on it: "Christopher Millard's last letter to me." It was actually the longest letter Christopher had written to him for some time.

Robbie's brother, Alec, had died the previous week and this had upset Christopher probably mainly because Alec had been supportive financially: "I have lost in him a good friend who subscribed over-generously to my Methuen case fund and also had for some time past allowed me £10 a year towards the excess rent which my bitch of a landlady has exacted (quite illegally I believe)." However he had never felt that he had been close to Alec: "I never was intimate with him and did not presume to think of going to the funeral. Indeed I imagine the funeral was fixed at an early hour on purpose to discourage people from attending. Vyvyan told me that he would be leaving Chelsea at dawn on the chance of getting there in time." Nevertheless despite the difficulties Walter had made the effort to attend: "You presumably must have gone up on the previous evening and spent the midnight hours in the crematorium with the corpse."

In fact Christopher had rather resented Alec's wealth, which he thought was excessive and unmerited. As a staunch Labour Party supporter Christopher was in favour of increasing taxes on such wealthy people, who were living lives of leisure on unearned income: "The Ross part of his fortune remains in the family; but in addition he had so much money that literally he didn't know what to do with it; and a few years ago made a present of a Rolls-Royce to every member in his family who wanted one – so as to avoid the necessity of investing his bank-balance and being liable for more income tax and super tax; and yet, I have no doubt, he would have been the first to protest against the Labour Party's proposed 10% 'sur-tax' on unearned incomes of over £500!"

Socialist politics were much in Christopher's mind at the time because he was planning to combine two of his interests by reading a paper to his Labour Party branch about "Oscar Wilde as Socialist & Prison Reformer" on Monday 21 November, even though he thought he did not have "anything very original to say." But he would never give that reading. Within a few days of writing to Walter he was admitted to a private ward at the Hospital of St John and St Elizabeth. He was well cared for there, but there was little that the doctors could do for him and on Tuesday 22 November he died after suffering an aneurism.

Rather unexpectedly it was his brother Baldwin who registered his death. He lived in Hampstead at 61 Fitzjohn's Avenue only a couple of miles away from Christopher's home, which was presumably why he was contacted by the nurses at the hospital, even though he had never got on well with his brother. Christopher had remained hostile towards him to the end stating unequivocally in his will that Baldwin should "abstain from taking any part in my funeral."

Hospital of St John and St Elizabeth

Three days later on Friday 25 November Christopher was buried at St Mary's Catholic Cemetery in Kensal Green with "the simplest possible ceremony and at the least possible expense." It was Father Joseph Lyon who led the funeral procession from the cemetery chapel to the grave on a day that was bright and sunny.

Chapel at St Mary's Catholic Cemetery, Kensal Green

It had been Christopher's "special desire that my funeral may be fixed at an hour and on a day when as many as possible of my comrades of the St Marylebone Labour Party may follow me to my grave" and as requested "'The banner bright the symbol plain'" was carried in front of his coffin and the song *The Red Flag* (written by the Irishman Jim Connell in 1889) was sung over his grave. Christopher had been particularly fond of this song, which was adopted as the anthem of the British Labour Party. He had frequently encouraged loud renditions in the pubs he had visited by buying rounds for everyone present and by leading the singing of the first verse that commemorated the martyrs who had died in the socialist cause: "The people's flag is deepest red,/It shrouded oft our martyred dead./And ere their limbs grew stiff and cold,/ Their hearts' blood dyed its every fold."

At his request no memorial was set over Christopher's grave and "no purchased flowers and none but wild flowers and evergreens" were placed either on his coffin or on the grave itself. Plot 10158 is still covered only by grass.

Section of St Mary's Catholic Cemetery where Christopher is buried

In Italy Charles Scott Moncrieff heard of his former lover's death and in response wrote a warm and sympathetic obituary which appeared in the early editions of *The Times* on Thursday 1 December, but which was pulled from the later editions probably because of its supportive comments on the *For Love of The King* case.

Paul Elwin was particularly thankful that his brother had been well looked after during his last days and that he had not died alone at his bungalow. A few months after Christopher's death, Paul Elwin published his own small book called *Intentions at the Eucharist*. It was intended as a guide to worshippers and gave them a framework for prayer combining an act of thanksgiving, of prayer for others, and of prayer for oneself. The mood of the book is typically compassionate and Paul Elwin might well have had his dead brother in mind in composing prayers for prisoners and for "the unemployed, the overworked, and the underpaid", as well as for those living in "wilful sin" and those who were "slaves to lust." Undoubtedly he had some sympathy with Christopher's commitment to the causes he had believed in and would leave his

243

possessions to the organisation closest to his own heart - The Community of the Resurrection.

On Tuesday 20 December Christopher's probate was issued to his solicitor Lawrence Arthur Wingfield (of 30 Grove End Road NW8 and 7 Queen Street EC4) and to Captain John Thomas O'Brien JP (of 16 Church Street NW8). He did not leave a great deal. His possessions were initially valued at £290 17s 6d, which was revised to £467 14s 1d once his books and manuscripts had been properly examined. Paul Elwin and Alphonse Symons were appointed to go through Christopher's papers and Alphonse arranged for the books to be sold. Once Christopher's debts were settled and his modest funeral expenses paid, all the money that remained, along with any other useful items, were duly given to the Marylebone branch of the Labour Party. The No. 2 Empire Typewriter and the No. 10 Roneo Duplicator which were on loan to him were also returned to the branch.

Even though his material possessions at his death were few, Christopher had left other, more important, legacies. One was his literary work - in particular his Wildean research. Another was his contribution to the causes he supported. And a third was his love and friendship.

Walter outlived his great friend by just a few years and died on 14 December 1931 aged sixty-nine. He had cherished his long friendship with Christopher and greatly felt his loss. Three years before Christopher's death he had written, "It is over 20 years since we first met. Through sunshine and storm, through good and ill fortune, the flame of our friendship has burnt steady and bright, and, please God, it will light and cheer us to the end." Following an Anglican service, Walter was buried with his sister in St Mary the Virgin churchyard in Merton. He left a substantial legacy to the vicar and churchwardens for the maintenance of the graves, though they are no longer visible. His will was proved on 29 January 1932 and one of his executors was his long-standing friend, the barrister Donald Charles Ludlow Cree (who was another keen sailor). Walter had visited him at Lincoln's Inn dressed in his nautical outfit and Donald remembered him warmly and wrote an appreciative obituary. He was probably unaware of Walter's attraction to men as he was definitely uncomfortable with Oscar's sexuality referring to him as "a perfectly beastly person" even as he acknowledged the value of his literary work. One of Walter's main concerns in his will was the future of his Oscar Wilde collection and Donald was given the responsibility of finding a home for it. He carried out this task rather reluctantly but eventually Walter's extensive Wildean library and his letters from Robbie and Christopher were presented to University College, Oxford. For many years they were held in the Bodleian Library but have recently returned to University College where they form (as Walter requested) the Robert Ross Memorial Collection named in tribute to Robbie for his "chivalrous and selfless devotion to and friendship in adversity for Oscar Wilde."

Charles Scott Moncrieff moved to Rome and by the summer of 1929 was already seriously ill with cancer. He died on 28 February 1930 at the Hospital of the Sisters of the Company of Mary at the age of forty and was buried in the English section of the Campo Verano where his bones now lie in an ossuary.

However Christopher's young friend, Michael Davidson, lived on for almost half a century. After Christopher's death he spent time in Berlin where he was amazed and delighted by the very different attitude towards homosexuality, but his increasing concern about the rise of Hitler's ideology led to his involvement with communism. On his return to London he found attitudes towards gay men largely unchanged and in 1936 he was arrested for gay sexual activity. Like Christopher he was convicted and he served four months with hard labour. But by the time of his death in 1976, things had begun to improve. The Wolfenden Report had appeared in 1957 and ten years later the Sexual Offences Act 1967 had finally decriminalised gay sexual activity in private between consenting men over twenty one years of age. True equality was still a long way off but at least things were moving in the right direction.

Christopher had not lived to see any of these changes and his life had often been far from easy though he had faced difficulties with a stubborn determination and persistence. Unlike his hero, Oscar Wilde, he was no genius, and it was evident to his friend, Robbie, amongst others, that he was no great writer, although he was careful and thorough in his research. He was not without his faults of course. He was something of a snob at times, despite his concern for the masses, and he displayed (like many of his contemporaries) both a casual anti-semitism and rather misogynistic views, despite his left-wing sympathies. He could be scathing and impatient at times and he often took the financial support of his family for granted.

But Christopher was certainly no coward and he rarely took the easy way out. He defended the causes he believed in and he negotiated a path through life as an openly gay man at a time when this was a brave path to follow.

It was fitting, then, that the chorus of *The Red Flag* rang out over his grave. Hopefully it was a spirited rendition.

"Then raise the scarlet standard high.
Within its shade we live and die,
Though cowards flinch and traitors sneer,
We'll keep the red flag flying here."

ANNOTATED BIBLIOGRAPHY AND NOTES

Works cited in the text itself are not duplicated here

General sources

Contemporary newspaper reports, census records, probate records, directories and civil registration records have all been extensively used throughout as has *The Clergy List* (the professional directory of the Church of England) and *Crockford's Clerical Directory* for clerical careers, and the Oxford Dictionary of National Biography (available at www.oxforddnb.com).

The only previous full length biography of Christopher is
Hyde, Harford Montgomery (1990) *Christopher Sclater Millard (Stuart Mason) Bibliographer and Antiquarian Book Dealer*, New York, Global Academic Publishers

Biographical material also appears in several other works.

Burdett, Osbert (1935) *Memory and Imagination*, London, Chapman & Hall pp.97-108
Davidson, Michael (1962) *The world, the Flesh and myself*, London, Arthur Barker mainly pp.135-139 and pp.146-148
Muir, Percy (1956) *Minding My Own Business*, London, Chatto & Windus pp.48-51
Powell, Anthony (1976) *Memoirs Vol 1 Infants of the Spring*, London, Heinemann pp.91-97
d'Arch Smith, Timothy (1967) Introduction to the new edition of Stuart Mason's *Bibliography of Oscar Wilde*, London, T. Werner Laurie
Another useful source is Christopher's obituary written by Charles Scott Moncrieff which appeared in the early editions of *The Times* on 1 December 1927 p.18

Two invaluable resources for contemporary gay history are
Cook, Matt (2003) *London and the Culture of Homosexuality, 1885-1914*, Cambridge, Cambridge University Press
Houlbrook, Matt (2005) *Queer London: perils and pleasures in the sexual metropolis, 1918-1957*, Chicago, University of Chicago Press

The biographies of Robert Ross by Borland, Maureen (1990) *Wilde's Devoted Friend*, Oxford, Lennard and Fryer, Jonathan (2000) *Robbie Ross: Oscar Wilde's Devoted Friend*, New York, Carroll and Graf have both been helpful for the material that related to him.

Two collections of manuscript material have been invaluable in the writing of this book. Indeed without them it would have been impossible to write.

The first is the collection of letters from Christopher to Walter Ledger (as well as some from Robert Ross to Walter and a few copies of Walter's own letters to Christopher) which are part of the Robert Ross Memorial Collection owned by University College, Oxford. I am very grateful to The Masters and Fellows of University College, Oxford for permission to read and quote from these.

The second collection is that held by The National Archives. Particularly useful have been MEPO 3/240, which is a Metropolitan Police Office file and includes correspondence and statements, and CRIM 1/149/1 which contains records from the trial of Thomas Crosland. Again I am grateful for permission to quote from this public sector information licensed under the Open Government Licence v2.0.

Cover

The image of Christopher reproduced on the front cover of the book was published in *Scottish Patriot* December 1904

Prologue

Michael Davidson's book was first published as Davidson, Michael (1962) *The world, the Flesh and myself*, London, Arthur Barker.
"exactingly fastidious" and "a grave and…" are from p.136
"the fun of literary and bibliographical detection" from p.138
"crushingly plain-spoken" from p.136
"tickled the palm" from p.137
"my new young man" from p.138

Chapter One Christopher's Father

The material on Magdalen College School comes largely from
Hare, Patrick (1982) *Victorian Masters: A Biographical Essay on the Nineteenth Century Headmasters of Magdalen College School, Oxford*, Oxford, Magdalen College School (which includes a photograph of Christopher's father) and Wintle, Frederick Thomas William (1840) *A History of His Own Times – By a Chorister* - the original manuscript is held by Magdalen College Archives (MC:F21/MS1/1) - as well as the website for the school alumni at oldwaynfletes.org
The quotes from the account by William Salter Millard appear in *Macmillan's Magazine* (1895) pp.81-93
There are details of the naval careers of John Yelland, James Robert Mosse and Sir Hyde Parker in Marshall, John (1823-1835) *Royal Navy Biography*.
"anything that savours..." from Christopher's letter to Walter 21 October 1905 included in the Robert Ross Memorial Collection owned by University College, Oxford.

Chapter Two Childhood

Lewis Carroll's letter to Magdalen appears in Cohen, Morton N. and Lancelyn Green, Roger (eds) (1979) *The Letters of Lewis Carroll*, Macmillan, pp.236-7. The account of the trip to see the Millards at Basingstoke is on pp.437-8 of volume 6 and the trip to Sandown is on p.423 of volume 6 of *Lewis Carroll's Diaries* edited by Edward Wakeling and published in 2001 by The Lewis Carroll Society.
The material on Basingstoke comes mainly from Parker, Malcolm (2007) *Images of England: Basingstoke*, Stroud, Tempus which includes a photograph of Christopher's home taken at around the time of his birth on p.33, a photograph which includes his father on p.40 and a photograph of the schoolroom at Queen Mary's School also on p.40. Most of these photographs are owned by Hampshire County Museums Service.
The information on Bradfield comes from Leach, Arthur F. (ed) (1900) *History of Bradfield College*, London, H. Frowde
"a parish that..." from James' obituary in *The Times* 22 September 1894

Chapter Three Oxford

The Oxford University Calendar, Oxford, University of Oxford published annually from 1810 gives some background information

There is information on academic careers in Nicolls, O. C. C. (1927) *A Register of the Alumni of Keble College*, Oxford, The Alden Press

The details of Christopher's theological studies at Oxford is based on 'The Study of Theology at Oxford' pp14-19 in *The Old and New Testament Student*, January 1890 vol. 10 no. 1

The Keble College website at www.keble.ox.ac.uk is the source of most of the information on the college's history.

Material on Jacobitism is drawn mainly from Pittock, Murray (1993) *Spectrum of Decadence* London Routledge

The details of Christopher's involvement are given in *Scottish Patriot*, December 1904

There is a biography of Alexander Teixeira de Mattos: McKenna, Stephen (1922) *Tex*, Thornton Butterworth and another biography consulted was Brundage, Anthony (1993) *The People's Historian: John Richard Green and the Writing of History in Victorian England*, Westport, Greenwood Press

Details of pupils at St Edward's School appear in *The Roll of St Edward's School 1863-1927* published in Oxford in 1927 by the St Edward's School Society.

Material on Catholicism draws largely on O'Malley, Patrick R. (2006) *Catholicism, Sexual Deviance and Victorian Gothic Culture* Cambridge, Cambridge University Press

The quote "noisy folly" is from Symons, A. J. A. (1952) *The Quest for Corvo*, London, Folio Society p.1

"his friendships with " from Davidson, Michael p.137

"I used to …" and "not a very…" from Christopher's letter to Walter Ledger 22 March 1905.

"the grey twilight…" from letter to Alfred Douglas from Oscar Wilde. The full quote is "Do go there to cool your hands in the grey twilight of Gothic things…" Appears in Rupert Hart-Davis (ed) *Selected Letters of Oscar Wilde*, London, Hart-Davis p.107

"too honest with himself …" is from Davidson, Michael p. 137

"I am glad you too …" from Christopher's letter to Walter 21 October 1905

Chapter Four Teaching

The history of St Thomas' church is given on www.stthomaswoodford.org

Dorothy's fashionable wedding was reported in the *Reading Mercury* of 27 April 1901

Hyde's suggestion about trouble at the school in Woodford Wells is on p.11

The 1901 photograph of Millard in academic dress is in the Robert Ross Memorial Collection - MS Ross 13/1*

"the only book…" from Christopher's letter to Walter 8 December 1924

"Please don't address …" from Christopher's letter to Walter 6 July 1919

"Pilgrimage of Love" from Christopher's dedication in his translation of Andre Gide's *Oscar Wilde*

"one nosegay" Robert Harborough Sherard (1905) *Twenty Years in Paris* London, Hutchinson p.455. He describes this and other visits to Oscar's temporary grave and the visit to the room where Oscar died pp.450-458

"a most charming person" from Christopher's letter to Walter 17 February 1905

"a beautiful personage" and "I quite fell …" from Christopher's letter to Walter 6 March 1905

"very pleasant" and "unbearable with his …" from Christopher's letter to Walter 14 February 1905

There is a copy of *The St Germain's Magazine* November 1904 in the Robert Ross Memorial Collection MS Ross 13/1** and "the author of …" and the following quotes about St Germain come from this.

Chapter Five Oscar and Walter

Most of the information about Walter in this chapter comes from his will (proved on 29 January 1932 in the Principal Probate Registry and held by HM Courts and Tribunal Service) and his obituary written by Donald Charles Ludlow Cree and published in the *Royal Institute of British Architects Journal* vol. 40 dated 5 August 1933, p.780

The transcript of *The Harlot's House* is now in the William Andrews Clark Memorial Library at the University of California, Los Angeles.

"I cannot get …" from Christopher's letter to Walter 30 November 1904

"Thanks so much …" from Christopher's letter to Walter 9 December 1904

"a considerable portion ..." and "due to Mr... from Walter's obituary
"I wish you ..." from Christopher's letter to Walter 15 December 1904
"I am sending..." from Christopher's letter to Walter 10 December 1904
"It seems between..." from Christopher's letter to Walter 22 January 1905
"beautiful copy of ..." and other quotes in paragraph from Christopher's letter to Walter 11 December 1904
"When you have ..." from Christopher's letter to Walter 13 December 1904

Chapter Six The Road to Prison

Most of the information on Huyshe comes from the *Rochester, Chatham and Gillingham Journal* 17 February 1905 which is extensively quoted here. The material and quotes relating to the charges Christopher faced, the alleged incidents and the resulting court cases comes from newspaper reports in the *Oxford Times* of 12 May, 19 May and 23 June 1906 and a Metropolitan Police report in a file at the National Archives MEPO 3/240
Sheila Rowbotham wrote a biography of Edward Carpenter published by Verso in 2008 *Edward Carpenter: A Life of Liberty and Love*
"The Curate of..." from Christopher's letter to Walter 17 February 1905
"reading a novel..." and other quotes in this and following paragraph from The *Rochester, Chatham and Gillingham Journal* 17 February 1905
"was always mad!" from Christopher's letter to Walter 17 February 1905
"I, too, am..." from Christopher's letter to Walter 28 October 1905
"Madly as ever" from Christopher's letter to Walter 8 November 1905
"excellent review" from Christopher's letter to Walter 6 March 1905
"So far the..." from Christopher's letter to Walter 25 February 1905
"an old parson ..." and "bar-'lady.'" from Christopher's letter to Walter 19 October 1905
"What humbugs the ..." from Christopher's letter to Walter [ides of] 15 March 1905
"I return to ..." from Christopher's letter to Walter 25 February 1905
"more than I ..." and "immense fascination" from Christopher's letter to Walter 3 March 1905
"I can put..." from Christopher's letter to Walter 25 February 1905
"a delightful week..." from Christopher's letter to Walter 27 April 1905
"Bravo! You have ..." and "No, my name ..." from Christopher's letter to Walter 5 October 1905
"sweet enough to..." from Christopher's letter to Walter 20 August 1905

"quaint" from Christopher's letter to Walter 21 September 1905

"a week on…" from Christopher's letter to Walter 20 August 1905

"with the author's love" from Christopher's letter to Walter 15 November 1905

"dull and uninteresting" and "run by a … "from Christopher's letter to Walter 19 February 1906

"If I can …" from Christopher's letter to Walter 24 February 1905

Christopher's *Chrysanthemum* poem is copied in his letter to Walter 2 November 1905

"I am not keen…" and "I am trying…" from Christopher's letter to Walter 15 December 1905

"I am not…" from Christopher's letter to Walter 27 August 1905

"You are so…" from Christopher's letter to Walter 21 October 1905

"Your designs are…" from Christopher's letter to Walter 28 October 1905

"Ex corde" from Christopher's letter to Walter 26 September 1905

"Yours with accumulating affection" from Christopher's letter to Walter 15 November 1905

"Toujours a toi" from Christopher's letter to Walter 24 November 1905

"Ever to thee" from Christopher's letter to Walter 30 March 1906

"Fancy two Lesbian…" from Christopher's letter to Walter 8 November 1905

"He is very insistent…" from Christopher's letter to Walter 29[?] September 1905

"Countless tas for …" from Christopher's letter to Walter 24 November 1905

"I have never…" from Christopher's letter to Walter 28 September 1905

"Your last letter…" from Christopher's letter to Walter 28 October 1905

"I am browsing …" from Christopher's letter to Walter 2 November 1905

Max Nordau's book *Degeneration* was first published in German as *Entartung* in 1892. It was translated into English in 1895. A second German edition was published in 1898 and these quotes are from pp.538-9 of the English translation of that second edition published in London by Heinemann in 1913. Most of the references to Oscar Wilde are on pp.317-322.

"As for my relations…" from Christopher's letter to Walter 24 December 1905

"The delirious delights…" from Christopher's letter to Walter 17 January 1906

"go the round…" from Christopher's letter to Walter 14 February 1906

"However, possess your..." from Christopher's letter to Walter 21 February 1906

"a dreadful person" from Christopher's letter to Walter 27 March 1906

"simply an ex..." and following three quotes from Christopher's letter to Walter 31 March 1906

"I will come..." from Christopher's letter to Walter 21 March 1906

"sunshine of Spring..." from Christopher's letter to Walter 25 December 1906

"A glorious day..." from Christopher's letter to Walter 12 April 1906

"I know absolutely" from *The Oxford Times* 12 May 1906

"I am in..." from Christopher's letter to Walter 7 May 1906

"some sudden obsession ..." from *The Oxford Times* 23 June 1906

"the shadow of..." p.98 from Burdett, Osbert (1935) *Memory and Imagination*, London, Chapman & Hall

"One of my friends..." and remaining quotes in the chapter are all from Christopher's letter to Walter 7 May 1906

Chapter Seven Charles

Most of the information about Charles Kenneth Scott Moncrieff (who incidentally never used a hyphen in his name) here and the following chapters comes from Scott Moncrieff, Charles Kenneth (1931) *Memories and Letters* edited by Scott Moncrieff, J. M. and Lunn, L. W., London, Chapman & Hall.

"I must sell ..." from Christopher's letter to Walter 21 September 1906

"wrote sympathetically to..." from Christopher's letter to Walter 12 November 1906

"Only just a..." from Christopher's letter to Walter 21 September 1906

"I have had..." and other quotes in this paragraph from copy of Walter's letter to Christopher 26 September 1906

"We are none..." from copy of Walter's letter to Christopher 26 September 1906

"I have no..." from copy of Walter's letter to Christopher 1[?] April 1906

"my collection of..." and following quote from copy of Walter's letter to Christopher 26 September 1906

"I would have..." from Christopher's letter to Walter 27 April 1907

"by the sea..." and following quote from Christopher's letter to Walter 1 November 1906

"It nearly breaks..." from Christopher's letter to Walter 27 April 1907

"I am on..." from Christopher's letter to Walter 7 December 1906

"I bitterly groan..." from Christopher's letter to Walter 19 August 1907

"trivial little works" from Robert Ross' letter to Walter 23 January 1908 in the Robert Ross Memorial Collection, University College, Oxford
"to see *The…*" and "delightful old town" from Christopher's letter to Walter 25 December 1906
"lines of grey …" from Charles' letter 30 April 1905 in *Memories*, p.19
"These spring winds…" from Christopher's letter to Walter 20[?] March 1907
"I have not…" from Christopher's letter to Walter 17 April 1907

Chapter Eight Exile and Return

"a quiet little…" and following quote from Christopher's letter to Walter 27 April 1907
"being here better…" from Christopher's letter to Walter 13 May 1907
"rather out of…" and following two quotes from Christopher's letter to Walter 19 August 1907
"old landlord of…" and following quote from Christopher's letter to Walter 27 April 1907
"It nearly breaks…" from Christopher's letter to Walter 27 April 1907
"translated by a…" from Christopher's letter to Walter 7 May 1907
"I bitterly groan…" from Christopher's letter to Walter 19 August 1907
"I hear from…" from Christopher's letter to Walter 7 May 1907
"My own collection…" from Christopher's letter to Walter 13 May 1907
"I suppose you…" from Christopher's letter to Walter 4 June 1907
"horrid" and following quote from Christopher's letter to Walter 24 May 1907
"which I like…" and following two quotes from Christopher's letter to Walter 19 August 1907
"a humble lodgement" from Christopher's letter to Walter 17 September 1907
"The speed and …" is on p.102 of Osbert Burdett's book
"He is rather…" from Christopher's letter to Walter 15 December 1905
"I shall be…" from Christopher's letter to Walter 15 October 1907
"dreadfully mauled" from Christopher's letter to Walter 11 November 1907
"They have inserted…" from Christopher's letter to Walter 23 May 1908
"I had a…" from Christopher's letter to Walter 4 July 1908
"rusticating… at a …" and following quote from Christopher's letter to Walter 21 July 1908
"What an awful…" from Christopher's letter to Walter 3 October 1908
"the remnants of…" from Christopher's letter to Walter 3 October 1908

"It is four…" from Christopher's letter to Walter 8 December 1908

"Mr Stuart Mason" from Robbie's speech quoted in Ross, Margery (ed) (1952) *Robert Ross: Friend of Friends*, Cape, pp.156-7

"one of my…" from Christopher's letter to Walter 3 December 1908

"more suited to…" from Christopher's letter to Walter 1 April 1909

"I am in…" from Christopher's letter to Walter 25 June 1909 "Bank 'Oliday" from Christopher's letter to Walter 2 August 1909

"found another Yiddish…" and following quote from Christopher's letter to Walter 24 August 1909

Chapter Nine Alfred Douglas

The material on Thomas Crosland comes mainly from Brown, W Sorley (1928) *The Life and Genius of T W H Crosland*, London, Cecil Palmer

Most of the material on Philip Bainbridge and the quotes from *Achilles in Scyros* are from Hesin, P. J. (2005) *The Transvestite Achilles* Cambridge Cambridge University Press.

Vandiver, Elizabeth (2010) *Stand in the Trench, Achilles*, Oxford, Oxford University Press also has a short section on Philip Bainbridge pp328-331

"dubious stories of…" *The Academy* 12 June 1909

"He floored Marshall…" from Christopher's letter to Walter 21 February 1910

"I am nearly…" from Christopher's letter to Walter 2 March 1910

"I want to…" from Christopher's letter to Walter 17 October 1910

"I fear it…" and following two quotes from Christopher's letter to Walter 30 November 1910

"it is a… and "for your Christmas…" from Christopher's letter to Walter 18 January 1911

"this is in…" from Christopher's letter to Walter 13 February 1911

"an appalling production" and following quote from Christopher's letter to Walter 26 April 1911

"peculiar genius" from Robert Harborough Sherard (1906) *The Life of Oscar Wilde* London, T. Werner Laurie p. 320

"silly" ibid p.306

"Willy give me …" ibid p.358

"just passed the…" from Christopher's letter to Walter 29 May 1911

"I have been…" from Christopher's letter to Walter 12 July 1911

"Saturday is my…" from Christopher's letter to Walter 15 October 1911

"indolent" from Christopher's letter to Walter 12 July 1911

"on the water…" from Christopher's letter to Walter 16 August 1911

"quite good" from Christopher's letter to Walter 15 October 1911

"It was crowded…" from Christopher's letter to Walter 2 November 1911

"You need have…" from Christopher's letter to Walter 29 November 1911

"the really interesting…" from Christopher's letter to Walter 29[?] December 1911

Chapter Ten Admiring Oscar

The account of the theatre protest is based on Burdett, Osbert (1935) *Memory and Imagination*, London, Chapman & Hal, pp.104-5

Most of the material on Lyki is from Lockhart, Robert Hamilton Bruce (1932) *Memoirs of a British Agent*, London, Putnam

"rather rushed" from Christopher's letter to Walter 29[?] December 1911

"very different from…" and following quote from Christopher's letter to Walter 2 December 1911

"it is far…" from Christopher's letter to Walter 19 January 1912

"Will you collaborate…" from Christopher's letter to Walter 16 January 1912

"I don't want…" and following quote from copy of Walter's letter to Christopher 18 January 1912

"I am delighted…" and following quote from Christopher's letter to Walter 9 November 1912

"I have so…" from Christopher's letter to Walter 19 January 1912

"Poor Vyvyan is…" from Christopher's letter to Walter 19 February 1912

"Germany has produced…" from Christopher's letter to Walter 7 September 1912

"NOW CONTROL YOURSELF…" from Christopher's letter to Walter 8 November 1912

"I wonder how…" from Christopher's letter to Walter 9 November 1912

"The *Athenaeum* turned…" from Christopher's letter to Walter 13 November 1912

"I hope you…" from Christopher's letter to Walter 12 November 1912

"I have been…" from Christopher's letter to Walter 18 November 1912

"the fair slim…" from Christopher's letter to Walter 3 November 1912

"I am going…" and following quote from Christopher's letter to Walter 15 November 1912

"Buckinghamshire and the…" from Christopher's letter to Walter 3 August 1912 "filthy book" from Christopher's letter to Walter 18 December 1912

"bugger and a ..." quoted in Borland p.175 which comes from p.38 of the Ross Deposition 1913 now in in the William Andrews Clark Memorial Library at the University of California, Los Angeles.

"I hope to..." from Christopher's letter to Walter 18 December 1912

"My intended Christmas..." from Christopher's letter to Walter 20 December 1912

"come and see..." from Christopher's letter to Walter 22 January 1913

"I don't seem..." and "A great deal..." from Christopher's letter to Walter 10 February 1913

"chucked the *Burlington*..." from Christopher's letter to Walter 1 April 1913

"The reading of..." and following three quotes from Christopher's letter to Walter 23 April 1913

"so pretty" from Christopher's letter to Walter 23 July 1913

"a jolly little..." from Christopher's letter to Walter June 1919

"a dull, flat" from Christopher's letter to Walter 16 May 1914

"much time for ..." from Christopher's letter to Walter 12 June 1913

"rather nice" and following quote from Christopher's letter to Walter 28 September 1907

"Both will be..." from Christopher's letter to Walter 19 July 1913

Chapter Eleven Charley

The material on the suffragettes in this chapter draws mainly on Crawford, Elizabeth (2006) *The Women's Suffrage Movement in Britain and Ireland: a regional survey* Elizabeth Crawford, London Routledge

The section on Harry Pankhurst is based on Pugh, Martin (2001) *The Pankhursts*, London, Allen Lane

The information on Charley draws heavily on newspaper reports including that of the *Leicester Daily Mercury* 4 February 1913 – from which all the material and quotes on his time at the George Hotel and the pillar-boxes incident are taken - as well as two important sources in the National Archives - MEPO 3/240 which is a Metropolitan Police Office file and includes correspondence and statements and CRIM 1/149/1 which contains records from the trial of Thomas Crosland.

"to appear bigger..." from Elizabeth Garratt's deposition 29 April 1914 in MEPO 3/240

"the smartest in ..." from Elizabeth Garratt's deposition 29 April 1914 in MEPO 3/240 "at a fried…" from Elizabeth Garratt's deposition 28 April 1914 in MEPO 3/240

"lived a decent…" from Elizabeth Garratt's deposition 29 April 1914 in MEPO 3/240

"whether Millard and…" and following quote from Charley's deposition 29 April 1914 in CRIM 1/149/1

"young men wearing…" from Hoare, Philip (1997) *Oscar Wilde's Last Stand* p.5

"effeminate" and other quotes in this paragraph from Metropolitan Police report 26 January 1915 in MEPO 3/240

"quite turned" and following quote from Robbie's letter to Christopher 6 September 1913 quoted in Borland's biography p. 194. The original is in the William Andrews Clark Memorial Library at the University of California, Los Angeles.

"a very jolly…" from Christopher's letter to Walter 16 September 1913

"kick up a …" from statement made by Aylmer Clerk 25 July 1914 in MEPO 3/240

"positive there was…" from Susan Humer's interview reported in MEPO 3/240

"purple people or…" from Robbie's letter to Christopher 13 September 1913 quoted in Borland's biography p. 196. The original is in the William Andrews Clark Memorial Library at the University of California, Los Angeles.

"a student at.. " and quotes in the rest of this and following paragraph from *Reynolds'* September 21 1913

"Please inform Mr…" from Metropolitan Police report 15 July 1914 MEPO 3/240

"merely excited" from *Reynold's* 21 September 1913

"Was there any…" and other quotes in this and following paragraph from *Reynolds's* 28 September 1913

"I fear your…" quoted in *The Daily Express* 30 June 1914

"I have especially…" and following quote from Robbie's letter to Christopher 13 September 1913 quoted in Borland's biography p. 197. The original is in the William Andrews Clark Memorial Library at the University of California, Los Angeles.

"collecting little out-of-the-way…" from Christopher's letter to Walter 13 October 1913

"a weird American…" from Christopher's letter to Walter 3 December 1913

"Ever so many…" and following two quotes from Christopher's letter to Walter 26 December 1913

Chapter Twelve Replaying Oscar

Again this chapter draws on newspaper reports and on MEPO 3/240 and CRIM 1/149/1 at the National Archives

The Marlborough Police Court Registers are held at London Metropolitan Archives. 1914 material appears in PS/MS/A01/022-027 and PS/MS/A02/005-007

"Dear Mother, Please..." quoted in *The Morning Post* 30 June 1914

"Millard and my ..." and quotes in following four paragraphs from Charley's deposition 6 May 1914 in CRIM 1/149/1

"he could not ..." and other quotes in this paragraph from deposition by Elizabeth Garratt 29 April 1914 in CRIM 1/149/1

"'Hullo young man...'" from deposition by Elizabeth Garratt 28 April 1914 in CRIM 1/149/1

The quoted letters from Alfred Douglas are in MEPO 3/240

"nowhere to turn" from Charley's deposition 13 May 1914 in CRIM 1/149/1

"this awful beastly..." from Charley's letter quoted in *The Daily Express* 13 May 1914

"taken the most..." from Christopher's letter to Walter 26 December 1913

"to a Charles..." from Christopher's letter to Walter 29 January 1914

"no particular news" from Christopher's letter to Walter 4 February 1914

"untruthful, of bad..." in Metropolitan Police report 15 July 1914 in MEPO 3/240

Alfred's letter to Christopher was quoted in *The Daily Citizen* 28 April 1914

The postcard to "My dear F" was quoted in *The Morning Post* 1 July 1914

The comment "traitor" written by George Ives is quoted in McKenna, Neil (2004) *The Secret Life of Oscar Wilde* London, Arrow p.363

"It seems almost..." from Christopher's letter to Walter 9 March 1914

"my lips with ..." and following quote from Charley's deposition 13 May 1914 in CRIM 1/149/1

"confessed on Saturday..." from Christopher's letter to Walter 9 March 1914

"the officer said..." from Charley's deposition 12 May 1914 in CRIM 1/149/1

"to pester from..." from Christopher's letter to Walter 17 March 1914

"gross abuse of..." from Christopher's letter to Walter 24 March 1914

"It is all..." from Christopher's letter to Walter 16 April 1914 "but heard only…" and following two quotes from Christopher's letter to Walter 28 April 1914

"bottling and botany…" from Christopher's letter to Walter 18 June 1914

"a short change…" from Christopher's letter to Walter 28 May 1914

"It is my…" from Christopher's letter to Walter 8 July 1914

"Shortly before the…" from Christopher's obituary by Charles Scott Moncrieff in early editions only of *The Times* on 1 December 1927 p.18

"minutely detailed" from *The Library Association Record* 15 October 1914

Other quotes from review in *The Library Association Record* 15 December 1914

"It is enough…" and following quote from Christopher's letter to Walter 2 January 1919

"debauched and degraded…" and following quote from Justice Avory quoted in Metropolitan Police report 15 July 1914 in MEPO 3/240

"The horror of…" from Christopher's letter to Walter 8 July 1914

"It is perfectly…" from Metropolitan Police report 28 July 1914 in MEPO 3/240

The information supplied by Christopher's neighbours, landlord and cleaner is recorded in the Metropolitan Police report 28 July 1914 in MEPO 3/240

Chapter Thirteen War

The information about Chipping Campden and Charles Ashbee is from MacCarthy, Fiona (1981) *The Simple Life*, London, Lund Humphries

Information about the White Cross League comes from a letter from Casimir A Bourne published in *The Spectator* 22 June 1912 pp.17-18 and Prochaska, F. K. (1980) *Women and Philanthropy in Nineteenth-century England*, Oxford, Clarendon, p. 215

Charles Scott Moncrieff's poems are reprinted in *Memories* pp. 83-5, 213-215

"I wonder where…" from Christopher's letter to Walter 6 August 1914

"I am frightfully…" from Christopher's letter to Walter 6 September 1914

"My companion-to-be has…" from Christopher's letter to Walter 6 August 1914

"I was immediately…" from Christopher's letter to Walter 6 September 1914

"I would much…" and quote in following paragraph from Christopher's letter to Walter 6 September 1914

"As for the…" and quote in following paragraph from Christopher's letter to Walter 14 October 1914

"a strong presentiment…" letter of 5 November 1914 in *Memories* p.65

"I'd rather spend…" letter of 12 November 1914 ibid p.71

"may go on …" letter of 14 November 1914 ibid p.72

"used to spend…" letter of 20 November 1914 ibid p.77

"an alleged habitual …" from Metropolitan Police report 11 November 1914 in MEPO 3/240

"a New Year's…" from report in *The Times* 24 November 1914

"not very hopeful…" from Christopher's letter to Walter 23 November 1914

"inner history" from Christopher's letter to Walter 20 December 1914

"as happy a…" and following two quotes from Christopher's letter to Walter 24 December 1914

"I am reading…" and following quote from Christopher's letter to Walter 30 December 1914

"Did you see…" and following quote from Christopher's letter to Walter 1 April 1915

"Two of my …" from Christopher's letter to Walter 23 November 1914

"The war seems…" from Christopher's letter to Walter 17 February 1915

"I admire your…" and following quote from Christopher's letter to Walter 1 April 1915

"respectable" and other quotes in the same paragraph are from Archibald Henry Bodkin's letters in MEPO 3/240.

"I have just…" from Christopher's letter to Walter 16 April 1915

"You will be…" from Christopher's letter to Walter 13 May 1915

"will now be…" from Christopher's letter to Walter 27 May 1915

"I have so…" from Christopher's letter to Walter 29 May 1915

"I went up…" from Christopher's letter to Walter 27 May 1915

"I am very…" from Christopher's letter to Walter 13 June 1915

"The latest news…" from Christopher's letter to Walter 23 July 1915

"returned to the…" and following quote from Christopher's letter to Walter 17 August 1915

"I persuaded him…" from Christopher's letter to Walter 18 August 1915

"in a frightful" and following quote from Christopher's letter to Walter 23 July 1915

"a holiday from…" and poems from Christopher's letter to Walter 3 August 1915

"being alone for …" from Christopher's letter to Walter 17 August 1915

"I should very…" copied in Christopher's letter to Walter 19 October 1915 "rescue" and "prey to the..." from the letter from Casimir A. Bourne published in *The Spectator* 22 June 1912 pp.17-18

"turned over a new leaf" and "irreclaimable" from the police report of 8 March 1915 in MEPO 3/240

"I wasn't able..." and following two quotes from Christopher's letter to Walter 18 August 1915

 "I saw the..." from Christopher's letter to Walter 13 September 1915

"found sooner or ..." letter from Charles 22 July 1915 in *Memories* p.92

"a proper Papist" from letter of 1 August 1915 ibid p.98

"very contented" from letter of 19 February 1916 ibid p.112

"Palmer, my publisher ..." from Christopher's letter to Walter 13 September 1915

"little half-yearly cheque..." from Christopher's letter to Walter 1 October 1915

 "Here is a..." from Christopher's letter to Walter 23 December 1915

Chapter Fourteen On the Run

Some of the material on Cecil Falcy is from www.greatwarlondon.wordpress.com

The Times 3 January 1916 reported the case involving Maurice Rothfarb

 "crowds of officers..." from Christopher's letter to 'R.' 1 January 1919 published in facsimile in 1983 as *Five letters and A Catalogue* with an introduction by Timothy d'Arch Smith. Victim Press London

"I am fairly..." from Christopher's letter to Walter 15 January 1916

"I may be..." from Christopher's letter to Walter 21 January 1916

"It was all..." and following four quotes from Christopher's letter to Walter 31 May-1 June 1916

"It was, moreover..." from Christopher's letter to Walter 28 August 1916

"delights of spring" and following quote from Christopher's letter to Walter 31 May-1 June 1916

"old fashioned commercial" and quote at end of same paragraph from Christopher's letter to 'R.' 9 June 1918 reproduced in *Five Letters and a Catalogue*

"We do everything..." and all quotes in this and following four paragraphs from Christopher's letter to Walter 31 May-1 June 1916

"I was so..." from Christopher's letter to 'R.' 13 June 1918 reproduced in *Five Letters and a Catalogue*

To One Falce is copied into Christopher's letter to Walter 31 May-1 June 1916

"I don't much…" from Christopher's letter to Walter 31 May-1 June 1916
"I fear I…" from Christopher's letter to Walter 25 June 1916
"the fact that…" and quotes in next two paragraphs from Christopher's letter to Walter 28 August 1916
The photograph referred to in the final paragraph accompanied Christopher's letter to Walter 16 October 1916

Chapter Fifteen A Dulce et Decorum Halo

The material on the Community of the Resurrection is from the *C.R. Diamond Jubilee Book 1892-1952* published by the Community in 1952 at Wakefield.
"It is a …" from Christopher's letter to Walter 21 October 1916
"Some things are…" and other quotes in paragraph from Christopher's letter to Walter 9 November 1916
"the picture of…" and following quote from Christopher's letter to Walter 21 October 1916
"'chucked' Oscar about 1893" from Christopher's letter to Walter 9 November 1916
"by the good…" from Christopher's letter to Walter 21 October 1916
"People are so…" and following quote from Christopher's letter to Walter 9 November 1916
"not at one…" from Christopher's letter to Walter 11 December 1916
"wet through" and rest of quotes on Christopher's time at Etaples and his discharge from his letter to Walter 5 April 1917
"pleasant enough to…" from Christopher's letter to Walter 30 May 1917
"catch it in…" from Christopher's letter to Walter 5 April 1917
"I do absolutely…" from Christopher's letter to Walter 18 June 1917
"I thought Kernahan's…" from Christopher's letter to Walter 30 May 1917
"If you really…" from Christopher's letter to Walter 18 June 1917
"drawn the teeth…" from Christopher's letter to Walter 5 April 1917
"I went to…" from Christopher's letter to Walter 1 July 1917
"every day from…" from Christopher's letter to Walter 16 October 1917

Chapter Sixteen Prison Rhymes with Sorrow

All the quotes from Christopher's prison letters to R. come from the 1983 facsimile publication of *Five letters and A Catalogue* with an introduction by Timothy d'Arch Smith. Victim Press London

Charley's army career is recorded in his service and pension records under the name Nehemiah Garratt regimental number 26482. Digital images are available at www.ancestry.com. All the quotes about this period of his life come from this source.

"almost adjoining the…" from Christopher's letter to Walter 16 October 1917

"I only wish…" and following quote from Christopher's letter to Walter 6 December 1917

"If Quaritch won't…" and following two quotes from Christopher's letter to Walter 12 December 1917

"I had been…" and following quote from Christopher's letter to R. 13 June 1918

"though his dreams…" and rest of quotes in paragraph from Charles' article *The Poets there are III : Wilfred Owen* in *New Witness* 10 December 1920 pp.574-5

"such conduct was…" and rest of quotes in this paragraph from *The Times* of 4 March 1918

"sent…around very…" and following quote from Robbie's letter to Walter 4 April 1918 in the Robert Ross Memorial Collection owned by University College, Oxford

"The only witness…" from Christopher's letter to R. 13 June 1918

"unprincipled powers such…" from Christopher's letter to R. 9 July 1918

"dangerous man" from Christopher's letter to Walter 4 April 1923

"Fortunately I now…" and following quote from Christopher's letter to R. 13 June 1918

"much as if…" from Christopher's letter to R. 9 July 1918

"a sufficiency to…" and following quote from Christopher's letter to R. 13 June 1918

"no man could…" from Christopher's letter to R. 4 October 1918

"I try by…" and following quote from Christopher's letter to R. 13 June 1918

"much better reading…" from Christopher's letter to R. 13 June 1918

"poor stuff tho'…" from Christopher's letter to R. 13 June 1918

"a jolly yarn…" from Christopher's letter to R. 13 June 1918

"really admirable character …" and following six quotes from Christopher's letter to R. 4 October 1918

"I am allowed…" and following quote from Christopher's letter to R. 13 June 1918

"He & his…" from Christopher's letter to R. 9 July 1918

"What do you…" from Christopher's letter to R. 13 June 1918

"Has there been…" from Christopher's letter to R. 9 July 1918

"Oxford was, no…" and following quote from Christopher's letter to R. 9 July 1918

"Oxford ought to…" and following quote from Christopher's letter to R. 4 October 1918

"It passes the…" and following quote from Christopher's letter to R. 9 July 1918

"both delightfully dignified…" and following quote from Christopher's letter to R. 9 July 1918

"I know the…" and following two quotes from Christopher's letter to R. 9 July 1918

"on a wooden…" and following two quotes from Christopher's letter to R. 4 October 1918

"the agent of…" quoted in Hoare, Philip p.152

"kicking the corpse…" from Robbie's letter to Cecil Sprigge quoted in ibid p.137

"The prosecution might…" Christopher's letter to R. 9 July 1918

"'Think what ills…'" and quotes from *Autumn* from Christopher's letter to R. 13 June 1918

"My time is…" and following quote from Christopher's letter to R. 4 October 1918

"I think to…" from Christopher's letter to R. 9 July 1918

"I am afraid…" from Paul Elwin's letter to Walter 23 December 1918

"devoted friendship and…" from Christopher's letter to Walter 2 January 1919

The suggestion that Alec did set up the trust fund is made in Maureen Borland's book. However the letter Christopher wrote to Walter on 7 November 1927 after Alec's death suggests only the £10 allowance was made.

"I feel too…" from Christopher's letter to Walter 2 January 1919

"My general health…" and following five quotes from Christopher's letter to R. 4 October 1918

"It is a …" from Christopher's letter to R. 29 December 1918

"old friend" from Christopher's letter to Walter 13 June 1921

"I was most…" and following two quotes from Christopher's letter to R. 9 July 1918

"I shall not… and following quote from report in *The Morning Advertiser* 1 July 1914

"It must be more..." and "has robbed me..." from Christopher's letter to Walter 2 January 1919

"Food is more..." from Christopher's letter to R. 29 December 1918

"a sort of..." and following two quotes from Christopher's letter to Walter 2 January 1919

"At present all..." from Christopher's letter to R. 1 January 1919

"lived his life..." Anthony Powell *Infants of the Spring* p91

"It is sufficiently..." and following quote from Christopher's letter to R. 1 January 1919

"When you come..." from Christopher's letter to Walter 2 January 1919

"My flower border..." from Christopher's letter to Walter 12 April 1919

"My garden grows..." from Christopher's letter to Walter 24 April 1919

"country cottage in..." from Davidson, Michael p.137

"speedily gathered a..." from Christopher's obituary by Charles Scott Moncrieff in the early editions of *The Times* on 1 December 1927 p.18

"I don't know..." from Christopher's letter to Walter 12 April 1919

"My friendships are..." from a letter written by Edward Fitzgerald to his friend John Allen dated 9 September 1834 quoted in Hayter, Althea (ed.) (1979) *Fitzgerald to his Friends: Selected letters of Edward Fitzgerald,* London, Scolar Press p,12

"far beyond" from Christopher's letter to Walter 3 January 1919

"to part with..." from Christopher's letter to Walter 2 January 1919

"I'm not really..." from Christopher's letter to Frank Harris 3 April 1919 reproduced in Hyde pp.68-69

The incident in Lewes is recounted in Christopher's letter to Frank Harris 7 May 1919 reproduced in Hyde pp.69-71

"little presents to..." Osbert Burdett p.107

"four very elementary..." from Christopher's letter to Walter 22 October 1919

"You will be..." and following quotes from Christopher's letter to Walter 10 July 1919

"first war play..." from Maltby, Henry Francis (1950) *Ring up the Curtain,* London, Hutchinson p.146

"a little memento..." from Christopher's letter to Walter 11 August 1919

"A.D. may be ..." from Christopher's letter to Frank Harris 16 June 1919 reproduced in Hyde pp.71-2

Chapter Eighteen Booksellling

Most of the information about Magdalen Millard comes from her will proved on 29 December 1921 in the Principal Probate Registry and held by HM Courts and Tribunal Service.

Walter's collection of Nelson memorabilia is described in his will held by HM Courts and Tribunal Service.

The bankruptcy of Alfred's brother Percy was reported in *The Times* 29 January 1920.

Dora Millard's will was proved on 8 February 1921 in the Principal Probate Registry and held by HM Courts and Tribunal Service.

The description of Christopher's image collection and of his iconography of Oscar Wilde comes largely from the article in *Nineteenth Century Contexts* December 2010 vol. 32 no. 4 by Daniel A Novak *Picturing Wilde; Millard's Iconography*

"My Catalogue No. ..." from Christopher's letter to Walter 15 October 1919

"teeming with his..." and following quote from Christopher's obituary by Charles Scott Moncrieff in the early editions of *The Times* on 1 December 1927 p.18

"Prices more reasonable..." quoted by Percy Muir in *Minding My Own Business* p.50

"book talk" and following quote from Christopher's letter to Walter 10 December 1919

"interrupt our book..." from Christopher's letter to Walter 15 December 1919

"I am really..." from Christopher's letter to Walter 24 December 1919

"a little Riccardi..." and following two quotes from Christopher's letter to Walter 24 December 1919

"mostly rubbish, I'm..." from Christopher's letter to Walter 16 March 1920

"They are a..." from Christopher's letter to Walter 29 January 1920

"what brutes they..." from Christopher's letter to Walter 29 March 1920

"recklessly went into..." and following two quotes from Christopher's letter to Walter 31 March 1920

"didn't have to..." from Christopher's letter to Walter 21 March 1920

"quite a nice..." from Christopher's letter to Walter 8 September 1920

"a very jolly..." from Christopher's letter to Walter 11 August 1920

"to tide me..." from Christopher's letter to Walter 8 September 1920

"Sorry to put..." from Christopher's letter to Walter 21 November 1920

"Uranian passages" and following quote from Vyvan Holland's letter to Christopher quoted by H. Montgomery Hyde in his biography p. 86. The original is in the William Andrews Clark Memorial Library at the University of California, Los Angeles.

"A.D.'s *Perkin Warbeck…*" from Christopher's letter to Walter 25 April 1921

"a presentation inscription…" from Christopher's letter to Walter 10 May 1921

"for 'a long…" and other quotes in this and following paragraph from Christopher's letter to Walter 23 May 1921

"the week-end in …" and following quote from Christopher's letter to Walter 13 June 1921

Christopher's comment, "I should have thought they might have been able to find space for it in the lavatory," is quoted by Anthony Powell in *Infants of the Spring* p.93

"I fear you…" and other quotes in this paragraph from Christopher's letter to Walter 14 November 1921

"I heard Douglas…" from Christopher's letter to Walter 30 November 1921

"the two pictures…" from Christopher's letter to Walter 15 January 1922

"a rather interesting…" from Christopher's letter to Walter 7 February 1923

"She is such…" from Christopher's letter to Walter 15 December 1921

"I am much…" from Christopher's letter to Walter 13 December 1921

"to fill in …" from Christopher's letter to Walter 12 January 1922

"wrote to a…" and following three quotes from Christopher's letter to Walter 16 January 1922

"The date 22.2.22…" and quotes in following paragraph from Christopher's letter to Walter 23 February 1922

"with a man…" and following quote from Christopher's letter to Anthony Powell 9 March 1922 reproduced in H. Montgomery Hyde's biography p. 163

Chapter Nineteen New Interests

Anthony's account of his association with Christopher appears in Powell, Anthony (1976) *Memoirs Vol. 1 Infants of the Spring*, London, Heinemann pp.91-97

Christopher's letter to Anthony that referred to the MacFisheries' designs was dated 5 April 1922 and is reproduced in H. Montgomery Hyde's biography p. 169

There is a biography of Brian Howard by Lancaster, Marie-Jacqueline (1968) *Brian Howard: Portrait of a Failure* London, Anthony Blond

"In conversation on ..." is from *Memoirs Vol. 1 Infants of the Spring* p.91

"You're really rather..." is Anthony's quote from Christopher ibid p.93

"the 'onlie begetter'..." from Christopher's letter to Anthony 15 March 1922 reproduced in H. Montgomery Hyde's biography p. 167

"I am collecting..." from Christopher's letter to Walter 23 February 1922

"some rather interesting..." and following quote from Christopher's letter to Walter 23 February 1922

"*very* sinister" - Brian Howard quoted by Anthony Powell in *Infants of the Spring* p118

"discovered" and other quotes about Brian Howard in this paragraph are from Christopher's letter to Anthony 28 February 1922 reproduced in H. Montgomery Hyde's biography pp. 160-1

"quite the right..." from Christopher's letter to Anthony 28 February 1922 reproduced in H. Montgomery Hyde's biography pp. 160-1

"a man calling..." from Christopher's letter to Walter 26 July 1922

"18 years ago..." and following quote from Christopher's letter to Walter 10 December 1922

"staggered" from Christopher's letter to Walter 7 February 1923

"heard Douglas cross-examined..." from Christopher's letter to Walter 19 July 1923

"I have searched..." from Christopher's letter to Walter 23 October 1923

"very silly and..." from Christopher's letter to Walter 26 October 1923

"It is over-subscribed..." from Christopher's letter to Walter 23 October 1923

Christopher refers to his letter to *The Sunday Express* in his letter to Walter 11 November 1924

"His secretary called..." from Christopher's letter to Walter 6 October 1923

Christopher's reference to the London fog is in his letter to Walter 11 December 1923

"I hope Douglas..." and following quote from Christopher's letter to Walter 11 December 1923

"You will find..." from Christopher's letter to Walter 16 December 1923

"special 10/6 dinner..." and following quote from Christopher's letter to Walter 19 January 1924

Paul Morand's *Ouvert la Nuit* was given the title *Open All Night* in Vyvyan's translation which was first published in July 1923 by Guy Chapman, London. The quote "cosmopolitan swine" is from p.224 and "swathed to their..." is from p.223

Chapter Twenty Politics

The information about Michael Davidson is from *The world, the Flesh and myself*.

"Please allow me…" is from Christopher's letter to Michael quoted in Davidson, Michael p.133

"horrified" from Christopher's letter to Walter 5 December 1924

The description of his re-decorating is from Christopher's letter to Walter 7 June 1924

"To-morrow I shall…" from Christopher's letter to Walter 7 June 1924

"stupidly slept in…" and following quote from Christopher's letter to Walter 5 December 1924

"had a very…" from Christopher's letter to Walter 2 January 1925

"The sumptuous way…" and following quote from Christopher's letter to William Andrews Clark 29 March 1924 quoted in H. Montgomery Hyde's biography p.80. The original is in the William Andrews Clark Memorial Library at the University of California, Los Angeles.

"I hope you…" and following two quotes from Christopher's letter to Walter 2 January 1925

"notoriously inaccurate and…", the quote from *The Observer* and "Robbie does not…" all from Christopher's letter to Walter 6 April 1925

"should be an…" and following quote from Christopher's letter to Walter 25 November 1925

Chapter Twenty One Defending Oscar

Nina Hamnett in her 1932 book *Laughing Torso* London, Constable recounts the episode acting out *Salome* on p. 98 whilst other details of the Bohemian group at The Plough Tavern come from Michael Davidson's book.

"six very interesting…" - the letter from Mabel Wodehouse Pearse is reproduced in Christopher's pamphlet called *Who Wrote 'For Love of the King'?*

"A WOMAN BLUFFS…" and following quote from Christopher's letter to Walter 1 July 1925

"a charming fellow…" from letter from Oscar to Robbie 2 February 1899

"insanity in his …" from letter from Oscar to Robbie 21 March 1899

Both of above reprinted in *The Complete Letters of Oscar Wilde* edited by Merlin Holland and Rupert Hart- Davis (2000) London, Fourth Estate, p.1121 and p.1134

"I used to…" from Christopher's letter to Walter 3 January 1926.

"It is awful…" from Christopher's letter to Walter 6 January 1926

"made a heroine of her" and "It is quite…" from Christopher's letter to Walter 18 January 1926

"The worst article…" and following quote from Christopher's letter to Walter 21 January 1926

"a few out-of-the-way…" from Christopher's letter to Walter 18 January 1926

"It is sad…" and "You need not…" from Christopher's letter to Walter 21 January 1926

"inscribed EDWARD SHELLEY…" from Christopher's letter to Walter 15 November 1926

"at the John…" from Christopher's letter to Walter 23 March 1926

The quoted comments made at Elkin Mathews come from the account in Percy Muir *Minding My Own Business* pp.50-51

"not good" and "not pure" in Newton, Arthur Edward (1912) *Oscar Wilde*, Pennsylvania, Daylesford, p.5

"general nastiness" ibid p.13

"disease" ibid p.22

"Methuen's statement of…" from Christopher's letter to Walter 23 March 1926

"pressing Methuen for…" and following quote from Christopher's letter to Walter 17 May 1926

The quotes from Michael's description of political activity during the General Strike appear in Davidson, Michael pp.146-7

"was hoping to…" from Christopher's letter to Walter 30 August 1926

"awful tosh" is quoted in *The Daily Mirror* 10 November 1926 p.19

"I had a…", "I am quite…" and following five quotes from Christopher's letter to Walter 15 November 1926

"nearly stone deaf…" from Christopher's letter to Walter 21 January 1926

"I cannot think…" from Christopher's letter to Walter 1 February 1926

The inscription in Michael's copy of the *For Love of the King* pamphlet beginning "Shall look out …" is quoted in Davidson, Michael p.147

Chapter Twenty two A Last Golden Interlude

There is a biography of Alastair by Victor Arwas (1979) *Alastair Illustrator of Decadence*, London, Thames and Hudson

The material about Varda is from *The Anthony Powell Society Newsletter* issue 31, Summer 2008 pp.3-6 and Nicholson, Virginia (2002) *Among the*

Bohemians: experiments in living 1900-1939 London, Viking p.263 includes the details of her singing in the early hours.

Christopher's will was proved on 20 December 1927 in the Principal Probate Registry and is held by HM Courts and Tribunal Service.

"the only copy..." from Christopher's letter to Walter 1 March 1927

"It is getting..." from Christopher's letter to Walter 4 March 1927

"suspicious from internal..." and "get her fingers..." from Christopher's letter to Walter 4 April 1927

"I really know..." and following three quotes from Christopher's letter to Walter 15 May 1927

"golden interlude" and following quote from Davidson, Michael *The world, the Flesh and myself* p.146

"abstain from taking..." and following three quotes from Christopher's will

"no purchased flowers..." from Christopher's will

"the unemployed, the..." from Millard, Paul Elwin (1928) *Intentions at the Eucharist*, London, A R Mowbray, p.15

"wilful sin" ibid p.3

"slaves to lust" ibid p.39

"It is over..." Walter Ledger in a letter to Christopher of 10 December 1924 which is quoted in Hyde p.88. The original letter (along with many other letters from Walter to Christopher almost all dating from 1922-1927) is in the William Andrews Clark Memorial Library in Los Angeles - Wilde L475L M 645 1924 Dec. 10

"a perfectly beastly..." and "chivalrous and selfless..." from Darwall-Smith, Robin (1999) *The Story of the Robert Ross Memorial Collection* in *The Wildean* no.15

(The) Avenue public house, Shaftesbury Avenue 118-9, 139

Avory, Horace 144-5, 154, 217

Bacon, Mrs Daisy 146

Baker, R. 136

Bagneux 45, 60

Bainbridge (Bainbrigge), Philip Gillespie 98-9, 187, 198

Baldwin, Stanley 217

(The) Ballad of Reading Gaol by Oscar Wilde 53, 93-4, 100-1, 165, 175, 180, 200

Ballads and Other Rhymes of a Country Bookworm by Thomas Hutchinson 218

Balliol College, Oxford 212

Balzac, Honore de 45

Banstead, Surrey 223

Barber, William 146

Barrie, Sir James Matthew 211

Basingstoke 7-8, 16-26, 28, 33, 205

Basingstoke Rectory 7-8, 17, 20, 23

(The) Battle of Trafalgar by James Elwin Millard 13

Baverstock, Alban Henry 36

Beaumaris Grammar School 17

Beaumont, Cyril William 203, 211

Beaumont Street 192

Beardsley, Aubrey 85, 216, 237-8

Beaverbrook, Lord 185

Bedford College, London 146

Beech Hotel, Wadhurst 47

Beecham, Thomas 99

Beerbohm, Max 208, 211

(The) Beggar's Opera 211

Bendz, Ernst Paulus 143

Benniworth, Lincolnshire 42

Beowulf by Charles Scott Moncrieff 219

Berkshire downs 89

Berkshire Militia 70

Berlin 245

Berneval 82, 86

Bibliography of Oscar Wilde 66, 77-8, 87, 99, 105-7, 142-3, 176
    And Grant Richards 83, 86
    And Methuen's interest 65, 87
    Collaboration with Walter 49, 52, 57, 60, 77, 83, 105
    Early plans 44, 51

Brightlingsea 220
Brighton 29, 136, 190
Bristol 17, 64, 230
British Museum 66, 91, 94, 114, 134, 222
British War Memorials Committee 185
British Worker 232
Brixton Prison 136, 149, 177
Brookfield, Charles Hallam Elton 107
Bryan, Cecil Henry Ferris 58-60, 67, 70-3
Bullen, Frank Thomas 181
Bullingdon Petty Sessions 70-71
Bulwer-Lytton, Robert 181
(The) Bungalow, 8 Abercorn Place 192-5, 201, 209
Burdett, Osbert 72, 84-5, 93, 173, 182, 196, 235
Burgoyne and Osbourne 146
Burlington Magazine 76, 101-2, 105, 109, 196
Burns, Robert 183
Bursledon 233, 239
Burnham on Crouch 206
Buszards, Oxford Street 201
Butterfield, William 34
Byron, Lord 224
Café Royal 118, 134-5, 138, 196, 218
Campden School of Arts and Crafts 157-8, 189
Campo Verano 245
Cannes 228
Carew, Mr 134-6
Carlton House Terrace 174
7 Carlton Street 86
Carpenter, Edward 57, 64, 158
Carrington, Charles 88, 104
34-38 Cartwright Gardens 163-4
Cassell, Sir Ernest 216
Castle Hotel, Ramsgate 111
Catholic Encyclopaedia 224
Catholic Emancipation Act 37
Catholic Literature Association 36
Catholicism 36-8, 94, 102, 203
    And Alan Alington 42
    And Alexander Teixeira de Mattos 32
    And Alfred Douglas 37, 98, 129, 135, 198

(handwritten margin note: GROLLEAU Cufparues 104)

HYDE WINTON MONTGOMERY 2 2

Lightning Source UK Ltd.
Milton Keynes UK
UKHW02f0137300618
325012UK00001B/134/P